The TRACE econometric model of the Canadian economy

Studies in social and economic policy
a series sponsored by the
Institute for the Quantitative Analysis
of Social and Economic Policy
University of Toronto

1   The TRACE econometric model of the Canadian economy
Nanda K. Choudhry, Yehuda Kotowitz, John A. Sawyer, John W.L. Winder

The TRACE econometric model of the Canadian economy

NANDA K.CHOUDHRY, YEHUDA KOTOWITZ, JOHN A.SAWYER, JOHN W.L.WINDER

University of Toronto Press

© University of Toronto Press 1972
Toronto and Buffalo
Printed in Canada
ISBN 0-8020-1806-8
Microfiche ISBN 0-8020-0125-4

Contents

Preface ix

1 Introduction 3

1 The purpose of the model 3
2 An overview of the TRACE model 6
  a Definition of variables
  b Aggregate demand
    Demand for commodities
    Money market and foreign exchange market
    Potential output and the utilization rate
  c Aggregate supply

2 The model 14

1 Estimation procedure 14
2 Notation and ordering of the equations of the model 14
3 Solution of the non-linear system of equations 15
4 The model: section by section 16
  A Personal expenditure on consumer goods and services
  B Government expenditure on goods and services
  C Business gross capital formation
    Residential construction
    Non-residential construction and machinery and equipment
    Value of the physical change in inventories
  D Foreign Trade
    Merchandise exports
    Exports of services
    Statistical discrepancy
    Imports of goods and services
    Interest and dividends
  E Gross national expenditure
  F Output
  G Prices and wages
  H Employment
  I Income

J   Taxes
K   Interest rates
L   International capital flows and exchange rate
M   Government revenue and expenditure account
N   Capital formation and saving account
5   Listing of the equations of the model 52

3   **Ex post forecasts: a test of the model** 70

4   **Policy multipliers under fixed and flexible exchange rates** 87

5   **Forecast for 1970: the methodology of ex ante forecasting** 113

6   **Conclusion** 123

    Appendices 126

1   Names, definitions, and sources of variables 127
    1   Explanations of terminology and sources 127
    2   Listing of variable names, definitions, and sources 128
2   Method of estimating the stock of capital 151
3   Estimates of interindustry input-output coefficients, 1956 and 1959,
    by T.I. Matuszewski, P.R. Pitts, and J.A. Sawyer 152
4   Import content of gross domestic product, 1959 157

    References 162

TABLES

1 Actual values and percentage 'forecast' errors (solution values minus actual values as percentages of actual values) for subsets of the sample period 71
2 Forecast errors in Y9R adjusted for forecast errors in BCF9R 82
3 Directions of change and turning points 84
4 Income shares, actual and ex post forecast values 84
5 Actual and ex post forecast values of yield on capital and implicit ratio to real implicit rental of capital services 85
6 Simulation results based on 1957 experiments 88
7 Simulation results based on 1960 experiments 95
8 Simulation results based on 1964 experiments 99
9 Convergence in 1957 simulations 108
10 Convergence in 1960 simulations 109
11 Convergence in 1964 simulations 110
12 Impact-year solution values for income shares, real capital yield, and ratio of capital yield to implicit rental price of capital services 111
13 Estimated 1969 and forecasts for 1970 from the TRACE model 114
14 Constant adjustments 116
15 Assumptions for alternative forecasts 117
16 Values of exogenous variables for the basic forecast 118
17 The forty-two industries 153
18 Scheme of inter-industry flow of goods and services matrix 154
19 Indirect import content of final demand expenditures directed towards the Jth industry, 1959 158
20 Composition of $100 million of final demand directed towards industries by categories, 1959 159
21 Primary direct and indirect import content of an expenditure of $100,000 (1949$) by a final demand category, assuming the 1959 industrial distribution 160
22 Import content coefficients for components of final demand, 1959 161

FIGURES

1 Aggregate demand and supply functions 12
2 Flow chart for simplified version of the model 13
3 Flow chart for residential construction sector 21

Preface

This University of Toronto project was initiated in the summer of 1966. The desire to build the model grew out of a series of informal seminars in econometrics in which the authors participated along with William C. Hood and was a result of our common interest in econometrics together with a feeling that there was a need to complement the econometric model building efforts within the Canada Department of Finance, the Bank of Canada, and the Economic Council of Canada with a model and forecasts which would be publically available. It is our commitment to publish all forecasts and policy analyses made from our model, provided we feel that their quality merits publication, that distinguishes our efforts from those of the government economists. In 1968 the project was brought into the recently formed Institute for the Quantitative Analysis of Social and Economic Policy of the University of Toronto.

The project was financed in an unusual manner in that research grants were obtained from both government agencies and business corporations. We gratefully acknowledge the support of the following: The Canada Council, Canada Department of Labour, Canada Department of Manpower and Immigration, Bank of Nova Scotia, Bell Canada Limited, Canadian Imperial Bank of Commerce, Canadian International Paper Company, Canadian Pacific Railway, Canadian Tax Foundation, Chemcell Limited, Dominion Foundries and Steel Limited, Dominion Stores Limited, The Eaton Foundation, Imperial Oil Limited, IBM Canada Limited, Manufacturers Life Insurance Company, Massey-Ferguson Limited, Noranda Mines Limited, North American Life Assurance Company, Ontario Paper Company, Shell Canada Limited, Sun Life Assurance Company, Thistlebee Research Incorporated, Wood Gundy Securities Limited, The University of Toronto.

The division of labour among the four authors was as follows: Choudhry devised the estimation procedures and the export demand and export price equations. Kotowitz was responsible for the supply side of the model (the production function, labour market, and other price equations), and the corporate profits and tax equations. The non-residential construction and investment in machinery and equipment equations were jointly developed by Kotowitz and Sawyer. Sawyer also served as project co-ordinator, supervised the assembly and modification of the computer programs required for the project, advised on the national accounting framework, was responsible for the consumption and import equations, and edited the present volume. Winder supervised the assembly of a machine-readable data bank for the project and was responsible for the residential construction, inventory, money market, balance of payments, and the personal income tax equations. Choudhry was on leave of absence for the academic year 1969-70; hence, he did not participate in the forecast for 1970 described in Chapter 5. Appendix 2 was prepared by Kotowitz and Appendix 4 by Sawyer.

The project has encouraged several University of Toronto students to write dissertations related to the model. In the Department of Political Economy there have been two PhD theses: C.B. Jutlah, "Income Tax Relationships: Estimation and Role in Economic Stabilization" (1970), and Rasiah Mahalingasivam, "Market for Canadian Refined Copper: An Econometric Study" (1969). In the School of Business, two MBA dissertations were written: N. Papadolias, "The Demand for New Automobiles in Canada, 1952-1966" (1968), and W.M. Putt, "An Econometric Study of Business Capital Formation in Canada" (1967).

A large number of graduate students in the Department of Political Economy and the School of Business worked at various times on the model. We would like to acknowledge particularly the assistance of Mr J.G.A. Vermeeren who has been the principal research assistant for the last two years and who supervised all the computations for the model. We also express our appreciation to Miss Lorell Triolo who has been project secretary since 1968 and who has typed the various working papers and the manuscript of this publication.

At an early stage in the project Professor Laurence R. Klein gave us advice. We also wish to express our appreciation to Professors R.G. Bodkin and Lawrence Officer who read the manuscript and made many helpful comments. Mr R.I.K. Davidson of the University of Toronto Press gave us editorial assistance. This book has been published with the help of a grant from the Social Science Research Council of Canada, using funds provided by the Canada Council.

January, 1971

The TRACE econometric model of the Canadian economy

1 Introduction

1. THE PURPOSE OF THE MODEL

The TRACE model is a nonlinear econometric model of the Canadian economy built using annual data. Its name derives from "Toronto annual Canadian econometric" model. The various versions are referred to by the year in which they were constructed. TRACE 1968 was the first version and was reported on by Choudhry, Kotowitz, Sawyer, and Winder (1968). There are two versions of TRACE 1969. Version A appeared in Choudhry, *et. al* (1969). TRACE 1969B, the one described in the present publication is identical with TRACE 1969A except for the export equations, the employment equation, and the equation for real inventory charge.

The purpose of the model is not to represent all the complexities of the real economic system but, through a set of mathematical functions, to generate time paths for economic variables which follow closely the real world paths of such variables and to relate these paths to policy instrument variables used by the Government of Canada. The TRACE model can be described as a multipurpose model built on the annual Canadian National Income and Expenditure Accounts. It is designed to forecast the majority of the figures appearing in the principal tables of the Accounts. More specifically, five uses of the present version of the model are envisaged: (i) a source of information on estimates of the structural parameters of the Canadian economy, (ii) conditional short-run forecasts, giving alternative forecasts for some alternative combinations of policy instruments which might be selected by the Government of Canada, (iii) policy analysis, i.e., simulations of past periods of time to attempt to assess the implications of alternative fiscal and monetary policy mixes which might have been used, (iv) a teaching device for use in courses in macroeconomics, and (v) a training project for econometric students.

The characteristics of the model changed as we changed the specification of the model to improve its tracking ability and the way in which government policy instruments enter into it. The earlier version of the model, TRACE 1968, had some serious deficiencies which TRACE 1969 tries to remedy. The price disaggregation introduced into TRACE 1969 enables the model to generate both current and constant dollar values for the major components of gross national expenditure. Most of the implicit indexes required for this purpose are endogenous variables in the model, although a few prices and a few components of gross national expenditure are exogenous variables.

The choice of an annual rather than a quarterly model may require some explanation. Since we envisage that ultimately the model may be used both for estimates of structure and for growth analysis, an annual model seemed appropriate. Some quarterly models contain a large number of functions which are essentially autoregressive and which may work well for short-run forecasting but which provide little information on the underlying structure of the economy and are generally not reliable for longer-run projections. Moreover, a quarterly model has to be confined to the postwar period. An annual model can draw on the variety of experience of the late 1920s and 1930s and avoid some of the problems of multicollinearity which exist when estimates are made only from postwar data. Unfortunately, however, data for some balance of payments series exist only for the postwar period and many monetary series do not exist prior to the establishment of the Bank of Canada in 1935. The balance of payment equations and the monetary equations were therefore estimated only for the postwar period. Simulations can therefore be performed only for the postwar period, although data for the prewar period were used to estimate many of the structural parameters. The years 1941-6 were not used for estimating the parameters because of the existence of wartime controls. We were conscious throughout of the possibility of changes in the structural relations over such a long period. Thus we tested for consistency of postwar experience with the full period results. When a break in the series was evident, we allowed for it by dummy variables or by estimating the relevant equation using data for 1947-66 only.

A few comments on some of the other econometric models of Canada may help to explain why the decision to build the TRACE model was made. The oldest model of Canada is one dating from 1947 and now in the Department of Finance in Ottawa. It was originally designed by Professor Lawrence R. Klein for the Department of Reconstruction and Supply in collaboration with T. Merritt Brown, Donald J. Daly, and Henry Grayson. (See Brown (1970), pp. 355-65.) Later versions of this model were constructed by Brown and Sidney May. (See Brown (1970), pp. 366-87, Brown (1964a), and May (1966).) The model is in its sixteenth version and has been used continuously for annual forecasting up to the present. It has remained a relatively small model with little articulation of specific policy instruments appearing in it. The forecasts from this model were always kept secret by the Government of Canada until long after the forecast period had passed into history. While in the mid-1960s various versions of the model were published and the current version was made available by the Department of Finance, complete data for the model were unavailable since a number of specially-constructed unpublised series were used. Persons outside the government were therefore unable to use the model for forecasts or simulations of the behaviour of the economy.

Other models of the Canadian economy have been constructed for specific purposes: Brown's model (1964b) of Canadian economic growth, Rudolf Rhomberg's model (1964) and Lawrence Officer's model (1968) of the Canadian economy under the fluctuating foreign exchange rate of the 1950s. None of these models were intended to be carried on as continuing models and none was designed to be used for short-term forecasting.

In the mid-1960s independent decisions were made to build four new models of the Canadian economy. One new model appeared at the Bank of Canada where Helliwell, Officer, Shapiro and Stewart (1969a) produced RDX1 and its successor RDX2 is currently being produced. These models are quarterly models containing a large amount of detail on the monetary and fiscal sectors of the economy in addition to a detailed explanation of the workings of the real sector of the economy. The models are being used for policy simulations (see Helliwell, Officer, Shapiro and Stewart (1969b, 1969c). If forecasts are made from them within the Bank of Canada, it appears that the forecasts will not be made public. RDX1 itself is publicly available, including both the computer program and data bank to do simulations with it, so that others can work with the model.[1] At Queen's University, Tsurumi and Prachowny (1968) produced a long-term growth model. (See also Tsurumi (1970).) At the Economic Council of Canada the decision was made to produce a model useful for medium-term projections. For various reasons work on it was delayed and a first version by Agarwala, Downs, Illing, and Tjan (1970) has just appeared. At the University of Toronto, the TRACE model was constructed.[2]

The simultaneous outpouring of these models in Canada resulted in part from a maturing of the field of econometric model-building in the United States as evidenced by the successful operation of the Klein-Goldberger model at the University of Michigan by Daniel Suits (1962), the development of a model at the Wharteon School of Finance and Commerce of the University of Pennsylvania by Michael Evans and Lawrence Klein (1968), and the construction of a large-scale model by Duesenberry, Fromm, Klein, and Kuh (1965) now located in the Brookings Institution. The usefulness of econometric models for policy analysis and forecasting was now clearly demonstrated and sufficient technical resources were now available in Canada to make the econometric model building operations referred to above feasible.

The TRACE model was constructed so that there would be a model which could be used by university economists for regular short-term economic forecasts which would be made public. The first of these forecasts, a forecast for 1970 made in 1969, is discussed in Chapter 5.[3] The TRACE model is the first Canadian econometric model from which a *published ex ante* forecast has ever been made.[4] In order to have informed debate on government economic policy, it is necessary to have regular forecasts of the effects of alternative government policies on the economic outlook. Since the Government of Canada gave no indication of its willingness to publish its forecasts, it was necessary to have a model in the public domain which could be used to evaluate government policies. To use an econometric model for this purpose requires that the analysts be thoroughly familiar with the model they are using. Obviously, the best situation is where the analysts are the model builders. The TRACE model was built to meet this need. An important by-product of the project has been, however, the contribution the project has made to the teaching of macroeconomics at the University of Toronto (and at other universities) where it has been used to display the structure of the Canadian economy. A model such as this, when operational on a computer system, provides for the economist the equivalent of the physicist's laboratory facilities for conducting experiments.

1 See Jump (1970) for an evaluation of the model.
2 Some comparison of the characteristics of RDX1, TRACE, and the Tsurumi-Prachowny model appears in Sawyer (1969).
3 The forecast was originally published in Kotowitz, Sawyer, and Winder (1969).
4 A forecast for 1971 from the TRACE model was made by Sawyer and is published in Jump, Sawyer, and Winder (1970). Forecasts from newly-developed quarterly models are also contained in this publication, for the real sectors by Gregory Jump and for the financial sector by John Winder.

2 AN OVERVIEW OF THE TRACE MODEL

Before looking at the complete model, it may be helpful to give a quick outline of its main characteristics. The model aggregates both transactors and market transactions. Transactors are aggregated into four sectors: (i) the personal sector, which includes households and private noncommercial institutions, (ii) the business sector, which includes business firms and government business enterprises, (iii) the government sector, which includes all government departments and other public institutions, and (iv) the rest of the world. Markets are aggregated into (i) an aggregate commodity (goods and services market), (ii) an aggregate money market, (iii) an aggregate labour market, and (iv) a foreign exchange market, although the supply side of each of these markets is not completely specified.

Some markets include lagged adjustments on both the supply and demand side and thus short-term solutions are different from long-run equilibrium values. Since variables dated at different points of time appear, once the initial conditions and values of exogenous variables are given the model will generate values of endogenous variables for future periods of time. Thus, the model may be termed a dynamic disequilibrium model in contrast to the static equilibrium models of many textbooks.

The model is dynamic in a second sense since the stock of physical capital, which affects production as well as the demand for commodities and labour, changes through time as capital formation augments it and depreciation diminishes it.

Some special features of the model deserve mention at this point. First, we attempted to specify both the aggregate supply function for the economy and the investment function in a manner that was consistent with a constant-elasticity-of-substitution (CES) production function. This enables the model, with some modifications, to be used for the analysis of medium-term growth. In particular, the patterns of substitution between labour and capital and the distribution of factor incomes can be traced over time. In this respect, the model is different from most econometric models which emphasize the short-run income determination from the demand side.

Second, the large volume of foreign trade and capital flows in the Canadian economy requires a considerable degree of detail in the specification of these sectors. This problem was also complicated by the existence of periods of flexible and fixed exchange rates within the estimation period. While these equations are not as elaborate as in the model of Lawrence Officer (1968), they are considerably more important and detailed than in most models of other countries. In particular, exports are disaggregated in considerable detail by commodity and destination and are made endogenous. Imports, exports, and export prices are all affected by Canadian prices and wages. This leads to an increased sensitivity of the aggregate demand for Canadian commodities to Canadian prices and thus increases the feedback of prices on output. The inclusion of the flexible exchange rate as well as the fixed exchange rate period within the same model enables us to analyse the differences of patterns of adjustment of the economy in these periods. (See Chapter 4.)

Third, we have disaggregated prices to an unusual extent in order to predict the major National Accounts components in both real and money values. The specification of the supply side of these disaggregated expenditure categories is incomplete, so these prices are mainly derived from the aggregate price level. Even this imperfect procedure does allow, however, for some explanation of the variation of the movement of the implicit price indexes of the various categories of gross national expenditure.

Since the model is large and complex, its basic structure is not easily seen. The large number of interdependent equations makes it almost impossible to analyse the aggregate behaviour of the model except by simulation. While this complexity of large-scale econometric models is unavoidable, and indeed is the main advantage of such models, it may nevertheless obscure the basic structure of the model. Unless all equations in the model conform to our basic view of the way in which the economy works, specific assumptions embedded in an individual equation or in some complex inter-relationship within the structure of the model may lead to peculiar results when simulations are performed with the complete model. The culprit may sometimes be identified by appropriate simulations but such simulations are expensive. We considered it therefore inadvisable to build up the model in a disaggregated fashion equation by equation. Rather we decided at the outset to construct a relatively simple aggregate macroeconomic model which will embody our view of the working of the economy. While this prototype model was not estimated, it served as a skeleton from which disaggregation into individual sectors and expenditure categories proceeded. The simulation results can therefore be cast within the framework of the simplified model and the crucial assumptions leading to specific simulation results can be identified. The simplified model thus explicitly connects our econometric model with the main line of macroeconomic theory.

We present below this simplified version of the model. The major simplification is the use of a single price index, the implicit price of gross national product at market prices, as the deflator for all flows expressed in dollars of constant purchasing power. Other simplifications include the aggregation of some expenditure categories, the aggregation of all production sectors, the ignoring of corporate saving, and the use of a single interest rate and a single tax rate.

Our general approach is to derive an aggregate demand and an aggregate supply relation.[5] Aggregate demand is a negative function of prices and many exogenous and predetermined variables. Aggregate supply is a positive function of prices and some predetermined and exogenous variables. The equality of short-term aggregate demand and supply determines the annual values of gross national product and its price and, simultaneously, the values of the other endogenous variables. Due to the existence of lagged adjustment functions, to capital formation, and to exogenous labour force growth, both aggregate demand and supply keep shifting and generating new values of output and prices in successive periods of time. We shall present the equations of the simplified model in a manner to demonstrate the structure of the aggregate demand and supply functions. This is a different ordering of the equations from that used in Chapter 2 where the model is presented block by block.

(a) Definition of Variables

A lower case letter indicates a quantity in constant dollars or in physical units (except

---

5 The reader may find it of interest to compare this presentation of our model with the expository model of Ball and Bodkin (1963).

for f which is used as the general symbol for a function). Upper case letters denote a quantity in current dollars, a price index, or a percentage. As a superscript F means foreign and S means quantity supplied. The subscript t indicates the year to which the value refers. Flows are measured over the length of a year. Stocks are measured at the end of the year. Greek letters refer to rates which may vary over time. B = index of import prices, c = personal expenditure on consumer goods and services, d = personal disposable income, E = foreign exchange rate, G,g = government expenditure on goods and services, GAP = utilization rate (a proxy for the proportion of productive capacity utilized), H = foreign exchange reserves, i = business gross fixed capital formation, J = index of world prices of exports, k = stock of producers' capital goods (including housing) at the end of the year, s = stock of goods in inventories at the end of the period, L = net capital inflow, M = stock of money at the end of the year, n = employment in man-hours per year, n^S = labour force in man-hours per year, P = implicit price index of gross national product (GNP), POP = population, q = imports of goods and services, R = rate of interest, R^F = rate of interest in the rest of the world, t = time, U = unemployment rate, v = value of the physical change in inventories, W = wage rate, x = exports of goods and services, Y, y, y^S = gross national product (GNP) at market prices, y^F = an index of GNP in the rest of the world, y^o = potential GNP, δ = rate of capital consumption, τ = rate of taxation. Endogenous variables are shown on the left-hand side of the twenty equations which comprise the simplified model. Exogenous variables are: B, J, n^S, R^F, y^F, t, δ, POP. Instrument variables in the model are: G, M, τ.

(b) Aggregate Demand

(i) Demand for Commodities

(1) Personal disposable income:

$$d = (1 - \tau)y_t.$$

(2) Personal expenditure on consumer goods and services:

$$c_t = f(d_t, R_t, c_{t-1}, POP).$$

(3) Government expenditure on goods and services:

$$g_t = G_t/P_t.$$

(4) Business gross fixed capital formation:

$$i_t = f(GAP_t, R_t, k_{t-1}, i_{t-1}).$$

(5) Value of the physical change in inventories:

$$v_t = f(c_{t-1}, c_{t-2}, y_t, s_{t-1}).$$

(6) Exports of goods and services:

$$x_t = f(y_t^F, P_t, J_t, E_t).$$

(7) Imports of goods and services:

$$q_t = f(y_t, GAP_t, P_t, B_t, E_t).$$

(8) Total aggregate demand: gross national product at market prices (constant dollars):

$$y_t = c_t + g_t + i_t + v_t + x_t - q_t.$$

(9) Gross national product at market prices (current dollars):

$$Y_t = P_t y_t.$$

The fixed capital formation and inventory change equations are stock-adjustment equations which imply a lagged adjustment of actual capital stocks to desired capital stocks. Desired stocks are a function of expected output or consumer spending.

(ii)   Money Market and Foreign Exchange Market

(10) Rate of interest:

$$R_t = f(M_t/Y_t, R^F).$$

(11) Inflow of capital (net):

$$L_t = f(R_t/R_t^F, i_t).$$

(12) Foreign exchange reserves:

$$H_t = H_{t-1} + P_t x_t - B_t q_t + L_t.$$

The model assumes exchange rates are fixed except for the years 1950-61 when the rate was floating. In those years, the endogenous variable is the exchange rate.

$$E_t = f(R_t/R_t^F, H_t - H_{t-1}). \tag{12a}$$

(iii) Potential Output and the Utilization Rate

(13) Stock of business fixed capital:

$$k_t = i_t + (1 - \delta)k_{t-1}.$$

(14) Potential gross national product:

$$y_t^o = f(k_{t-1}, n_t^S, t).$$

(15) Utilization rate:

$$GAP_t = (y_t/y_t^o).$$

A production function (equation 14) is used to define potential (full employment) output. The utilization rate, an indicator of whether full capacity is being utilized, is the ratio of actual to potential output.

Equations 1-15 can now be summarized by substituting for the values of c_t, g_t, i_t, v_t, x_t, and q_t in equation 8 from equations 2-7, to give

$$y_t = f(d_t, R_t, GAP_t, y_t, P_t, E_t; c_{t-1}, k_{t-1}, i_{t-1}, c_{t-2}, s_{t-1}; G_t, POP_t, J_t, B_t, y_t^F).$$

Substituting again for d_t, R_t, and GAP_t from equations 1, 10, 14, and 15, and assuming E_t is exogenous, we get the short-run aggregate demand function:

$$y_t = f(P_t; c_{t-1}, k_{t-1}, i_{t-1}, c_{t-2}, s_{t-1}, H_{t-1}; G_t, POP_t, J_t, B_t, y_t^F, E_t, M_t, R_t^F, \tau, n^S, t).$$

This demand function has a negative slope because of the direct effect of prices on imports, on the real value of government expenditure, and on exports, and the indirect effects of prices on the real value of money. Exports are a negative function of prices because export prices (which are endogenous in the complete model) depend on Canadian prices (cost effect) and foreign demand for Canadian exports is a negative function of their price relative to competing sources. Imports are a positive function of Canadian prices. Therefore, a price increase will reduce aggregate demand in the absence of an exchange rate adjustment. Since government expenditure on goods and services is given in money terms, any increase in prices will result in a corresponding proportional decrease in real government expenditure. Finally, an increase in prices, given the nominal quantity of money, results in a proportional decrease in the real money supply. This raises the rate of interest and thus reduces the level of business gross capital formation.

Since the elasticity of each effect separately on the respective components of aggregate demand turned out to be equal to or smaller than one[6] and since price directly affects only part of aggregate demand, the total elasticity of the aggregate demand curve with respect to prices is quite small. As imports, exports, and government expenditure do not appear with a lag, the elasticity of the aggregate demand curve is increased only slightly in the long run due to the indirect effects of lagged investment and consumption. Figure 1 illustrates this relation between aggregate demand and price.

The mechanisms described are complicated somewhat in the case of a flexible exchange rate. An increase in price will generate a deficit in the balance of trade which will be somewhat offset by the reduction in real income, but the higher interest rate

6 This conclusion is based on the empirical results presented in Chapter 2.

resulting from the decrease in the real money supply (since the nominal supply of money is exogenous) will increase the inflow of capital. Whether a devaluation or an appreciation will result depends on the relative strengths of these effects. An appreciation will increase the impact on income and therefore will lead to a higher elasticity of the aggregate demand curve with respect to prices, while a devaluation will reduce this elasticity. We comment further on the relative magnitudes of these effects in Chapter 4.

The aggregate demand function shifts upward to the right in each period due to population growth, growth in foreign income and prices, and growth in the policy variables (government expenditure on goods and services and the money supply). Aggregate demand growth is also dependent on the rate of growth of the capital stock, since the utilization rate, which depends on productive capacity, enters into the import and captial formation equations.

(c) *Aggregate Supply*

(16) Employment:

$$n_t = f(y_t^S, k_{t-1}, t, n_{t-1}).$$

(17) Unemployment rate:

$$U = [(n_t^S - n_t)/n_t^S].$$

(18) Wage rate (nominal):

$$\dot{W}_t = f(\dot{P}_t, U_t^{-1}).$$

where the dot operator ($\cdot$) denotes the rate of change in the variable, i.e.,

$$\dot{W}_t = (W_t - W_{t-1})/W_{t-1}.$$

(19) Prices:

$$\dot{P}_t = f[\dot{W}_t, \dot{B}_t, (y_t^S/n_t), \dot{P}_{t-1}].$$

Employment is determined by the amount of labour input required to produce the desired output (y_t^S), given the stock of capital in place and the production function. The rate of change of money wages is determined according to a Phillips curve. The price equation is a marginal cost function derived on the assumption that labour will be hired until its marginal revenue product is equal to its marginal cost, subject to a constant-elasticity-of-substitution production function and import competition.

Equations 16-19 are four equations with five endogenous variables n_t, y_t^S, W_t, U_t, and P_t. They can be solved for aggregate supply as a function of the price level, lagged endogenous variables, and the exogenous variables B, n^S and t.

From our simulation experiments (Chapter 4), it appears that the slope of the short-run aggregate supply function is almost horizontal up to a level of output $(\mathbf{y}_1)$ equivalent to about 6 per cent unemployment from which point it curves upwards becoming asymptotically vertical at the level of output $(\mathbf{y}_2)$ equivalent to zero unemployment (see Figure 1).

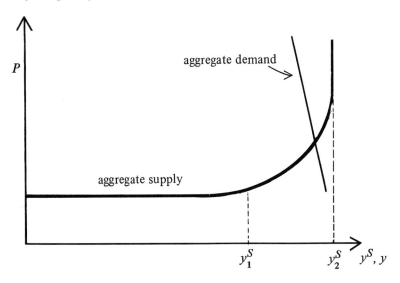

Figure 1 Aggregate demand and supply functions

Prices and output are determined in any year by the intersection of the short-run aggregate demand and supply functions, i.e.,

$$y_t^S = y_t \tag{20}$$

Growth of the labour force (n^S), technology (t), and capital (k) shift the aggregate supply curve downward and to the right in each period. Price and wage inflation in any period have an opposite influence on the supply curve for the following period in that they establish a new higher short-run supply price for any level of aggregate output. This is because equations 18 and 19 are in terms of rates of change and therefore the aggregate supply curve is a function of last period's level of prices and wages. The net effect will typically be a rightward shift in aggregate supply.

Since aggregate demand is shifting rightward as well, the level of real output is constantly increasing. The rate of change in the price level depends, of course, on the relative strengths of the shifts in aggregate demand and supply. Typically, the relative rightward shift in demand would appear to be greater. In part, this is because previously realized inflation does not affect the position of the aggregate demand curve and, in part, it is because accommodating or expansionary monetary and fiscal policies have their short-run impact on the position of the aggregate demand schedule, not the aggregate supply schedule.

The high degree of simultaneity within the model is illustrated in the following flow chart (Figure 2) for the simplified version of the model presented above.

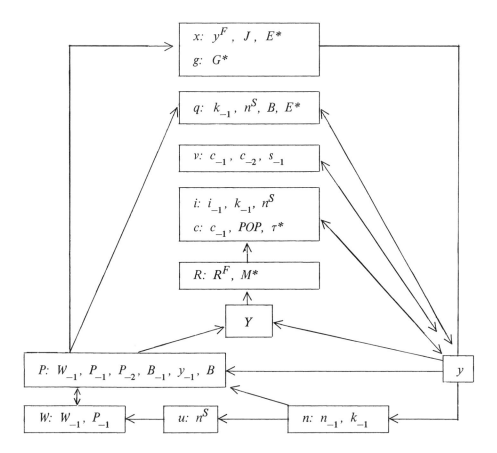

*Variables appearing above or to the left of the colon in any box are current endogenous. Policy instruments are denoted by an asterisk and predetermined variables by a subscript. Remaining variables are current exogenous. For the years 1950-1961 of floating exchange rate, E^* is replaced by E with the following linkages:

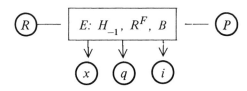

Figure 2 Flow chart for simplified version of the model.

2 The model

1. ESTIMATION PROCEDURE

All equations, with the exception of the export and foreign exchange equations, were estimated by two-stage least squares. For this purpose, principal components of the set of exogenous and lagged endogenous variables which enter into the model were computed for the complete period 1928-66 (excluding 1941-6) and for the period 1947-66. Equations which were estimated for the complete period were estimated by regressing at the first stage the endogenous variables on principal components 1, 2, 3, 4, 5, 6, 7, 8, 9, 11, 12, 14, 15, and 16. The postwar equations were estimated using principal components 1, 2, 3, 4, 5, 6, 7, 8, 9, 11, 14, 15, 17, and 19. The choice of principal components was based on an attempt to obtain a balance between explaining all the systematic variation of the endogenous variables in the model and attempting to avoid the error of including some of the stochastic variation in the calculated values from the first stage. Some principal components were omitted because they did not seem to contribute significantly to the explanation of key endogenous variables in the model. Inclusion of a longer list would, particularly for the post-war period, have used up too many degrees of freedom and would have resulted in the error of explaining all the variation, both systematic and stochastic, in the endogenous variables. At the second stage of the regression, endogenous variables were replaced by the calculated values from the regression on the above-mentioned set of principal components. We did not include directly the exogenous variables which enter into a specific equation as regressors in the first stage. Such exogenous variables entered indirectly through the set of principal components.

2. NOTATION AND ORDERING OF THE EQUATIONS OF THE MODEL

The equations of the model are presented at the end of this chapter. The model is presented in the form in which it is used in computer programs for solution of the system of simultaneous equations comprising the model. Each equation has been normalized so that a single endogenous variable appears on the left-hand side of an equation and there is one equation for each endogenous variable in the model. The equations are therefore not always presented in the form in which they were estimated. Equations in which exponential terms appear were estimated in the logarithms of the variables. In section 4 where the model is explained equation by equation, our system of notation is explained using equation A.1, the consumer durable goods expenditure equation, as an example.

The model contains 67 stochastic equations and 120 identities. The number of essential identities in the model is 52; the remaining 68 identities serve only a convenience function in defining intermediate variables thus making it possible to write some equations in a more concise manner. In 14 of the stochastic equations the dependent variable is a function of only exogenous variables or lagged endogenous variables. The values of the dependent variables in these 14 equations can be obtained without reference to the rest of the system and then used in solving the remaining equations. The remaining 53 stochastic equations[1] and most of the identities form a block of simultaneous equations. The remaining identities can be solved after this simultaneous block is solved. These latter identities are present in the model simply because of the desire to obtain estimates of the values of some variables implied by the solution of the model. Calculation of a residual quantity such as personal saving, even though it means introducing some additional variables into the model, provides a useful check on the reasonableness of the results from the whole model.

The fact that 53 of the 67 stochastic equations are in a single simultaneous block within which there is no recursive ordering of sub-blocks indicates the very high degree of simultaneity in the model. This means that a change in any one of the equations affects almost all the endogenous variables of the model. It also complicates the task of detecting and correcting those equations whose incorrect specification is responsible for divergences between simulation results and actual values of variables. To some extent, of course, some of these divergences are due to random disturbances and cannot be removed by respecifying the systematic part of the stochastic equations.

3. SOLUTION OF THE NON-LINEAR SYSTEM OF EQUATIONS

Various computer programs are available for solving systems of non-linear equations by methods such as Newton's or Seidel's.[2] Care must be taken in ordering the equations but the general experience has been that if the equations are ordered in an approximately causal ordering, as the economist would naturally order them, the solution converges quickly. The listing of equations at the end of this chapter is in the actual order used in solving the system.

In making conditional forecasts, the assumption is made that the stochastic disturbance term in the structural equations takes on its expected value. This term is assumed to have an expected value of zero and a normal distribution. Where the equation is of the form

$$y_t = a + \beta x_t + u_t$$

where x and y are endogenous or exogenous variables and u is the disturbance term, u_t is set equal to zero when forecasting. In multiplicative specifications, such as the production function, of the form

$$y_t = a x_t^\beta e^{u_t}$$

---

1 Nine of these equations are functions of only exogenous variables or lagged endogenous variables during the period of the fixed foreign exchange rate.

2 The solution program used was originally written by Michael Hartley for the Economics Research Unit of the Wharton School of Finance and Commerce of the University of Pennsylvania and was adapted for our use by J.G.A. Vermeeren. A discussion of solution procedure can be found in Evans and Klein (1968, pp. 39-49).

the expected value of e^{u_t} is $e^{0.5\sigma^2}$, where σ^2 is the variance of u_t, provided the expected value of u_t is zero and u_t is normally distributed.[3] Hence, for multiplicative equations an additional constant term appears in the form $EXP(0.5*X)$, where X is the estimate of the variance of the disturbance term (the square of SDR).

4. THE MODEL: SECTION BY SECTION

A. *Personal Expenditure on Consumer Goods and Services*

All three consumption functions are expressed in constant dollars per person and estimated using data for 1928-66 (excluding 1941-6). The equation for personal expenditure on consumer durable goods follows an approach of T. M. Brown (1952) developed to reflect habit persistence and lags in consumer behaviour. The form of the equation is

$$c_t/POP_t = a + \beta(c_{t-1}/POP_{t-1}) + \gamma(y_t/POP_t) + \delta(Q_t/P_t) + \lambda R_t$$

where c is personal expenditure on consumer durable goods in billions of constant (1957) dollars, POP is population in millions, y is personal disposable income in billions of constant (1957) dollars, Q is the implicit price index of personal expenditure on consumer durable goods (1957 = 1.0), P is the implicit price index of total personal expenditure on consumer goods and services (1957 = 1.0), R is a long-term rate of interest expressed as a percentage.

Translating this equation into our Fortran variable names following the principles explained at the beginning of Appendix 1 and inserting the estimated values of the parameters we obtain equation A.1:

$$DUR3RC = 0.119 + 0.419*DUR3SC + 0.104*PDI3RC - 0.134*PD2/PC2$$
$$(2.89) \quad (3.46) \qquad\qquad (6.00) \qquad\qquad (3.75)$$

$$- 0.00793*LIC. \tag{A.1}$$
$$(2.51)$$

The definitions of all variables are listed in Appendix 1. Some comments on our system of variable names may be helpful. The system that we have adopted in place of the usual algebraic symbols has resulted from experience on our part with various problems concerning units of measurement and the need, in order to reduce errors, of a single version of the model which would be used for all purposes. This meant that our variable names had to meet the constraints imposed by the Fortran language used for our computer programs. We feel, however, that these disadvantages are far outweighed by the convenience in working with a model whose equations are written in a machine-readable language. Anyone doing simulations on a computer with an econometric model must learn to work with variable names written in this form if he wishes to make changes in the model specification in the process of his experiments. Thus, the writing of the equations of a model in a machine-readable language such as Fortran

3 See Aitchison and Brown (1957, p. 8).

is becoming increasingly common. All the models in Project LINK (an international project to link the national econometric models of various countries) are now written in standardized machine-readable variable names instead of in algebraic form. (The equations of the models in Project LINK will be published using these standardized names in a forthcoming book. The Canadian model in Project LINK is the TRACE model.)

The reader should now read the first section of Appendix 1 where he will find an explanation of how the name DUR3RC is derived for personal expenditure on consumer durable goods per person in thousands of constant (1957) dollars. Since price indexes are normally thought as having a base equal to 100 whereas our indexes are base equal to 1.0, we have written them as, for example, PC2 to indicate that one multiplies the value in our data bank by 10^2 to put the index into the conventional form in which it appears in the published statistical data sources. Since PC2 has only 2 letters for the basic name, the digit 2 is actually in the fourth position in the 6-character field available for the variable name. We have found the incorporation of the unit of measurement into the variable name has been very convenient and it has reduced the number of errors resulting from misunderstanding units of measurement, particularly when a transformation is performed on a variable.

To read the equations it is necessary to know the Fortran symbols for certain algebraic operations. Exponential terms such as e^x are written in Fortran as EXP(X). The operation of multiplication is indicated by an asterisk; thus, a multiplied by y is written $a*Y$. The operation of raising a variable to a power is indicated by a double asterisk; thus, x^2 is written $X**2$. The operation of division is indicated by a slash; thus, x divided by y is written X/Y. Parentheses are used, as in ordinary algebra, to indicate the set of variables on which the operations are performed.

Some further explanation of the way in which the equations are presented in the listing at the end of this chapter is in order. The numbers 1, 2, or 3, appearing in the sixth column of Fortran statements are continuation numbers to indicate when an equation is continued on a following line. The values appearing in parentheses underneath estimates of coefficients are ratios of the coefficient value to the standard error of the coefficient.[4] If certain assumptions are made about the error term in the specification of the equation, as is well-known, these may be interpreted as t-statistics. The value for RBSQ is the coefficient of multiple determination adjusted for degrees of freedom. SDR is the standard deviation of regression (or standard error of estimate) given in the units of the dependent variable of the equation, except where the regression was run on the logarithm of the dependent variable. DW is the Durbin-Watson statistic and PD indicates the period for which data were used to estimate parameters of the equation. OLS indicates that ordinary least squares was used; otherwise two-stage least squares was used.

In equation A.1 the long-term interest rate enters with a coefficient that is statistically significantly different from zero but whose magnitude is so small that the presence of this term in the equation does not create a strong link between the commodity and money markets. The relative price of durable goods to the total price of consumer goods and services plays a significant role in explaining durable goods ex-

---

4 Where two-stage least squares estimation was used, the standard errors are the asymptotic standard errors.

penditure. The long-run marginal propensity to consume durables exceeds the short-run propensity as a result of the habit persistence hypothesis incorporated into the specification of the equation. This contrasts with an inventory effect of an increase in the stock of durables which would lead to the long-run propensity being less than the short-run propensity as has been found by Houthakker and Taylor (1966, pp. 15-16).

The nondurables and services equations are modifications of the Houthakker-Taylor (1966) specification.[5] For commodities of which consumers do not hold physical inventories of any significance, Houthakker and Taylor interpret their model as relating to the psychological stocks of consumer habits. Equations A.2 and A.3 are estimated from this specification with the modification that personal disposable income is used as the explanatory variable instead of total expenditure on consumer goods and services. The general form of the Houthakker-Taylor specification as modified for equations A.2 and A.3 is

$$c_t/POP_t = a + \beta(c_{t-1}/POP_{t-1}) + \gamma(y_{t-1}/POP_{t-1}) + \delta\left[(y_t/POP_t)\right.$$
$$\left. - (y_{t-1}/POP_{t-1})\right] + \lambda(Q_{t-1}/P_{t-1}) + \mu\left[(Q_t/P_t) - (Q_{t-1}/P_{t-1})\right].$$

where the c, Q and P now refer to consumer nondurable goods in equation A.2 and services in equation A.3.

Translated into our notation and inserting the estimated values of the parameters we obtain

$$\begin{aligned} ND3RC = \ &0.076 + 0.519*ND3SC + 0.181*PDI3SC + 0.217*PDI3RD \\ &\quad\quad\quad (6.83) \quad\quad\quad (6.16) \quad\quad\quad\quad (5.50) \end{aligned}$$

$$\begin{aligned} &- 0.0313*PND21/PC21 \\ &\quad (0.87) \end{aligned} \tag{A.2}$$

$$\begin{aligned} SER3RC = \ &-0.00228 + 0.767*SER3SC + 0.0853*PDI3SC + 0.189*PDI3RD \\ &\quad (0.45) \quad\quad (8.66) \quad\quad\quad\quad (5.50) \quad\quad\quad\quad (6.03) \end{aligned}$$

$$\begin{aligned} &- 0.0390(PSR2/PC2 - PSR21/PC21). \\ &\quad (0.70) \end{aligned} \tag{A.3}$$

The relative price terms of the original specifications did not perform well in either equation and only one price term was left in each. Both parameter estimates are statistically insignificant but their presence makes it possible for the effect of shifts in relative prices to be captured by the model. From these equations the short-run marginal propensity to consume nondurables is 0.17 and to consume services is also 0.17; the respective long-run (stationary state) marginal propensities are both 0.37.[6]

Including expenditure on durable goods the sum of three short-run marginal pro-

5 The Houthakker-Taylor specification for the case of discrete time periods can be derived directly without the use of calculus, as has been shown by Winder (1971) and Schweitzer (1970). Winder has also related this specification to stock-adjustment models of the usual type which specify a desired stock relationship and a gradual rate of adjustment of actual to desired stock.
6 The short-run marginal propensity to consume in the Houthakker-Taylor specification is $2(\delta - \gamma/2)/(1 + \beta)$. See Houthakker-Taylor (1966, p. 15).

pensities to consume is 0.44, which seems low, while the sum of the long-run marginal propensities to consume is 0.92. The same specification when fitted to data for the period 1947-66 gives a LRMPC of 0.85. Since the average propensity to consume and the long-run marginal propensity to consume should not be significantly different, we used the parameter estimates based on the full period. The average propensity to spend the full period was 0.94. It may be that the high degree of collinearity of variables in the post-war period gave rise to the unsatisfactory estimate for the post-war period.

B. *Government Expenditure on Goods and Services*

Government expenditure on goods and services consists of three major components: (i) civilian wages and salaries (WSG9), (ii) military pay and allowances (MPA9), and (iii) other expenditure (GNW9). No distinction is made between expenditure on current and capital account. All three components are taken as exogenous variables in nominal dollars.

Government non-wage expenditure (GNW9) is deflated by the implicit price index of final expenditure on goods and services by Canadians (PYI2). (See equation G.4.) The deflator for wages and salaries and military pay and allowances (PGW2) is derived residually in the sample period as the weighted difference between PYI2 and the implicit price index of total government expenditure on goods and services (PG2). For forecasts and simulations, however, PGW2 becomes an exogenous variable and PG2 is a weighted average of PGW2 and PYI2 (equation B.3).

Government real expenditure on goods and services (equation B.2) is therefore an endogenous variable in the model. For forecasts and simulations the model assumes that governments determine wage and salary rates and employment levels and budget other expenditures in nominal dollars. The price of their non-wage and salary expenditure is, however, beyond their control. In so far as they fail to predict PYI2 correctly, their actual real expenditure will be different from anticipated expenditure. Hence, they will miscalculate the real multiplier effects of changes in nominal non-wage and salary expenditure (GNW9).

C. *Business Gross Capital Formation*

(i) Residential Construction

The specification of the equations in the residential construction sector reflects in part the valuable work done in this area by Lawrence Smith and therefore is similar in some respects to the corresponding sector of RDX1.[7] Professor Smith utilized the rather extensive body of research studies relating to particular aspects of mortgage markets

7 See especially, Smith (1969a), and Helliwell, Officer, Shapiro, and Stewart (1969a, pp. 6-8). The reader may wish to compare the flow charts in each of these publications with our own. The distinction between the single and multiple dwelling unit sectors of the housing market which we have tried to make is the basis of Smith (1969b). The adjustment mechanism by which monetary influences are transmitted to the real economy via the residential construction sector through the mortgage investment behaviour of mortgage lending institutions has been developed more fully in Smith and Sparks (1970).

and residential construction in order to develop a complete housing and mortgage market model for Canada, with particular emphasis placed upon the role of financial variables. While it therefore seemed eminently sensible to start with Professor Smith's work, we have in fact modified his structures to such an extent that he is, of course, in no way responsible for the result.

The modifications were designed to produce a series of equations more compatible with our own over-all model. This involved not only the transition from a quaterly to an annual basis but an attempt to economize on equations and variables. We were not prepared to cope with the financial and institutional detail that constitute much of the richness of Smith's work. We have therefore ignored such things as construction costs and restricted ourselves mainly to interest rates and demand variables which appear elsewhere in our model. The basic theme remains: interest sensitive mortgage flows influence housing starts and therefore residential construction spending. The actual empirical formulation of this nexus has been restructured for our model.

Constant dollar expenditure on new residential construction is determined by completions of single and multiple dwelling units in the same year (equation C.7). Real expenditure per dwelling unit is two-thirds greater for single than for multiple units completed. Completions of single units depend upon starts of single units in the same and preceding years (equation C.6). The coefficients sum to 0.996 rather than unity. After adjustment for this slight discrepancy the implication is that about 87 per cent of single completions within any year were started within that same year. Completions of multiple units are similarly dependent upon current and lagged starts (equation C.5). In this case the coefficients sum to 0.968. After adjustment for this discrepancy from unity the coefficients imply that 46 per cent of multiple unit completions within any year were started within that same year.

Starts are related to mortgage approvals measured in real dollars (equations C.3 and C.4): current National Housing Act (NHA) approvals made directly by Central Mortgage and Housing (CMHC), current and lagged NHA approvals made by institutional lenders, and current approvals of conventional mortgages. The implicit price deflator for residential construction was used in every case to obtain constant dollar approval series. It was not possible to distinguish between approvals for single and multiple units; single starts are therefore regressed upon the total of each type of approvals, as are multiple starts. This aggregation problem may account for the negative coefficients for conventional approvals in the equation for single starts and lagged NHA approvals by institutional tenders in the equation for multiple starts.

Direct NHA mortgage approvals by CMHC are exogenous. Other NHA approvals by approved lenders (equation C.1) depend upon population, the maximum rate on NHA loans and the differential between this rate and the long-term interest rate in the model, unemployment, a three-period weighted average of the rent-cost index relative to the implicit deflator of residential construction, and the beginning-of-period stock of residential construction. Conventional mortgage approvals (equation C.2) also depend upon population, the long-term rate and its differential with the NHA maximum rate, with the GAP (utilization rate) variable instead of the unemployment rate. In each case the specification is essentially a reduced form which does not distinguish between the demand for and the supply of mortgage loans. On balance it is evident that conventional mortgage approvals have been influenced relatively more by supply considerations than have approvals of NHA loans by institutional lenders. Figure 3 summarizes these relations.

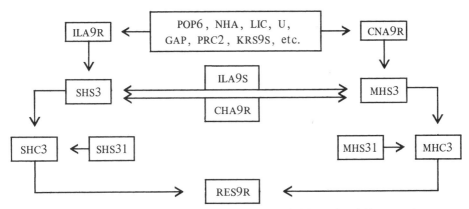

Figure 3 Flowchart for residential construction sector. Definitions of variables: CHA9R = NHA mortgage approvals by CMHC, deflated by PRS2, ILA9R = NHA mortgage approvals by institutional lenders other than CMHC, deflated by PRS2, CNA9R = conventional mortgage approvals, deflated by PRS2, SHS3 = single housing starts, SHS31 = single housing starts lagged one year, MHS3 = multiple housing starts, MHS31 = multiple housing starts lagged one year, SHC3 = single housing completions, MHC3 = multiple housing completions, PRS2 = implicit deflator for residential construction, POP = population, LIC = long-term interest rate, NHA = maximum rate on NHA loans, U = unemployment rate, GAP = utilization rate, PRC2 = rent-cost index, KRS9S = stock of residential construction at the end of the previous period, RES9R = constant dollar residential construction expenditure.

(ii) Non-residential Construction and Machinery and Equipment

Following Kotowitz (1968a) and Jorgenson (1967, pp. 140-7) we derive the demand for capital services from the hypothesis that firms maximize the present value of the firm subject to a production function and the condition that the rate of change of capital stock (net investment)

$$dk_t/d_t = i_t - \theta k_t \tag{1}$$

under a fixed set of current and forward prices for output, labour services, and investment goods, where k_t is the flow of capital services in period t, i_t is real gross fixed capital formation in period t, θ is the depreciation rate (assumed to be a constant).

The flow of capital services is assumed to proportional to the stock of capital at the beginning of the period (i.e., at the end of the previous period).[8]

Let the production function be a constant-elasticity-of-substitution (CES) function.[9]

$$y_t = [a(k_t e^{\delta t + \beta U_t})^{-\rho} + b(n_t e^{\lambda t + aU_t})^{-\rho}]^{-1/\rho} \tag{2}$$

where y_t is output in period t, n_t is the flow of labour services (manhours paid) in

8 See Appendix 2 for an explanation of how we estimated θ and calculated the stock of capital.
9 See Walters (1963).

period t, U_t is the unemployment rate in period t and measures short-run departures from full use of capital in place and labour paid, ρ is a substitution parameter, t is a time trend representing the rate of technological progress, a, β are utilization parameters, δ, γ are capital-augmenting and labour-augmenting parameters, respectively, and $\sigma = 1/(1 + \rho)$ where σ is the elasticity of substitution between labour and capital.

From the CES production function, the marginal product of capital is

$$\partial y_t/\partial k_t = a(y_t/k_t)^{1+\rho} \, e^{-\rho(\delta t + \beta U_t)} \,. \tag{3}$$

(In the limiting case where $\rho \to 0$ and $\sigma \to 1$, we have the Cobb-Douglas function and

$$\partial y_t/\partial k_t = a(y_t/k_t) \text{ and } \sigma = 1.)$$

Maximizing the present value of the firm subject to the two constraints, it can be shown that

$$\partial y_t/\partial k_t = C/P \tag{4}$$

where C is the implicit rental price of capital services supplied to the firm by itself, and P is the price of output.

Jorgenson shows that in the absence of a tax on business net income

$$C = Q(R + \theta) - (dQ/dt) \tag{5}$$

where Q is the price of capital goods, R is the cost of capital (the rate of interest).

If a proportionate tax on business net income exists,[10] then

$$C = [\![\, [(1 - uv)/(1 - u)] \, \theta \; + \; [(1 - uw)/(1 - u)] \, R$$
$$- \; [(1 - ux)/(1 - u)] \, (dQ/dt) \cdot (1/Q) \,]\!] \, Q \tag{6}$$

where u is rate of taxation of business net income, v is the proportion of depreciation which may be charged for tax purposes, w is the proportion of the cost of capital which may be charged for tax purposes, x is the proportion of capital loss which may be charged for tax purposes.

If $v = w = x = 1$, this expression for C reduces to the previous one. That is, a proportionate tax on business income does not affect the implicit rental price of capital service if all depreciation, costs of capital and capital losses may be charged for tax purposes. This, however, is not the situation. The schedule of allowable depreciation charges differs from a schedule of real depreciation rates. In our model, θ is the real rate of depreciation and it is a constant because of our assumptions that capital is homogeneous in quality regardless of vintage and that capital evaporates exponentially. For tax purposes, depreciation based on declining balances of actual costs is used, and various times accelerated or deferred depreciation rules have been used as an

10 For a formulation which allows for a tax credit on investment expenditure see Hall and Jorgenson (1967).

instrument of policy (see Helliwell (1968, pp. 122-34). The variable v_t would have to take into account both the difference between real depreciation and historical cost depreciation and the countercyclical changes in depreciation rules. For a macro-model some weighted average of the various depreciation rates would have to be produced if v_t was to be estimated directly. Alternatively one might try to estimate an implicit v_t (as does Jorgenson (1965, pp. 58-9)) by dividing the National Accounts "capital consumption allowances" by "current replacement cost." The latter is θ multiplied by the net stock of depreciable assets at the beginning of the period (k_t) multiplied by Q_t. This approach immediately encounters problems using Canadian data. We have only the breakdown of capital consumption allowances by form of organization (corporation, individuals and unincorporated business, and government business enterprises) from the National Accounts. On the other hand, our estimates of the stock of capital are by type of capital formation (residential construction, non-residential construction, and machinery and equipment) cross-classified by business non-agriculture and agriculture (including fishing). Moreover the National Accounts figures include "miscellaneous valuation adjustments." The closest we can come is to aggregate all business capital (including residential construction) and match that against corporate and individual and unincorporated business capital consumption allowances. This would provide a very crude approximation to v_t.

This raises a basic problem on sectoring. Financial statistics are available for form of organization. Production and employment statistics are by establishment classification. At the aggregate level, the business and corporate sectors do not correspond. There is no neat solution to the problem, although a system of enterprise rather than establishment statistics may be necessary for models interrelating financial and real statistics.

The cost of capital is "the maximum return that will obtain its use.[11] "To put the matter in the language of business finance, the discount rates used in computing present values are representative of the firm's cost of capital. For firms not able or willing to use new outside funds, the implicit cost of capital is the discount rate which serves to ration the available funds among the competing uses."[12]

Helliwell illustrates this in the simplest case[13] assuming the firm obtains finance by selling a security which entitles the buyer to receive whatever returns may accrue from an investment at the end of the period. The present value of this return will depend on the expected value and variance (or standard deviation) of the probability distribution of the uncertain return from the project. The discount rate will be a function of the variance of the distribution. The relevant discount rate (cost or capital) for comparing alternative investment programs, according to Helliwell, is the share market's discount rate (the average cost of capital).[14]

The investment program which maximizes the net market value of the firm is the one in which the marginal efficiency of investment (as defined by Keynes (1936, p.66)) is equal to the *marginal* cost of capital. Hence, for calculation of the effect on an established investment program of tax-induced changes in cash flows (e.g. changes in depreciation allowances), Helliwell uses the marginal cost of capital.[15]

11 Helliwell (1968, p. 4).
12 *Ibid.*, pp. 3-4.
13 *Ibid.*, p. 9.
14 *Ibid.*, p. 24.
15 *Ibid.*

In the Jorgenson model, R is the time rate of discount at which (i) the price of capital services is discounted and (ii) the price of capital goods is discounted. It is also the rate of time discount applied to the stream of future net receipts of the firm.[16] It would appear, therefore, to be the average cost of capital.

For the economy as a whole, as well as for individual firms, the average cost of capital is not the discount rate on a certain return, which is what is measured by the rate of interest on government bonds (after adjustment for expected changes in prices). If the allowance for uncertainty (the variance of the probability distribution of returns) varies in a way that is not closely correlated with the rate of interest, then the use of the interest rate as a proxy for the cost of capital will not be satisfactory.

Jorgenson avoids this problem by assuming perfect capital markets and certainty about future net receipts.[17] The rental of capital services correctly reflects interest, depreciation, and the change in the price of capital goods so that the firm is indifferent in choosing between renting and owning. The cost of capital reflects perfectly the availability of funds.

Miller and Modigliani (1967) retain the assumptions of perfect capital markets and rational behaviour but drop the assumption of certainty. Their analysis concerns large corporations and their assumptions are not unreasonable in this case. For smaller firms, availability conditions are very important, as they admit. For macroeconomic analysis, the relevant question would seem to be what proportion of investment expenditures is made by large corporations? If the proportion is very large, the assumption of perfect capital markets may be a workable hypothesis.

Miller and Modigliani derive an average cost of capital in the face of uncertainty by introducing a "risk equivalent class" where the expected value of the probability distribution of earnings is used in conjunctions with a market capitalization rate for the expected value of the uncertain pure equity earnings stream for this class of firm. The market's capitalization rate is not observable but is to be inferred by regressing the observed sum of market values of all the firms' securities against the expected level of average annual earnings generated by the assets the firm currently holds over a cross-section of firms within a class. What does one do for the economy as a whole for a macro-model?

The introduction of income tax complicates the problem. Interest payments may be charged as a cost of business reducing the amount of profits against which income tax is charged. If the business is unincorporated, the relevant rate is the personal income tax rate, otherwise the corporate tax rate is used. If we exclude residential construction, most business investment programs are carried out by corporations; hence, we might assume the corporate rate is relevant and by-pass this sectoring problem.

The impact of the deduction for tax purposes on the cost of capital depends on the proportion of debt capital to total capital. Miller and Modigliani define the weighted average cost of capital as $\rho(1 - uL)$ where ρ is the reciprocal of the capitalization rate for unlevered, pure equity streams, i.e., the marginal cost of equity capital, u is the corporate tax rate, L is the target debt to total capital ratio. They assume that the difference between the cost of equity and debt capital is accounted for only by the tax rate. They both depend, not on the market rate of interest for bonds, but on the

16 Jorgenson (1967, pp. 40-4).
17 *Ibid.*, p. 136.

rate ρ, which is a sufficient parameter. In a general equilibrium system, the cost of equity capital is directly connected to the interest rate. Miller and Modigliani are of the opinion that there is no reason to believe they will always move closely together over time. Their empirical findings, however, are that the average cost of capital for an industry conforms quite closely in its movements with the average yield on AAA bonds in the industry, which, they remark, is probably the most popular surrogate for the cost of capital in investment studies. Their study is, however, only for a three-year period. They suggest that this parallelism resulted from both series being dominated by factors affecting the supply of and demand for capital in general. Changes in investors' tastes for risk-bearing or in their evaluation of riskiness of this industry were apparently not large enough to cause any significant divergence of movement.

In Jorgenson's model the term w_t takes into account implicitly the fact that only interest on debt capital is deductible for income tax. He estimates w_t by dividing the total net monetary interest paid by the cost of total capital. The latter is the value of the capital stock, presumably Q_t x k_t x R_t. For R_t, he uses the long-term rate on US government bonds. Presumably, to allow partly for uncertainty, one should use the long-term corporate rate. No figure on interest paid is available from the Canadian National Accounts. One could try Taxation Statistics for corporations. This raises again, however, the problem of corporate sector versus business sector, since our capital stock figures refer to the business sector whereas the total interest charged against profits would refer to the corporate sector.

If one tries to follow the Miller-Modigliani approach, one could use Taxation Statistics to estimate an actual L (and assume it equalled the target L). It would then be necessary to estimate ρ for the business sector. This appears to be an almost impossible task.

A word on retained earnings is in order. The assumption of perfect capital markets presumably means that no distinction is made in computing the cost of internal and external finance.

Do businessmen take into account capital gains arising from changes in the price of investment goods? Jorgenson assumes not and drops the term dQ/dt from the model, his argument being that they are regarded as transitory and do not affect the long-run demand for capital.[18]

Under Canadian law, capital gains are not taxable; hence, $x_t = 0$.

Given all these formidable problems, we did not attempt a definition of C that allowed for the effect of taxation or capital gains. We used the simpler formulation

$$C = Q(R + \theta). \tag{7}$$

From equations 3 and 4,

$$C/P = a(y_t/k_t)^{1+\rho} e^{-\rho(\delta t + \beta U_t)}. \tag{8}$$

If we assume the factor of proportionality between capital services and the capital stock is unity, and if we interpret y_t as expected output, y_t^*, then k_t can be interpreted as the desired stock of capital at the end of the period, k_t^*.

18 Jorgenson (1965, p. 59).

$$k_t^* = [a(P/C)]^{1/(1+\rho)} \, y_t^* \, e^{[\rho/(1+\rho)]^{(\delta t + \beta U_t)}} = [a(P/C)]^{\sigma} \, y_t^* \, e^{-(1-\sigma)(\delta t + \beta U_t)} \qquad (9)$$

(In the Cobb-Douglas case $k_t^* = \beta(P/C) \, y_t^*$.)

On the assumption of pure competition and that capital is rewarded according to its actual marginal product, the actual rate of return on the capital in place at the beginning of the period (i.e., at the end of the previous period) will be

$$\partial y_t / \partial k_{t-1} = a(y_t/k_{t-1})^{1+\rho} \, e^{-\rho[\delta(t-1) + \beta U_t]} = \pi$$

where in this expression y_t and k_{t-1} are interpreted as actual output and capital stock, respectively, and π is the actual real rate of return on capital. It is assumed that actual output differs from expected output and hence desired and actual capital stocks differ.

We express the difference between the desired stock of capital at the end of the period and the actual stock at the beginning of the period in the form

$$k_t^*/k_{t-1} = [\pi/(C/P)]^{1/(1+\rho)}(y_t^*/y_t) \, e^{(\sigma-1)\delta} = [\pi/(C/P)]^{\sigma} (y_t^*/y_t) \, e^{(\sigma-1)\delta} \qquad (11)$$

The problem of obtaining a measure of expected output must now be solved. Let us assume that expectations about output are a function of deviations of the utilization ratio (GAP) from unity and of the normal annual rate of growth of output, x.

$$y_t^* = y_t \, e^{[a(GAP_t - 1) + x]}. \qquad (12)$$

An a greater than unity implies that any deviation from potential output is expected to continue whereas a negative value of a corresponds to an expectation that any deviation from potential output, in either direction, is followed by a return towards potential output.

The desired capital stock at the end of the period

$$k_t^* = i_t^* + (1-\theta)k_{t-1} \qquad (13)$$

where i_t^* is the desired gross fixed capital formation. Thus,

$$[i_t^* + (1-\theta)k_{t-1}]/k_{t-1} = (i_t^* - \theta k_{t-1} + k_{t-1})/k_{t-1} = (i_t^*/k_{t-1}) - \theta + 1$$
$$= [\pi/(C/P)]^{\sigma} \, e^{[a(GAP_t - 1) + x]} + (\sigma-1)\delta. \qquad (14)$$

Since $i_t^*/k_{t-1} - \theta$ is a small fraction,

$$\ln[(i_t^*/k_{t-1}) - \theta + 1] \approx (i_t^*/k_{t-1}) - \theta, \text{ and}$$

$$i_t^*/k_{t-1} = [\theta - a - (1-\sigma)\delta + x] + \sigma \ln[\pi/(C/P)] + aGAP_t. \qquad (15)$$

As has been pointed out by de Leeuw (1962) and Jorgenson (1965, pp. 46-55), there is a lag between changes in the demand for capital services and actual investment. This lag is the sum of the length of time it takes to evaluate and initiate an investment project, appropriate the funds, let the contracts, issue the orders, and finally put capital goods in place. Hence, actual investment is assumed to be a distributed lag function of desired investment in previous periods.

$$i_t = \gamma i_t^* + (1 - \gamma) i_{t-1}. \tag{16}$$

Thus, we obtain

$$i_t/k_{t-1} = \gamma[\theta - a - (1 - \sigma)\delta + x] + \gamma\sigma \ln[\pi/(C/P)]$$
$$+ a\gamma\mathrm{GAP}_t + (1 - \gamma)(i_{t-1}/k_{t-1}). \tag{17}$$

The signs of the Greek letter parameters can be specified: $0 < \gamma < 1, 0 < \theta < 1$, $a > 0, \delta > 0$, and $\sigma > 0$. Hence, when the four parameters of the investment functions are estimated, we would expect the last three to be positive. If θ and δ are small, the first parameter is likely to be negative.

The investment functions were estimated both in the ratio form shown above and in absolute levels with the right-hand side multiplied through by k_{t-1}. The latter provided a better fit to the most recent years and were selected for the model because of the intended use of the model for forecasting 1970 (see Chapter 5). Data for the period 1928-66 (excluding 1941-6) were used to estimate equations C.9 and C.15. When the equations were estimated for the period 1947-66, closer fit was obtained for the end years of the sample period. When this set of parameter estimates was used in simulations, however, the system tended to explode when subjected to disturbances because of the high value of the coefficient of lagged capital formation. Hence, the parameter estimates for the full period were used.

For equations C.9 and C.15, the real rate of return on capital (π) was measured by corporation profits deflated by the GNP price deflator (PY2) and divided by the real stock of machinery and equipment and non-residential construction. The implicit rental price of capital services (C) was also deflated by the GNP price deflator. The deflator cancels out therefore since it appears both in the numerator and denominator of the ratio $[\pi/(C/P)]$.

The equations used were therefore C.9 and C.15:

$$\mathrm{BME9R} = -0.205*\mathrm{KMB9S} + 0.0242*\mathrm{KMB9S}*\mathrm{ALOG}$$
$$\phantom{\mathrm{BME9R} =} (2.30) \phantom{*\mathrm{KMB9S}} (1.24)$$

$$[\![\mathrm{CPG9}/[\mathrm{KCB9S} + \mathrm{KMB9S}]/[\mathrm{PME2}*(\mathrm{LIC}*0.01 + 0.12)]]\!]$$

$$+ 0.578*\mathrm{BME9S} + 0.289*\mathrm{GAP}*\mathrm{KMB9S} \tag{C.9}$$
$$(4.25) \phantom{*\mathrm{BME9S}} (3.20)$$

$$\mathrm{BNR9R} = -0.119*\mathrm{KCB9S} + 0.00178*\mathrm{KCB9S}*\mathrm{ALOG}$$
$$\phantom{\mathrm{BNR9R} =} (4.28) \phantom{*\mathrm{KCB9S}} (0.33)$$

$$[\![\mathrm{CPG9}/[\mathrm{KCB9S} + \mathrm{KMB9S}]/[\mathrm{PNR2}*(\mathrm{LIC}*0.01 + 0.035)]]\!]$$

$$+ 0.704*\mathrm{BNR9S} + 0.146*\mathrm{GAP}*\mathrm{KCB9S}. \tag{C.15}$$
$$(8.40) \phantom{*\mathrm{BNR9S}} (4.35)$$

The resulting equations have the correct signs for the parameters. It is important to note that the cost of capital does appear in these equations in such a way that increases in the cost of capital (represented by LIC) do reduce capital formation. The statistical significance of the coefficient of the term containing the cost of capital is, however, very low and does not give us strong evidence to accept the theory of investment behaviour advanced in the specification of the equation. It should also be noted that increases in the price of capital goods (PME2 or PNR2) also act to lower capital formation. But the same qualification with respect to statistical significance applies.

From the equations actually used in the model, some of the parameter values can be estimated. In the equation for BME9R, $\hat{\gamma} = 0.42$, $\hat{a} = 0.69$, $\hat{\sigma} = 0.057$. If we assume $\hat{\theta}$ is equal to the value used in calculating the stock of capital (0.12) and that $x = 0.04$, we obtain $\hat{\delta} = -0.04$. In the equation for BNR9R, $\hat{\gamma} = 0.30$, $\hat{a} = 0.49$, $\hat{\sigma} = 0.006$, $\hat{\theta} = 0.035$, $\hat{\delta} = -0.01$. In the latter equation, the estimate of $(\gamma\sigma)$ has a t-value of only 0.33 and hence is not statistically different from zero. Its actual value is also close to zero. Hence the second equation is very close to being a function of GAP and lagged BNR9R. When the equations were estimated in ratio from as specified in equation 17, the derived parameter estimates were somewhat more realistic, although the over-all fit of the equation was no better. The value of δ should be very close to zero, if, as one might expect, technical progress was purely labour-augmenting. The estimate of δ is however affected by errors in estimating the real depreciation rate, specification error, and the use of corporate profits rather than the proper share of capital in calculating π.

Since the BME9R and BNR9R equations are very crucial to the dynamic properties of the model, some comments on alternative theories of investment behaviour are in order. Jorgenson and Siebert (1968) examined four alternative theories: the "neoclassical theory" a variation of which we have used in the TRACE model, the "accelerator theory," based on output or capacity utilization, the "expected profits theory" based on the market value of the firm, and the "liquidity" or internal funds theory. Their principal conclusion is that "the neoclassical theory of investment is superior to theories based on capacity utilization or profit expectations and these theories are superior, in turn, to a theory based on internal funds available for investment." (P. 708.)

The neoclassical theory of investment behaviour is based on an optimal time path for capital accumulation and implies, as we have explained above, a theory of the cost of capital. This theory has been developed by Modigliani and Miller (1967) whose hypothesis is that the cost of capital is shown to be independent of the financial structure of the firm or of dividend policy, except for the modification required by the fact that interest payments are deductible for tax purposes. In contrast, in the liquidity theory of investment behaviour the supply schedule of funds is horizontal up to the point where internal funds are exhausted and vertical at that point.

The testing of alternative theories of investment behaviour by Jorgenson and others in the United States is, however, based on an economy which is almost a closed economy. For an open economy such as Canada, it is crucial to ask whether long-term capital inflows, and particularly direct investment, should enter directly into the BME9R and BNR9R equations. Alternatively, for Canada, consideration might be given to "the 'staple theory' which holds that variations in the level and prospects for Canada's natural-resource-intensive exports dominate the rhythm of long-term growth and that one effect of a period of strong exports is to pull more direct investment in the country."[19]

These peculiar aspects of the capital formation functions were neglected in a study by T. A. Wilson (1967) which was based on a modified version of de Leeuw's model (1962), a "liquidity theory" model. In the Wilson quarterly model the variables are an output or capacity requirement variable, the cost of capital, and the availability of internal funds. Similarly, Evans and Helliwell (1969) have developed a quarterly model of investment behaviour whose variables are an accelerator variable, a cash flow variable (the sum of corporate retained earnings and depreciation allowances) which enters directly into the determination of desired capital stock, and a bond index which plays a cost or constraint role.

In TRACE 1968 we used the following function for the aggregate BCF9R = BME9R + BNR9R:

$$BCF9R = 14.20 + 7.19 \, GAP + 6.45 * (WRBOR) + 2.60 * (LDU9/PBC2)$$
$$(7.65) \quad (5.17) \qquad (13.75) \qquad\qquad (5.23)$$

$$+ 1.66 \, (UCP91/PBC21)$$
$$(5.24)$$

$$RBSQ = 0.971, \, SDR = 0.218, \, DW = 2.00, \, PD = 47\text{-}66,$$

where WRBOR is the real wage rate in the business non-agricultural sector, LDU9 is United States direct investment in Canada, PBC2 is the implicit price index for BCF9, UCP91 is lagged undistributed corporation profits.

We rejected this function in favour of the one used in TRACE 1969 because the latter one gave, in our opinion, more adequate play to market forces represented by changes in the cost of capital. The two hypotheses give opposite results to changes in interest rate in Canada. In TRACE 1968 an increase in interest rates led to an increase in LDU9 and a direct increase in BCF9R. In TRACE 1969 the interest rate increase still leads to an increase in LDU9 but the impact on BCF9R depends on the cost of capital. An increase in the cost of capital leads to a decrease in BCF9R. The poor performance of the cost of capital in equations C.9 and C.15 may, however, reflect the resultant of the two forces pulling in opposite directions. High interest rates (and hence a high cost of capital) may directly tend to discourage a given investment project and hence business capital formation as whole. On the other hand, a high interest rate in Canada may encourage capital inflows from abroad and hence, through the availability effects, capital formation in Canada.

(iii) Value of the Physical Change in Inventories

The real change in non-farm business inventories is estimated from data for the full period 1928-40, 1947-66. The explanatory variables are beginning of period real stock

19 Caves and Reuber (1969, p. 17).

of inventories, real gross domestic product, and lagged change in real expenditure on durables. The real stock of inventories was built up from an estimate of base-year stock by accumulating net investment over the years.

Inventory investment represents a highly volatile component of final demand and the importance attached to its explanation is reflected in the extensive literature on alternative models.[20] Given the fact that we were concerned with inventory investment as one sector in a large model and given the availability of data for a sample period long enough for purposes of an annual model, we were effectively constrained to an aggresive approach rather than disaggregation by motives for holding stocks or by stage of fabrication.

The hypothesis underlying our formulation is essentially that the desired stock of inventories (IKB9R*) is related to transactions demand, measured by gross domestic product (YGD9R) and backlog (together possibly, with speculative) demand, as measured by the lagged change in expenditure on durables (DUR9S − DUR9T) as a proxy for the change in unfilled orders.

$$IKB9R^* = a_0 + a_1 \, YDG9R + a_2(DUR9R - DUR9S).$$

The flexible-accelerator mechanism then gives the relation of this demand to actual inventory investment (DHB9R)

$$DHB9R = \gamma(IKB9R^* - IKB9S).$$

The constant a_0 is included to allow for error in our benchmark: its estimated value of 1.372 is an indication of the overstatement of our benchmark. This benchmark was taken from Brown (1964b, p. 230) who converted the estimates by Scott (1959) from 1949 to 1957 dollars. The 1947 base-year figure of 6.135 billion 1957 dollars excludes livestock but includes other business and farm inventories. The estimate of a_0 therefore implies that the rest of the farm inventory component, which should have been excluded, amounted to 1.372 billion 1957 dollars.

The estimate of a_1 is 0.275, very close to the approximate sample period average of 0.268 obtained by taking the ratio of average stocks (adjusted for benchmark error as implied by the estimate of a_0) to average gross domestic product. The estimate of a_2 is 1.203.

The current dollar value of physical change in business non-farm inventories is a function of the inventory valuation adjustment and the real change in non-farm business inventories. Additional variables are the real value of beginning of period stock of inventories and the proportional rate of change of prices in the business sector; the latter as an indicator of the magnitude of price effects involved and the former as a measure of the volume of stocks to be revalued. This equation has been estimated only for the postwar period. Separate estimation of real and nominal inventory investment

20 For excellent discussions of this literature and more or less complete bibliographies, see, for example, Courchene (1967) and Evans (1969, pp. 200-20). Both authors present valuable research results of their own. Courchene has demonstrated that motives for holding inventories are best considered with reference to the stages of fabrication and that the aggregate approach can, therefore, be misleading at best. Since our over-all constraints and the unavailability of data effectively limited us to aggregation, we are vulnerable to the possible pitfalls of this approach.

corresponds with the practice in the National Accounts of avoiding the implicit price deflector which is extremely volatile and complicated in this case.

D. *Foreign Trade*

(i) Merchandise Exports

Merchandise exports, following the Bank of Canada classification,[21] have been disaggregated into (*a*) farm and fish products, (*b*) forest products, (*c*) metals and minerals, (*d*) chemicals and fertilizers, (*e*) automobiles and parts ot the United States, and (*f*) other manufactured goods. Categories (*a*), (*b*), (*c*) and (*f*) were further disaggregated by destination: (i) United States, (ii) United Kingdom, and (iii) rest of the world.

Demand functions of the following form were specified for each of the categories:

$$X_{ij} = \beta_0 + \beta_1 Q_j - \beta_2 [P_{ij}/(R_{ij})(E_j)]$$

where i refers to the ith commodity group, j refers to the region of destination, X_{ij} is exports of the ith commodity to region j in constant Canadian dollars, Q_j is an index of production in region j, P_{ij} is the Canadian export price of the ith commodity to region j, R_{ij} is the price of the ith commodity in region j, E_j is the foreign exchange rate: the number of Canadian dollars per unit of region j's currency.

In the case of the rest of the world equations, however, the price of the commodity in the United States was used for R_{ij} and the Canadian-US foreign exchange rate was used for E_j.

The specification worked for nine of the equations: farm and fish products to the United States, forest products to the United States and the United Kingdom,[22] all three metals and minerals equations[23] and all three equations for other manufactured goods. Exports of farm and fish products to the United Kingdom and to the rest of the world were made exogenous. Exports of automobiles and parts to the United States were also made exogenous since it was found that a combination of dummy and a geometric trend term (0 for the years prior to the Canada-US automobile agreement, 1/4 for the first post-agreement year, 1/2 for the second, 1 for the third and all subsequent years) explained nearly all the variance in this variable. Exports of forest products to the rest of the world were made a function only of industrial production in the rest of the world. The specification did not work for chemicals and fertilizers and an alternative specification described below was followed.

The supply side of the export market was brought in by specifying Canadian supply prices to the United States for each category of exports.

$$P_{iu} = a_0 + a_1 (R_{iu})(E_u) + a_2 WRB + a_3 T$$

21 See the Bank of Canada, *Statistical Summary*. Export equations following this classification have also been developed by Officer and Hurtubise (1969).

22 In the latter equation the price of paper in Sweden was used as an indicator of the price competition for Canadian exports in the United Kingdom market.

23 In equation D.9, PMU2 was inadvertently punched instead of PMW2 which is the correct variable and the variable used in the regression. The two price series move somewhat differently and the XMW9R equation's performance was therefore adversely affected in our simulation experiments.

where the subscript u indicates the United States, *WRB* is the wage rate in the business non-agricultural sector in Canada, T is time.

Prices of exports to other regions were made a function of the export price to the United States, time, and/or the lagged price to that region.

As can be seen from equations G.23 to G.34, these specifications worked reasonably well. In the P_{iu} equations, the trend term was not used for farm and fish products and the equation for price of other manufactured goods was reduced to a function only of time.

For chemicals and fertilizers, a reduced-form type of equation was used for total exports to all countries. Exports were made a function of the export price to the United States (which is exogenous in the model), the Canadian wage rate, and time. The export price for all chemicals and fertilizers was made a function of the price to the United States and the lagged total price. No activity level variable appears in the equation. It is clear that considerable work needs to be done on the linkages between the US and the Canadian chemical industries before a satisfactory explanation of the distribution and pricing behaviour with respect to chemical and fertilizer products of Canadian origin can be advanced.

Together the "export demand" and "export price" equations serve to integrate the export sector with the main body of the TRACE model instead of leaving it as a nearly decomposable subset. The demand equations measure the effects of foreign income (activity) levels and Canadian export prices (in relative terms) on Canada's exports. Canadian export prices in turn depend on foreign prices as well as cost-push elements such as the wage rate in the business non-agricultural sector. Thus exports affect aggregate income (output) through the income identity and the latter affects exports through the effect of wage rates on export prices. In periods of flexible exchange rates there is yet another linkage available since the rate of exchange not only determines export quantities and prices but would itself depend on the payments position.

It may be worthwhile to analyse briefly the behavioural properties of the export subsector. Ignoring commodity group and destination subscripts for simplicity, we have a system of two equations: (i) the quantity of exports is a function of activity in the importing country, competing price, and the rate of exchange, and (ii) export price is a function of competing price, the rate of exchange, and the domestic wage rate. The competing price (R_{ij}) has been treated as exogenous. If we also abstract from the simultaneity between the export quantities and prices on one hand and the exchange rate and domestic wage rate on the other - the former characterizes situations of fixed or pegged exchange rates, the latter holds if the linkage between the wage rate and export incomes is slender - then the export sector is very nearly casual recursive in nature. That is, in the price-quantity plane, while the demand curve for exports is negatively sloped with respect to price, the supply curve appears horizontal (parallel to the quantity axis).

Of greater interest however, may be the response of export quantity and prices to some exogenous change - say devaluation of the exchange rate (rise in E). In the price-quantity plane, this situation would be represented by a change in the slope of the export demand function and an upward shift in the supply (price) function. The net result, however, would be no longer unambiguous and would depend upon the magnitude of the shift in the two functions. This property holds irrespective of whether we are looking at the effect of devaluation on the quantity of exports or export earnings measured in Canadian dollars (current) or foreign exchange earnings from exports.[24] All that we can say if the export quantity rises as a result of devaluation, *ex post* earnings measured in domestic dollars also rises. The same, however, is not necessarily true of export earnings measured in foreign exchange.

(ii) Exports of Services

The following components of exports of services were treated as exogenous in current dollars: (*a*) gold production available for export in United States dollars, (*b*) tourist and travel expenditures in Canada in Canadian dollars, and (*c*) freight and shipping receipts in Canadian dollars.

The constant dollar quantities were derived as follows: (*a*) gold production available for export was assumed to be the same in both current and constant dollars, (*b*) tourist and travel expenditures were deflated by the implicit price of personal expenditure on consumer nondurables and services, and (*c*) freight and shipping receipts were deflated by the implicit price index of merchandise exports and tourist and travel expenditures.

Interest and dividends received from abroad in current dollars were derived from an autoregressive function in which this year's receipts were an exponential function of last year's receipts. The deflator for these receipts is the implicit price of imports of goods and services. This deflation procedure follows closely the practice in the National Accounts.

(iii) Statistical Discrepancy

Equations D.29 and D.30 contain a statistical discrepancy item which absorbs (*a*) the discrepancy between the sum of merchandise exports as published by the Bank of Canada and the Dominion Bureau of Statistics trade statistics and the adjusted figure used in the balance of payments and the National Accounts, (*b*) the discrepancy resulting from the use of different deflators for the components of exports of goods and services than are used in the National Accounts. The price indexes used to deflate the various categories of merchandise exports are unofficial indexes obtained with the assistance of the Bank of Canada and the Dominion Bureau of Statistics but their use would result in a different constant dollar exports figure if the adjustments were not made. Moreover, the deflators used for gold, tourist and travel expenditures, and freight and shipping differ from those used by the National Accounts. In *ex ante* forecast situations it is necessary to forecast the amount of this statistical discrepancy.

24 $\partial x_{ij}/\partial E_j = -\beta_2/R_{ij}[(\partial P_{ij}/\partial E_j) \cdot E_j^{-1} - P_{ij}E_j^{-2}]$ (*a*)

$\partial(x_{ij}P_{ij})/\partial E_j = [-(\beta_2/R_j)[(\partial P_{ij}/\partial E_j)E_j^{-1} - P_{ij}E_j^{-2}]] P_{ij} + x_j(\partial P_{ij}/\partial E_j).$ (*b*)

Since $\partial P_{ij}/\partial E_j$ is positive, if $\partial x_{ij}/\partial E_j$ is positive, $\partial(x_{ij}P_{ij})/\partial E_j$ is also positive.

$\partial(x_{ij}P_{ij}E_j^{-1})/\partial E_j = E_j^{-1}[\partial(x_{ij}P_{ij})/\partial E_j] - (x_{ij}P_{ij})E_j^{-2}.$ (*c*)

(iv) Imports of Goods and Services

Imports of goods and services (equation D.35) are estimated using an equation of the form

$$\text{NMP9R} = \beta_0 + \beta_1 \left[a_0 \text{DUR9R} + \ldots + a_7 \text{X9R} \right] + \beta_2 \text{VPC9R} + \beta_5 (\text{PIM2/PY2})$$
$$+ \beta_3 \text{GAP} + \text{API9R}.$$

The as were estimated by input-output analysis following the method detailed in Appendices 3 and 4. The βs were then estimated by two-stage least squares using data from which the estimated imports of automobiles and parts attributable to the Canada-United States automobile pact (API9R) had been excluded. The latter quantity is then added as an exogenous variable.

(v) Interest and Dividends

Interest and dividends received from abroad are estimated from an autoregressive function (equation D.31). Interest and dividends paid abroad (equation D.33) are a function of the interest rate, dividends paid by Canadian companies, and a trend term. The deflators used correspond closely to those used in the National Accounts.

E. *Gross National Expenditure*

Gross national expenditure at market prices in constant dollars is obtained by summing the components from sections (A) to (D) of the model (equation E.1). In *ex post* forecasts and other simulations the residual error of estimate is given its actual value as an exogenous variable. In *ex ante* forecasts it was given the value zero although evidence on its serial correlation properties might be used to forecast its value. The current dollar gross national expenditure, Y9, is obtained from equation E.2 by multiplying the constant dollar estimate, Y9R, derived by the model by an estimate of the implicit price index of GNE, PY2, derived from equation G.8. A statistical discrepancy (ERA9) will exist if PY2 as derived from the model is not a properly weighted average of all the component price indexes. This discrepancy does not enter into the computations but is simply recorded as an error measure. It was felt that at the present stage of the development of the TRACE model this procedure for estimating Y9 would produce a more accurate estimate than the alternative procedure of multiplying each component of Y9R by the appropriate component price index and summing the components. Since, as is explained in section G, the component prices are functions of an aggregate price index, rather than the aggregate being a weighted average of the components which is the optimal procedure, we derived Y9 by multiplying Y9R by PY2.

F. *Output*

Real output is divided into three main components: (i) output in the government[25] and personal sectors as measured by real wages, salaries, and supplementary labour income and imputed rent on government-owned buildings,[26] (ii) output in agriculture, fishing, hunting and trapping, and (iii) business non-agricultural output. This last item is defined as (see equation F.7): total real gross domestic product less items (i) and (ii) and less real indirect taxes and subsidies, where real gross domestic product is defined as (see equation F.6): real gross national expenditure less real interest and dividends from abroad plus real interest and dividends paid abroad less the real residual error of estimate.[27] Real output in the government and personal sectors is assumed to be determined exogenously. While some elements of government expenditure are clearly endogenous, changes in its over-all magnitude are largely a policy variable and were therefore assumed to be exogenous. We did not deem it necessary to disaggregate this output component, as it is unlikely that any of its components influence directly any of the other endogenous variables in the model. However, caution must be exercised in forecasting because of changes in classification when activities which were performed by the private sector are taken over by the government, e.g., hospital care. Output of the personal sector changes slowly and was treated exogenously.

Real output in agriculture is estimated exogenously for short-term forecasting or analysis because no effective way was found to introduce weather and other physical factors affecting yields into the production function. For long-run analysis, however, a Cobb-Douglas production function gave fairly good results.[28] This leaves business real non-agricultural output as the key endogenous variable on the production side. We postulated that it is determined by the interaction of aggregate demand and aggregate supply, where both are functions of the price level and other variables. We have seen how aggregate demand is derived. We can now examine aggregate business non-agriculture supply as a function of the price level and other variables.

The derivation of a short-run aggregate supply function can be seen by looking at a four-equation model in which there is (1) a production function where output (y) is a function of labour (n) and capital (k) employed, (2) a marginal productivity condition where the marginal product of labour (f_n) multiplied by the price of output (P) is equal to the money wage rate (W), (3) a supply of labour function where supply (n^S) is a function of the money wage rate, the price of output, and population (POP), and (4) an equilibrium condition for the labour market.

$$y = f(k, n) \tag{1}$$

$$W = Pf_n(k, n) \text{ where } f_n = \partial f/\partial n \tag{2}$$

$$n^S = f(W, P, POP) \tag{3}$$

$$n^S = n. \tag{4}$$

---

25 The government sector includes public non-commercial institutions such as hospitals and universities. Government business enterprises such as Air Canada are included in the business sector.

26 Capital consumption allowances for private non-commercial institutions are not available separately. Hence, this part of gross national product is included in the output of the business non-agricultural sector rather than in the personal sector where it belongs. Thus, business non-agricultural output is biased upwards. This bias is not large, however, and was unavoidable because of lack of relevant data.

27 The residual error of estimate variable in the model, REY9, is taken from the expenditure side. In equations F.5 and F.6 the error from the income side should be deducted. Algebraically this is equivalent to adding the error from the expenditure side.

28    $\ln(\text{YA0RM}) = -1.183 + 0.208 \ln(\text{KA0RM}) + 0.036\text{T}$
            (4.57) (0.98)   (2.61) $\bar{R}^2 = 0.838$, PD = 28-66.

If we assume that in the short run *POP* and k are predetermined, we have four equations with five endogenous variables y, w, p, n^S, n, which upon combining and substitution for W, n, and n^S we can express as an aggregate supply function:

$$y = f(P, k, POP). \tag{5}$$

This equation together with the aggregate demand function then gives a solution for the values of output (y) and prices (P). If equilibrium prevails and in the absence of estimation problems, it does not matter if we interpret equation 1 as a short-run production function and equation 2 as a labour demand function or whether we interpret equation 1 as a labour demand function and equation 2 as a cost or supply function. The results are, of course, identical.

This is not so in a dynamic context and in the presence of estimation problems. For if rigidities which prevent adjustments occur, their nature must be specified and appropriate slack variables defined. Also, in small samples, the use of consistent estimating techniques such as two-stage least-squares, does not eliminate simultaneity bias and thus the estimated parameters of the two interpretations of equations 1 and 2 will not be the same.

We followed mainly the second approach; that is, we estimated equation 1 as a labour demand function and equation 2 as a desired supply price equation. That is, equation 1 was estimated with n as the dependent variable and equation 2 was estimated with P as the dependent variable. We assumed that in the short-run, given the predominance of imperfect competition in both labour and product markets, prices and wages are relatively rigid and that short-run departures from equilibrium are maintained by adjustments of various stocks. These are mainly underemployed capital and unemployed as well as underemployed labour. We tried to identify undesired inventory accumulation, but these attempts were unsuccessful. The form of this adjustment process is described in section G.

In addition to the short-run aggregate supply function thus derived we have also estimated and used a long-run production function to measure potential output. The ratio of the actual level of output in business non-agriculture to its potential value is defined as the utilization rate, GAP (equation F.11), which is a key variable in our model. For the purposes of analysis of equilibrium paths, the variable GAP must be set at a specified constant level consistent with the specified level of the unemployment rate (U). Either the long-run production function or the implicit long-run production function derived from the short-run labour demand function can then be used.[29]

We attempted to construct the production sector of the business non-agriculture sector of the economy around a factor-augmenting constant-elasticity-of-substitution (CES) production function with derived demand for labour and capital functions as well as a derived price equation. This would enable us to obtain consistent short- and long-run patterns of income distribution which are difficult to explain by simpler relations. We found, however, that, because of extreme multicollinearity between capital, labour and time, it was impossible to distinguish the CES function from its special

---

29 As will be seen later, the results of the two equations are very close, but not identical; so only one may be used. We retained both even though their use may lead to slight inconsistencies in the long run because it improves the short-run fit of the model.

case, the Cobb-Douglas, in the production function proper, or in the derived labour demand relation, even though it is distinguishable for the derived price and capital demand equations.

Thus, consider the factor-augmenting CES production function:

$$y = [a(k\,e^{\delta t + \beta U})^{-\rho} + b(n\,e^{\lambda t + aU})^{-\rho}]^{-1/\rho} \tag{6}$$

where t is a time trend representing rate of technological progress and U is the unemployment rate measuring short-run departures from optimal use of capital in place (k) and labour (manhours) paid (n).

Converting into natural logarithms and expanding around $\rho = 0$ by a Taylor expansion we get:[30]

$$\ln(y/n) = b + a\ln(k/n) + [\lambda + a(\delta + \lambda)]t + [a + a(\beta - a)U - 1/2\rho ab\,[\ln(k/n)]^2$$
$$- 1/2\rho ab(\delta - \lambda)(\ln k/n)t - 1/2\rho ab(\beta - a)(\ln k/n)U - 1/2\rho ab\,[(\delta - \lambda)t$$
$$+ (\beta - a)U)]^2 + \ldots$$

It is immediately apparent that the equation contains too many multicollinear terms to be estimated reliably. Even if $\lambda = \delta$ and $a = \beta$ the degree of multicollinearity is high and the coefficient of $[\ln(k/n)]^2$ is not likely to add much to the explanation. This in fact turned out to be the case.

The same problem occurs if equation 6 is manipulated so as to express n as a function of the other variables. It should be pointed out, however, that the bias caused by using a Cobb-Douglas production function instead of a CES production function for medium-term projections is very small if labour and capital in efficiency units grow at about the same rate over time. This appears to have been the case in Canada over the relevant period.[31]

Thus the production function used to generate potential output in the business non-agriculture sector (YBP9R) is a Cobb-Douglas production function estimated in the form:

$$\ln(y/n) = \ln A + b_1 \ln(k/n) + \lambda t + b_2 U_1 + b_3 U_1^2 + b_4 U_2 + b_5 U_2^2 + b_6 D, \tag{8}$$

where U_1 = unemployment rate 1928-40, U_2 = unemployment rate 1947-66, and D = 0 (1928-40), 1 (1947-66). The addition of these variables was necessary to eliminate short-run cyclical effects in calculating long-run potential output. These effects may arise from lags in adjustment or errors in the measures of labour and capital employment.[32] The separation of pre- and postwar cyclical effects was indicated because adjustments to cyclical conditions are likely to be different, in a long depression, from those of a relatively prosperous economy. It is notable that the elasticity of output with respect to capital is high (about 0.52) both in relation to capital's share in gross domestic product of the business non-agricultural sector (about 0.40) and the implicit

---

30 See Kotowitz (1968b) for a more detailed explanation.
31 See Kotowitz (1969).
32 See Appendix 2 on measurement of capital.

coefficient derived from the labour demand function (about 0.42). Various changes in specification did not reduce the coefficient. From this point of view the implicit production function derived from the labour demand function is probably superior for long-run analysis.

Equation 8 is used to generate potential output (YBP9R) by assuming that capital in place at the end of the previous period and the potential amount of manhours available for this sector (SMB9) are fully employed. The potential number of workers available to business non-agriculture is assumed to be equal to 0.96 of the labour force less 0.96 (EA6 + EG6)/(1 - 0.01U), where EA6 is agricultural employment and EG6 is employment in the government and personal sectors. This assumes that a level of unemployment of 4 per cent for all sectors is equivalent to full employment. Thus, the constant term in equation 8 is raised by 4 per cent. Standard manhours are obtained by the same assumption applied to the estimated standard hours (equation H.3) and multiplying standard hours by number of workers available. Thus equation F.10 for potential output is derived from coefficients derived from the regression described by equation 8 using actual unemployment rates in the various years. For equation F.10, the actual unemployment rate is replaced by 4.0 and the constant adjusted as described above.

We assume constant returns to scale in the production function because the meaning of non-constant returns to scale in an aggregate production function is ambiguous, and because multicollinearity in time series does not enable us to distinguish returns to scale from technical progress.

G. *Prices and Wages*

The main price in the model is the price of real output in business non-agriculture, PYB2 (equation G.5). The starting point for the derivation of the equation is the assumption that in the short-run producers attempt to equate the marginal revenue product of labour to its marginal cost.

$$P^*(1 + 1/\eta)(\partial y/\partial n) = W(1 + 1/\epsilon) \tag{9}$$

where P^* is the desired price of output, $\partial y/\partial n$ is marginal product of labour, η is elasticity of product demand, and ϵ is elasticity of labour supply. $1/1(1 + 1/\eta)$ can be called degree of monopoly and $1 + 1/\epsilon$ the degree of monopsony.

Solving for $\partial y/\partial n$ from the production function (equation 6) we get:

$$P^* = (1 + 1/\eta)^{-1} (1 + 1/\epsilon) Wb^{-1} y^{-(1+\rho)} n^{(1+\rho)} e^{\rho\lambda t + \rho aU} \tag{10}$$

and converting to natural logarithms:

$$\ln P^* = A + \ln W - 1/\sigma \ln(y/n) + \rho\lambda t + \rho aU \tag{11}$$

where $\sigma = 1/(1 + \rho)$ = elasticity of substitution between labour and capital, and $A = \ln(1 + 1/\epsilon) - \ln(1 + 1/\eta) - \ln b$.

We do not have independent measures of the degree of monopoly or monopsony.

However, it is likely that they change slightly over time and that there is some cyclical variability in them. It is, however, extremely difficult to evaluate the directions of this variability on *a priori* grounds. The exact result depends on the nature of the shift in the demand curves facing the firms as well as on the slope of the supply curve of labour, which is complicated by the existence of unions which bring the labour market elements of bilateral monopoly. The results are likely to be absorbed by the coefficient of the unemployment rate (U), affecting it in an unknown way. This coefficient is also likely to absorb biases due to other imperfections of the data.[33] Also, it is not known to which extent firms really take into consideration in their pricing decisions very short-run fluctuations in the relevant variables. Thus, the sign and size of the coefficient of U in the equation cannot be predicted. In our regressions it turned out highly insignificant and was therefore dropped.

Equation 13 does not take into consideration the high degree of competition from foreign sources. Eastman and Stykolt (1969, p. 102) have argued that some Canadian producers "price up to the tariff and share the market with other producers rather than face the sort of competitive price reductions necessary to attain minimum-optimum scale and drive out competitors." In the long run changes in the relation between local and foreign prices cause interindustry shifts, but in the short run they mainly affect profits. The price equation becomes:

$$\ln P_t^* = \gamma(A + \ln W - 1/\sigma \ln(y/n) + \rho\lambda t) + (1 - \gamma)\ln PIM \qquad (12)$$

where PIM is the implicit price of imports of goods and services as a proxy for relevant foreign prices and $(1-\gamma)$ is the fraction of output priced at foreign prices. Expressing equation 12 in first differences and assuming departures from desired prices and an adjustment process of the form:

$$\Delta \ln P_t = \beta(\Delta \ln P_t^*) + (1 - \beta)(\Delta \ln P)_{t-1} \qquad (13)$$

we get:

$$\Delta \ln P_t = \beta\gamma\rho\delta + \gamma\beta\Delta \ln W_t - \gamma \beta/\sigma \Delta \ln(y/n)_t + \beta(1 - \gamma)\Delta \ln PIM_t$$
$$+ (1 - \beta)\Delta \ln P_{t-1}. \qquad (14)$$

To account for price controls during 1951 which prevented price rises in that year and for the lagged price rise upon their removal, a dummy variable (DKW) of the form 1 for 1951 and −1 for 1952 was added to equation 14 to give the final price equation (G.5) for the business non-agriculture sector.

The results appear in broad conformity with the theory. The value of the wage rate coefficient is somewhat too high in relation to γ and β; thus, the implied wage rate impact is somewhat larger than one (about 1.18) but not significantly. Two estimates of the elasticity of substitution (σ) can be obtained from equation G.5: 0.61 and 0.73; both estimates are in line with most time series studies. The shares of prices determined by foreign influences appears to be somewhat high (about 0.4 in the long

33 For a more detailed discussion see Kotowitz (1968b)

run). We suspect that this is due to an overestimate of $1 - \beta$. We decided, however, to utilize the result for forecast purposes. However, care must be taken in interpreting the equation in a long-term context.[34]

All other price changes were assumed to be functions of changes in PYB2 or PY2, the price of gross national product at market prices (equation G.8) as well as cyclical and trend variables. The different weights of PIM2 in these equations reflect different proportions of imported goods in each sector. Because these proportions varied significantly between the pre-world war II period and the postwar, some of these equations were estimated using postwar data only. The disaggregation obtained here helps us to obtain separate deflators for different categories of national expenditure and thus follow the National Accounts procedure closely, avoiding serious aggregation errors. They also incorporate the effects of different rates of technological progress and interindustry movements in the economy, but care must be taken in long-run analysis as these equations describe events in the sectors in reduced form, rather than structural manner. Thus extrapolation involves stringent assumptions. From a structural point of view one might do better by estimating separate supply functions for each sector; unfortunately there were no reliable capital and labour sectoral statistics and their construction was beyond our means.

The price of imported goods and services in United States dollars is exogenous to the model.[35] The Canadian dollar price is obtained by multiplying the US dollar price by the foreign exchange rate (equation G.36). (In order to express both of these prices as indexes equal to one in 1957, the foreign exchange rate is also expressed as an index (equation G.20).)

The wage rate is assumed to behave according to the standard Phillips curve analysis. The proportional rate of change of wages per manhour in the business non-agricultural sector is assumed to be a function of the inverse of the rate of unemployment and of the rate of change of consumer prices (equation G.1). Other linear and non-linear specifications were tried but gave inferior results. It was impossible to identify any time lag pattern although quarterly models suggest the existence of a lag.

Additional variables suggested in the literature such as profits and the change in the unemployment rate were added to the basic relation but did not improve the results. While the change in the unemployment rate was significant when added, it has a positive rather than a negative sign. We interpreted it as a movement along the labour demand curve. That is, the change in unemployment is a result of unaccounted-for shifts of the labour supply curve. The persistence of this sign in spite of estimation by

---

34 If $(1-\beta)$ were 0.20 instead of 0.28 the long-term effect of the wage change would be about 1.0.
35 The fact that the price of imported goods is exogenous in US dollars and therefore remains constant can cause a problem in some simulations. The equations determining PC2 are such that the elasticity of PC2 with respect to PY2 is less than one. Thus, since PDI9 is deflated by PC2, a monetary disturbance which initially increases PY2 and Y9 but which leaves Y9R constant, will cause PDI9R to increase. Hence, C9R will increase and aggregate demand increases as PY2 increases giving an upward sloping demand curve. Under a flexible exchange rate regime, the increase in domestic prices will lead to an exchange rate depreciation which will increase PIM2 and probably result in PC2 rising sufficiently so that the increase in PDI9R will not occur. Under a fixed exchange rate, however, PIM2 will not change and since in the present version of the model the resultant decrease in exchange reserves does not induce open market transactions which offset the initial monetary disturbance, the perverse effect on the slope of the aggregate demand curve persists.

two-stage least squares can be attributed to an imperfect solution of the simultaneity problem, probably due to omission of a relevant predetermined variable from the wage equation. This interpretation is supported by the relatively low degree of explanation of the wage change variable. We therefore decided to omit the change in unemployment as an explanatory variable in this equation.[36] While at first glance the equation suggests a considerable degree of money illusion, it is likely that much of the direct price effect is included in the constant term, as the period covered had a mild inflationary trend throughout. We had to confine our estimation to the period 1949-66. Attempts to estimate the relation for the full period did not work well, probably because the rate of unemployment variable is of very poor quality before 1935.[37]

One price index that requires some explanation is PSI2, the deflator for indirect taxes less subsidies. The nature of PSI2 is revealed if we make the simplifying assumptions that there are no interest and dividends paid to or received from abroad, that there are no subsidies, and that the only indirect tax is an *ad valorem* sales tax on goods and services. Under these assumptions it can be shown that PSI2 is a currently-weighted (Paasche) index of the sales tax rate times the prices of the goods. Hence, PSI2 increases if prices increase or if the sales tax rate increases. For the sample period, PSI2 was computed as an exogenous variable. For long-run projections from a base year t to the period $t + k$, the definition of PSI2 should be

$$\text{PSI2}_{t+k} = \text{PYG2}_{t+k} * (1 + r_{t+k})\text{PSI2}_t$$

where r is the proportionate increase in the tax rate since the base period and $\text{PYG2}_t = 1.0$. PSI2_t is the actual value of PSI2 in period t.

Unfortunately, however, our estimate of PSI 2 from the available data forces it to absorb the statistical discrepancy between the Dominion Bureau of Statistics measurement of real output from the expenditure side and their estimate built up by adding the real output originating in each industry.[38] From our data, the rate of growth in PSI2 is lower than one would expect in relation to the growth in PYG2 and tax rates. This suggests that the statistical discrepancy is growing over time.

Equations G.1 and G.5, which explain WRB and PYB2, have been used by R.G. Bodkin (1970) as a subsystem to suggest the considerable conflict between the goals of full employment and stable prices, even under fairly favourable assumptions regarding external prices and productivity growth. Bodkin abstracted these two equations from the complete model, linearized, and eliminated the effects of lagged adjustment to obtain a steady state solution. The result was the following trade-off equation

$$\dot{P} = 0.01935 + 0.12042(1/U) - 1.17661\dot{A} + 0.54796\dot{B},$$

where $\dot{P}$ is the rate of change in PYB2, U is the unemployment rate, $\dot{A}$ is the rate of change in YBORM, $\dot{B}$ is the rate of change in PIM2. He observes from this equation,

36 Lipsey (1960) interpreted the presence of the change in the unemployment rate in the wage adjustment equation as reflecting aggregation error resulting from different rates of excess demand in different labour markets.
37 The same problem appears to have plagued other researchers, see e.g., Bodkin *et. al* (1967).
38 See Dominion Bureau of Statistics (1963, pp. 135-44).

for example, that if imports prices are stable ($\dot{B}$ = 0.0) and productivity growth is 3 per cent per annum ($\dot{A}$ = 0.03), then stable domestic prices ($\dot{P}$ = 0.0) imply an unemployment rate of 8 per cent. On the other hand, a slightly lower target of 1 per cent per annum increase in prices implies an unemployment rate of about 4½ per cent. If the rate of increase in import prices increases or if productivity decreases, the unemployment rate associated with a given amount of domestic inflation is much higher.

The equation for PRS2, the price level of residential construction, was estimated without a constant. Since the equation was run with the percentage rate of change as the dependent variable, the specification does not really call for a constant, and constant terms in various versions of the equation were generally not statistically significant.

For economic stabilization policy it is necessary to calculate the dynamic multipliers of various policy instruments. We do this in Chapter 4 where it is shown that the short-run trade-offs are different for different instruments and change in accordance with whether the economy is operating under a régime of fixed or flexible foreign exchange rates. That some trade-off between the rate of inflation and the unemployment rate exists is clearly implied by the results of the simulation experiments of Chapter 4 and is also apparent from the alternative *ex ante* forecasts of Chapter 5.

H. *Employment*

The demand for labour is composed of three sectoral components in the same manner as real output: (i) personal and government employment, (ii) agriculture, and (iii) business non-agriculture. Employment in the government and personal sectors is assumed to be exogenous.

The number of manhours worked in agriculture (EMA9) (equation H.6) is derived from a Cobb-Douglas production function as follows:

$$\ln(\text{EMA9})^* = \ln a + b_1 \ln(\text{YA9R})^* - b_1 \ln(\text{KA9S}) - b_2 t \qquad (15)$$

where * designates desired level (unobserved), YA9R is real output, and (KA9S) is capital in place at the beginning of the year and t is time.

We assume that expected real output in agriculture (YA9R)* is a positive function of time and of the level of agricultural income per manhour divided by the wage rate in the business non-agriculture sector of the economy, both lagged one period. This is because expected output is a function of the number of families engaged in agriculture. Migration of families from farms to the cities is a function of the level of farm income per employed member of the family relative to wages in the rest of the economy. Thus expected output incorporates elements of the supply of labour (and capital) to agriculture. This is clearly not an entirely satisfactory procedure for the long run as there is no explicit specification of the demand and supply of agricultural products and their relation to government policies and other exogenous variables. However, the reduced form of the equation does capture the major elements of the short-run demand-supply interaction of agricultural employment.

The final form of the equation is obtained by substitution for $\ln(\text{YA9R})^*$ of $c_1 t +$

c_2 $\ln[\text{YA91}/(\text{WRB01}*\text{EMA91})]$ and by assuming a Koyck-type lagged adjustment function for the dependent variable.

The implicit structural coefficients of the production and off-the-farm migration functions derived from this reduced form are of reasonable magnitude. The long-run gross share of capital in value added (β) is about 29 per cent. The elasticity of farm population relative to income differentials between farmers and urban labourers is greater than 7 per cent,[39] i.e., a 1 per cent change in the ratio of urban wages to farm income will cause a farm population decline of over 0.07 per cent. The equation also revealed a structural change during world war II, a once and for all reduction of labour demand during the war and a strong negative trend in the postwar. In view of the fact that the direct estimate of the production function does not show these changes they must be interpreted as changes in hours[40] and in off-the-farm migration pattern: many of the soldiers did not return to farms in the postwar period and the rate of off-the-farm migration accelerated.

Employment in agriculture is obtained by dividing manhours by hours worked per year. Since no separate estimate was available for hours worked in agriculture, we used hours worked in the business non-agriculture sector as a proxy variable. This introduces an error into the dependent variable in the demand for manhours equation, but the results were better than when the demand for workers was estimated directly.

Employment in the business non-agriculture sector was estimated by derivation of a demand for labour function from a Cobb-Douglas production function and the addition of a lagged adjustment function as follows:

$$\ln n^* = -(1/\beta)\ln A + (1/\beta)\ln y - [(1-\beta)/\beta]\ln k - (1/\beta)\lambda t. \qquad (16)$$

The desired demand for employees (L^*) is obtained by the identity $\ln L^* \equiv \ln n^* - \ln HSB$, where HSB = standard hours worked per year in business non-agriculture and is assumed to be a function of time of the form $\ln HSB = a + \delta t$. Thus equation 16 becomes

$$\ln L^* = -(1/\beta)\ln A - a + (1/\beta)\ln y - (1-\beta)/\beta \ln k - [(1/\beta)\lambda + \delta]t. \qquad (17)$$

As actual output may diverge from expected output, and as costs of hiring and firing are not negligible, and as the pool of manpower available for hiring is limited, we must assume that actual employment will adjust to desired employment with a lag which depends on the available labour pool as measured by the lagged rate of unemployment. The lower the rate of unemployment, the less of the desired employment change can be realized.

$$\ln L_t = \gamma \ln L_t^* + (1-\gamma)\ln L_{t-1} + \theta U_{t-1} + \gamma. \qquad (18)$$

39 This is because c_1 measures the effect of migration of both capital and labour. It is likely that labour migration is greater than capital migration, so c_2 underestimated the impact of income differentials on labour migration.
40 The hours equation H.2 also demonstrated the same shifts, but the magnitudes are smaller so they do not fully explain the changes in labour demand.

Substituting from equation 17 and reorganizing we get:

$$\ln L_t - \ln y_t = -\gamma/\beta \ln A - a + \gamma + [\gamma(1 - \beta)/\beta] [\ln y_t - \ln k_{t-1}]$$
$$+ (1 - \gamma)(\ln L_{t-1} - \ln y_t) - \gamma(\lambda/\beta + \delta)t + \theta U_{t-1}. \qquad (19)$$

The reason for estimating the demand for employees directly, rather than estimating the demand for manhours first and then dividing by the number of hours worked to derive employment is that the level of unemployment and therefore the level of employment are crucial variables in the model. As the estimate of hours worked per year is not very good, we found it better to estimate employment directly, rather than create additional error in employment by relying on weak hours data.

The employment equation was estimated for the postwar only in order to minimize error. The result for the complete period as well as those for the demand for manhours was very close to the equation used but the residuals for recent years were somewhat inferior. As the model is to be used for prediction as well as for analytical purposes, we decided to use the postwar equation. The implied coefficient of the production and adjustment functions appear to be reasonable: the competitive labour share in gross private output is about 58 per cent and about 50 per cent of the adjustment is made within one year. The pattern of labour productivity in the short run and the long run is consistent with theory and observation. The partial elasticity of business employment with respect to business output is 0.86 within one year and about 1.7 in the long run holding capital constant. As capital stock in the employment relation is lagged one period, growth of capital is assumed not to affect employment in the same year. However, in the long run, the growth of capital stock will offset the required increase in employment.

The supply of hours worked per week in business non-agriculture, equations (H.2 and H.3) is explained by a negative time trend measuring the long-term income effect and by a negative impact of unemployment measuring the substitution effect of higher marginal wage rates at higher employment levels. An attempt to measure these effects directly rather than by proxy variables gave inferior results, mainly because average wage rates underestimate the cyclical variability of marginal wage rates, a measure of which is not available, and because they include elements of income as well as substitution. The estimate of hours was constructed by us as a weighted average of industry indexes. Because of changes in coverage and variation in weights which occured in the raw data but which could not be properly incorporated in our estimate, the quality of the dependent variable is not high.

Some of the equation results are notable. No clear income effect is apparent for the period 1928-40 probably because no clear trend in income existed. Hence the dummy variable TTB which appears in the equation has a non-zero value only in the postwar period; in the prewar period it is zero. The income effect in the postwar period was approximately −0.3 per cent per year; that is, the income elasticity of the supply of hours was approximately −0.1 per cent during this period, as is indicated by the shift variable DMB. A marked positive shift of about 14 per cent in hours of work is apparent during the second world war. This result was consistent for most other regressions tried. It is difficult to interpret. The substitution effect measured by the unemployment effect turned out to be consistent for the full period. The non-linearity exhibited is marked: the marginal effects of increases in unemployment increase rapidly with the unemployment rate. This is probably because of the tendency to spread employment as much as possible in time of slack, as well as the entry of housewives and students into the labour force on a part-time basis when family income falls.

In the standard manhours equation (H.8), actual employment (not employment as calculated by the model solution) is used. Hence SMB9 is calculated outside the model (i.e., it is an exogenous variable) for simulations over past periods of time. In forecasts, however, it is calculated endogenously using calculated employment. The standard hours equation (H.3) is the hours equation (H.2) with unemployment set at the full employment level of 4 per cent.

I. *Income*

The wage bill in business non-agriculture is given by the identity wage bill = wage rate * employment * average hours (equation I.2). Gross corporate profits are then assumed to be a fraction of the non-wage part of the business non-agriculture income sector as well as a function of *GAP* and a time trend to allow for cyclical and secular variations in the proportion of corporate profits in non-wage business income. As can be expected the share of corporate profits shows a positive secular trend and is positively affected by business conditions. There is, however, no simple way of judging about the cyclical variability of corporate profits relative to GNP or to GDP generated in the private sector as the wage share itself fluctuates cyclically. We will develop that further in the section reporting the simulation results.

Following Lintner (1962), we assume that dividend policy is a function of current net disposable corporate income and lagged dividends. Attempts to include tax policy and investment expectation variables in the dividend equation along the lines suggested by Brittain (1964) and Smith (1963) were not successful. The long-run corporate marginal propensity to save implied by the dividend equation is 0.31.

Net national income at factor cost is obtained in equation I.10 by subtracting indirect taxes less subsidies and capital consumption allowances from gross national product at market prices. (Subsidies and capital consumption allowances are exogenous variables in the model.) Personal income is derived in equation I.14 by subtracting undistributed corporate profits, corporate income taxes and a number of exogenous variables from national income and adding transfer payments and interest on the public debt. Equation (I.10) and (I.11) estimate interest on the public debt and contributions to social insurance and government pension funds. Personal disposable income is then obtained by subtracting personal taxes. Expressed in constant dollars per person, this becomes the principal variable in the consumption functions. If the model generates incorrect figures for personal disposable income, consumption estimates are directly affected. Personal saving is derived as a residual.

J. *Taxes*

Personal income taxes (equation J.1) are a function of personal income, employment, the exemption level, the utilization ratio (*GAP*) and a representative personal income tax rate. The latter is the effective rate implied by the tax schedule, calculated as the ratio of tax payable to taxable income, assuming the individual has taxable income of $4,250. Personal income per employed worker less the exemption level is taken as an index of taxable income per taxpayer. There are obvious problems of aggregation resulting from cyclical changes in the distribution of taxable personal incomes, given a progressive structure of rates.[41] We have not included changes in the distribution of personal income within the model. On the hypothesis that such changes are systematically related to variation in the level of economic activity, we have tried to capture some of this effect through the inclusion of the utilization ratio in the function. The number of taxable persons is therefore taken to be function of employment and the utilization ratio. The exponential function we have employed appears to yield a satisfactory representation of this non-linear relation.

Corporate income taxes (equation J.3) are a function of *GAP*, net profits, the cut-off rate for the low corporate tax rate, and the high and low corporate tax rates. The function essentially reflects the corporate tax structure with the utilization ratio included to capture cyclical changes in the distribution of firms by taxable profit category.

Total indirect taxes (equation J.4) are related to the sum of consumer expenditure on durable and non-durable goods, the sum of the investment expenditure on machinery and equipment and the sum of investment expenditure on residential and non-residential construction. The lagged realized rate of indirect tax is applied to each such sum in an attempt to capture some of the variation in the over-all rate structure.

The dummy variable takes on values 0.3 in 1963, 0.42 in 1964, 0.84 in 1965. Prior to 1963 the values are zero; after 1965 the values are unity. These values are taken to be representative of the gradual implementation of the sales tax on building materials introduced in 1963. Multiplication by this dummy variable contemporaneously phases in construction expenditure as part of the indirect tax base. During the transition period, however, the lagged realized rate of indirect taxation is higher than the rate which is really applicable to construction expenditure. The change in the dummy variable is therefore included to bring about an adjustment for this effect. From 1967 on, the change variable becomes zero.

K. *Interest Rates*

The short-term interest rate (SIC) determined by the model is the rate on three-month Canadian treasury bills. The demand for money function, normalized on the treasury bill rate, was estimated for the postwar period (equation K.1). Data prior to the establishment of the Bank of Canada in 1935 were not available.

With the development of the Canadian money market the treasury bill rate has come to be reasonably representative of short-term interest rates within the country. This is particularly true for annual data since any transitory eccentricities of the tender rate which might appear in a monthly, or even a quarterly series, will substantially average out.

Real cash balances per dollar of real gross national product (applying, in effect, the

41 For a very good discussion of these problems and an empirical investigation incorporating
disaggregation by income classes, see Jutlah (1970, Chapter 3). It is hoped that it will be possible
to incorporate Jutlah's work on corporate as well as personal income taxes in later versions of
the model.

implicit price deflator for GNE to both current dollar GNP and the nominal money stock) are negatively related to the Canadian treasury bill rate and positively related to the US treasury bill rate and the depreciation of the Canadian dollar. The specification of the equation is not completely adequate but the signs of the coefficients on interest rates and the change in the exchange rate are consistent with interpretation as a Canadian-US yield differential, with the US yield augmented by any depreciation in the value of the Canadian dollar. Since our data are annual we cannot hope to pick up in any very sensitive way the role of exchange rate expectations operating upon decisions relating to short-term (quarterly horizon) financing. What is essentially implied is that during a year in which the Canadian dollar did in fact depreciate there was, on balance, a contemporaneous prevailing expectation that devaluation was going to take place.

For such an adjusted yield differential to represent appropriately the opportunity cost of holding Canadian cash balances, Canadian securities would have to be closer substitutes than US securities for Canadian cash balances. Thus a widening of the differential, which would lead to the holding of more Canadian relative to US issues, would also reduce the demand for Canadian cash balances. Such a difference in the degree of substitutability is quite probable, given the predominance of the chartered banks in the market for Canadian treasury bills and the role which these issues serve in helping them meet their secondary reserve requirement.

Equation K.2 for the long-term interest rate is a Koyck distributed lag on the short-term (treasury bill) rate. This formulation is based on the familiar expectations model of the term structure of interest rates whereby long-term rates are interpreted as averages of expected short-term interest rates plus (possibly) a risk premium.[42] Extrapolative expectations were assumed to be related to a sufficiently recent past to be ignored in a specification designed for use with annual data.[43]

However, the long-run equilibrium solution of this equation is

LIC = 2.5 + 0.75 SIC.

The 0.75 coefficient of SIC is not consistent with the hypothesis stated above; which would require that this coefficient be unity; rather the magnitude of the coefficient implies that the risk premium varies inversely with LIC.[44]

L. *International Capital Flows and Exchange Rate*

Behavioural equations (L.1 and L.2) have been specified for United States direct investment in Canada (LDU9) and for the net movement of long-term Canadian secur-

42 See, for example, Meiselman (1962).
43 Shapiro (1967) found from quarterly data for the years 1955-62 that LIC depended on past values of SIC up to a 16-quarter lag (p. 457); but that the effect of extrapolative expectations was negligible after 4 quarters and not apparent at all after 6 (see Figure 2, p. 458).
44The equilibrium solution is strikingly close to that obtained by Johnson and Winder (1962) from monthly data from April 1952 to December 1961.

LIC = 2.5 + 0.67 SIC.

(For the long-rate they used the mid-month 20-year theoretical bond yield to December 1957, and thereafter the yield on 3¼ per cent Canadas, October 1, 1979.)

ities to the United States (CIF9).[45] The value of business capital formation in Canada is the principal explanatory variable in US direct investment in Canada. Caves and Reuber (1969, p. 16) acknowledge the correspondence between the size and composition of direct investment flows and the pattern of capital formation currently under way in Canada. They also acknowledge the determinants of the rate of flow of direct investment to Canada to be harder to identify in specific, statistical terms than those of portfolio or short-term flows. They found quarterly changes in direct investment in Canada to be associated with current quarterly changes in Canadian gross national product but were reluctant to draw any conclusion as to cause or effect. It seems plausible to us to take the decision to undertake real investment as the primary decision, with financing secondary. The actual investment expenditure could then well be synchronized, (for annual data) with capital inflow; they would be associated aspects of a prior decision. Our model explains decisions relating to the undertaking of real investment but not financing decisions *per se*. However, given the established role of US firms in the Canadian economy, they will ordinarily share in any general expansion of investment and in turn finance part of their share by an inflow of capital. Our equation L.1 captures the relationship which emerges on the average. Individual cases may diverge substantially from this pattern, of course, and there may well be lags that would not show up in annual data (see Caves and Reuber (1969, p. 34)).

Other variables suggested by Caves and Reuber, such as lagged exports or gross national product or the utilization rate are either not separately identifiable when annual data are used, or at least not when investment expenditure is already included in the equation. We did not directly test the importance of liquidity of the parent US firms or their investment prospects elsewhere. It may be that we have captured some of these effects through our domestic inflationary and monetary variables. Direct US investment will also be greater the higher is the Canadian price level in relation to the US price level (in terms of the respective implicit deflators for GNE), after adjustments for changes in the exchange rate. In effect, a net inflationary bias of the Canadian relative to the US economy spurs US direct investment in Canada. The statistical significance of this effect is, however, marginal. The percentage rate of growth of the Canadian money supply is also a determining factor. The more rapid this rate of growth, the less the reliance which is placed upon US funds for any given net inflationary bias of the Canadian economy. The net impact of expansion of the Canadian money supply on US direct investment in Canada thus depends upon the net inflationary effect, if any, associated with such expansion. Such net impact therefore cannot be assessed from this single equation; it depends upon the model as a whole. As the model is presently constructed, moderate domestic monetary expansion has little or no inflationary influence. The dummy variable in the equation is zero for all years except 1964-66 when it is unity; it is designed to pick up the inhibiting effect of various policies of the US government designed to discourage investment abroad by US firms for balance of payments reasons.

The net movement of long-term Canadian securities to the United States is also a function of business capital formation in Canada and the net inflationary bias of the Canadian relative to the US economy (measured in the way described above but now of somewhat greater statistical significance). However, in the case of this portfolio in-

---

45 The general form of the equations in this section have been influenced by Rhomberg (1964).

vestment, the net inflationary bias reduces rather than increases the inflow of capital. To the extent that inflation reduces the real cost to borrowers (i.e., reduces the real rate of interest, given nominal rates) who repay predetermined amounts in dollars of reduced purchasing power, there would appear to be a tendency to rely more on the Canadian capital market when this effect is relatively stronger in Canada.

The remaining explanatory variables are differentials in nominal interest rates. The differential between the Canadian and US nominal long-term rates of interest has the expected impact of increasing the inflow of long-term capital when the Canadian rate is relatively high. This differential in nominal rates together with the net inflationary bias variable (in effect as a proxy for a differential in expected rates of inflation) essentially constitutes a differential in real rates of return. The role of the net inflationary bias variable is somewhat complicated by the fact that the Canadian-US differential in nominal short-rates also appears.

The role of the short-term interest differential is somewhat complicated. Although the statistical significance of the variable is marginal, its inclusion substantially improves the significance of the other differentials. If the long-rates related to maturities much in excess of the average term to maturity of the securities associated with the capital inflow, inclusion of the short differential as well as the long may effectively provide a more representative rate differential. The short differential alone ought to be relevant for short-term capital movements which, in the present version of our model, are determined residually by the balance of payments identity. It is possible that short and long term capital flows are complementary. It is also possible that the short-term capital inflows create expectations of exchange rate revaluation (since such revaluation is shown in the exchange rate equation). Expectations of exchange rate revaluation would decrease the expected real cost of funds to Canadian borrowers and therefore augment the net movement of long-term Canadian securities to the US. This effect would, of course, not be operative during the years of fixed exchange rate and this may be part of the reason for the marginal performance of the variable.

The remaining interest rate differential is the excess of the US long- over the US short-term nominal rate. A widening of this differential tends to reduce the net movement of long-term Canadian securities to the United States, evidently because it is associated with the reduced attractiveness of fixed nominal income securities generally so far as US investors are concerned. The reason for this would be that the widening of the differential is associated with a movement toward generally lower nominal rates throughout the term structure of US yields. In effect, the differential is a proxy for the marginal long-term nominal yield which is typically less than the average long-term rate when the long-term rate is following the short-term rate downward. Given the long and short differentials between Canadian and US interest rates, the US long-short differential would therefore be expected to reduce the inflow of US long-term portfolio investment.

The determinants of portfolio investment according to equation L.2 are essentially similar to those identified by Caves and Reuber (1969, p. 13-6). They stress the importance of the volume of new projects undertaken by government as well as by business, but would probably accept the volume of business capital formation as a causal variable in this instance. Canadian-US long-term interest rate differentials and the Canadian long-short spread (as a measure of interest rate expectations) are also found important by Caves and Reuber. The three coefficients of the interest differentials in our equation L.2 are essentially equal in absolute value. Reorganizing terms, we could therefore interpret these as yielding the international long-rate differential and a long-short differential as a measure of interest expectations, except that this differential would also be international - the excess of the US long-rate over the Canadian short-rate. We are not inclined to interpret the result in this way, however, because the direct test of the Canadian long-short differential did not perform as well as the reported version of the L.2 equation. We do not have the value of the exchange rate in our equation, (although Caves and Reuber found it significant) since we would not capture short-run expectational effects with annual data.

The exchange rate equation (G.19) is estimated from data relating only to the years 1950-61, the period of the fluctuating exchange rate. Because the principal components used elsewhere in the model for the derivation of two-stage least squares estimates were derived from longer time periods, the ordinary least squares version of this equation has been employed.

When the Canadian-US short-term interest rate differential widened, the Canadian dollar appreciated, because of the influence of associated increases in short-term capital inflows. Short-term capital flows appear, however, as a separate variable. The role of the short-term capital flow variable must therefore be interpreted in terms of its partial impact, which is to say, as the role of that part of short-term capital movements not induced by the response to short-term interest differentials. Moreover, the short-term capital flow variable must be interpreted in relation to the given value of change in reserves. Now it is clear from the balance of payments identity that in this case total short-term capital flows and/or the change in foreign exchange reserves must cover the excess of (IMP9 − X9 − F9) over (LDU9 + CIF9 + LN9) which is the size of the trade deficit not financed by long-term capital flows.[46] Part of this remainder will be financed by the fraction of short-term capital flows responsive to the interest rate differential. The remainder, the effect of which is picked up by S9 in the exchange rate equation, represents a residual demand for US dollars which, as expected, tends to depreciate the Canadian dollar. Any increase in foreign exchange reserves also leaves the Canadian dollar less valuable than it would otherwise have been.

In the current version of the model, the change in foreign exchange reserves is taken as exogenous and short-term capital movements (equation L.3) are determined by the balance of payments identity throughout the postwar period. In effect, therefore, short-term capital movements are a residual over the postwar period. During the period of the fluctuating exchange rate, changes in this residual feed back into the rest of the model through the exchange rate equation. The specification therefore seems quite appropriate for a period of fluctuating exchange rate, during which time changes in reserves of foreign exchange could reasonably be taken as exogenous in the sense that they would arise only through direct action of the Bank of Canada via the Exchange Fund Account.

With the return to the fixed exchange rate in 1962, the exchange rate of course

---

46 The current account balance of the balance of international payments, CR9 (equation L.5) differs from the balance shown in the National Accounts, CRA9 (equation D.38) by the net inflow of inheritances and migrants' funds, F9, which is regarded in the National Accounts as a capital, rather than a current, transfer.

becomes an exogenous variable.[47] In the present version of the model we have therefore dropped the exchange rate equation for the years 1962-6. The consequence of this is that the effect of interest rates and other variables on long-term capital flows carry through the balance of payments identity to the residual category of short-term capital flows and stop there; there is no feed-back into the rest of the model again.

We have continued to handle the change in reserves of foreign exchange from 1962 on as an exogenous variable although it might more appropriately be treated as endogenous. Rather than estimate a separate function from the limited data available for the years 1962-6 it would be preferable to normalize the exchange rate equation on DR9. With the exchange rate itself exogenous, and the interest differential (SIC - SIU) determined by the rest of the model, this normalized equation would express DR9 as inversely related to S9. The balance of payments identity would express a direct relation between DR9 and S9, given the other capital flows as determined by the rest of the model. These two relations thus would yield solutions for S9 and DR9, neither of which would feed back into the rest of the model. Interest in this approach would be in the behaviour of DR9.

In recent years there has been an agreement to limit the accumulation of foreign exchange reserves. Forecasts and simulations with DR9 endogenous would indicate the magnitude of the policy challenge involved in living within these agreements. To acknowledge this constraint explicitly, we should retain the assumption that the change in foreign reserves was exogenous (in the sense of being subject to direct policy action) and accordingly normalize the exchange rate equation on the Canadian-US short-term interest differential instead.

This latter approach requires at the same time that we normalize the demand for money equation on the money supply. Making the money supply endogenous in this way is one means of introducing the constraint upon Canadian monetary policy which has characterized recent years (as described at somewhat greater length in the section on interest rates).

M. *Government Revenue and Expenditure Account*

This is a summary account which pulls together the information on government expenditures and revenues as given by the model, plus the values of some exogenous variables, to derive an estimate of the government deficit.

N. *Capital Formation and Saving Account*

This is another summary account that gives total national capital formation and national saving as estimated by the model. Since the two sides of the account are built up independently, a statistical discrepancy (ERB9) exists between total capital formation and total saving, which by definition should equal each other, apart from the residual error of estimate in the National Accounts.

---

47 Our solution program requires that an exogenous variable be given a different name from an endogenous variable. Hence in the fixed period EXC (endogenous) = XXU (exogenous). In the floating rate period the behavioural equation G.19 is operative with EXC as the left-hand variable.

5. LISTING OF THE EQUATIONS OF THE MODEL

```
                          TRACE 1969
              ANNUAL ECONOMETRIC MODEL OF CANADA
                 INSTITUTE FOR POLICY ANALYSIS
                    UNIVERSITY OF TORONTO
------------------------------------------------------------------
```

A.   PERSONAL EXPENDITURE CN CONSUMER GOODS AND SERVICES

(A.1) CONSUMER DURABLE GOODS IN CONSTANT (1957) DOLLARS
PER PERSON

$$DUR3RC = 0.118452 + 0.418709 * DUR3SC + 0.103648 * PDI3RC$$
$$\qquad\quad (2.89) \qquad (3.46) \qquad\qquad (6.00)$$
$$1 \qquad\quad - 0.134115 * PD2/PC2 - 0.007931 * LIC$$
$$\qquad\qquad (3.75) \qquad\qquad (2.51)$$
$$\qquad\quad RBSQ=0.982 \qquad DW=1.68 \quad SDR=0.006721 \quad PD=1928-40,47-66$$

(A.2) CONSUMER NON DURABLE GOODS IN CONSTANT (1957) DOLLARS
PER PERSON

$$ND3RC = 0.097509 + 0.519056 * ND3SC + 0.181740 * PDI3SC$$
$$\qquad\quad (2.38) \qquad (6.83) \qquad\qquad (6.16)$$
$$1 \qquad\quad + 0.216714 * PDI3RD - 0.031274 * PND21/PC21$$
$$\qquad\quad (5.50) \qquad\qquad (0.87)$$
$$\qquad\quad RBSQ=0.996 \qquad DW=2.51 \quad SDR=0.0075639 \quad PD=1928-40,47-66$$

(A.3) CONSUMER SERVICES IN CONSTANT (1957) DOLLARS
PER PERSON

$$SER3RC = -0.002276 + 0.766955 * SER3SC + 0.085335 * PDI3SC$$
$$\qquad\quad (0.45) \qquad (8.66) \qquad\qquad (3.11)$$
$$1 \qquad\quad + 0.189428 * PDI3RD - 0.039033 * (PSR2/PC2-PSR21/PC21)$$
$$\qquad\quad (6.03) \qquad\qquad (0.70)$$
$$\qquad\quad RBSQ=0.997 \qquad DW=2.17 \quad SDR=0.00596 \qquad PD=1928-40,47-66$$

(A.4) CONSUMER DURABLE GOODS IN CONSTANT (1957) DOLLARS

$$DUR9R = DUR3RC * POP6$$

(A.5) CONSUMER NON DURABLE GOODS IN CONSTANT (1957) DOLLARS

$$ND9R = ND3RC * POP6$$

(A.6) CONSUMER SERVICES IN CONSTANT (1957) DOLLARS

$$SER9R = SER3RC * POP6$$

(A.7) CONSUMER DURABLE GOODS

$$DUR9 = DUR9R * PD2$$

(A.8) CONSUMER NON DURABLE GOODS

$$ND9 = ND9R * PND2$$

(A.9) CCNSUMER SERVICES

$$SER9 = SER9R * PSR2$$

(A.10) PERSONAL EXPENDITURE ON CONSUMER GOODS AND
SERVICES IN CONSTANT (1957) DOLLARS

C9R $\quad$ = DUR9R + ND9R + SER9R

(A.11) TOTAL PERSONAL EXPENDITURE ON CONSUMER GOODS AND
SERVICES

C9 $\quad$ = DUR9 + ND9 + SER9

B. GOVERNMENT EXPENDITURE ON GOODS AND SERVICES

(B.1) GOVERNMENT EXPENDITURE ON GOODS AND SERVICES

G9 = WSG9 + GNW9 + MPA9

(B.2) GOVERNMENT EXPENDITURE ON GOODS AND SERVICES
IN CONSTANT (1957) DOLLARS

G9R = G9/PG2

(B.3) PRICE LEVEL OF GOVERNMENT EXPENDITURE ON GOODS AND SERVICES

PG2 = G9/ ((WSG9 + MPA9)/PGW2 +GNW9/ PYI2)

C. BUSINESS GROSS CAPITAL FORMATION

(C.1) INSTITUTIONAL LENDERS N.H.A. MORTGAGE APPROVALS IN 1957
DOLLARS
ILA9R $\quad$ = -3.335578 + 0.438404 * POP6 + 0.269074 * (NHA-LIC)
$\qquad$ (2.29) $\qquad$ (2.25) $\qquad$ (4.02)
1 $\qquad$ +0.042533 * U + 0.342807 * (PRC2/PRS2 + PRC21/PRS21 +
$\qquad$ (2.56) $\qquad$ (2.13)
2 $\qquad$ PRC22 / PRS22)/3.0 - 0.136295 * KRS9S - 0.300715*NHA
$\qquad$ (1.68) $\qquad$ (4.07)
$\qquad$ RBSQ=0.8092 $\quad$ DW=2.29 $\quad$ SDR=0.06078 $\quad$ PD=49-66

(C.2) CONVENTIONAL MORTGAGE APPROVALS IN 1957 DOLLARS

CNA9R $\quad$ = 0.183945 * POP6 - 0.320477 * LIC - 0.273731 * (NHA -
$\qquad$ (8.41) $\qquad$ (5.81) $\qquad$ (5.16)
1 $\qquad$ LIC) - 0.998759 * GAP
$\qquad$ (6.01)
$\qquad$ RBSQ=0.9248 $\quad$ DW=1.99 $\quad$ SDR=0.051695 $\quad$ PD=49-66

(C.3) MULTIPLE HOUSING STARTS

MHS3 $\quad$ = 6.486649 + 47.940368 * CHA9 / PRS2 + 27.631234 *ILA9R
$\qquad$ (2.23) $\qquad$ (5.41) $\qquad$ (3.84)
1 $\qquad$ + 89.744601 * CNA9R - 14.586405 * ILA9S
$\qquad$ (12.21) $\qquad$ (2.21)
$\qquad$ RBSQ=0.9740 $\quad$ DW=2.47 $\quad$ SDR=3.572 $\quad$ PD=49-66

(C.4) SINGLE HOUSING STARTS

SHS3 $\quad$ = 42.995247 + 55.211573 * CHA9 / PRS2
$\qquad$ (7.79) $\qquad$ (3.28)
1 $\qquad$ + 69.426399 * ILA9R - 17.080895 * CNA9R
$\qquad$ (5.07) $\qquad$ (1.22)
2 $\qquad$ + 20.450255 * ILA9S
$\qquad$ (1.63)
$\qquad$ RBSQ=0.7219 $\quad$ DW=1.24 $\quad$ SDR=6.7934 $\quad$ PD=49-66

(C.5) MULTIPLE HOUSING COMPLETIONS

```
MHC3     = 0.448707 * MHS3  + 0.519916 * MHS31
            (4.49)             (4.98)
          RBSQ=0.9450     DW=1.94    SDR=4.8825      PD=49-66
```

(C.6) SINGLE HOUSING COMPLETIONS

```
SHC3     = 0.863238 * SHS3  + 0.132937 * SHS31
            (17.80)            (2.68)
          RBSQ=0.8746     DW=1.77    SDR=4.0951      PD=49-66
```

(C.7) RESIDENTIAL CONSTRUCTION EXPENDITURE IN CONSTANT
       (1957) DOLLARS

```
RES9R    = 0.295652  + 0.010723 * SHC3  + 0.006436 * MHC3
            (3.61)      (9.61)             (10.65)
          RBSQ=0.9476     DW=1.53    SDR=0.04905     PD=49-66
```

(C.8) RESIDENTIAL CONSTRUCTION EXPENDITURE

```
RES9     = RES9R * PRS2
```

(C.9) BUSINESS NON AGRICULTURE INVESTMENT IN MACHINERY
       AND EQUIPMENT IN CONSTANT (1957) DOLLARS

```
BME9R    = -0.20456 * KMB9S + 0.024156* KMB9S * ALOG (CPG9/(KCB9S+
            (2.295)            (1.24)
1           KMB9S)/(PME2*(LIC*0.01+.12))) + 0.577583 * BME9S
                                             (4.25)
2         + 0.289281 * GAP* KMB9S
            (3.20)
          RBSQ= .966     DW= 1.22   SDR=0.165      PD= 28-40,47-66
```

(C.10) BUSINESS NON AGRICULTURE INVESTMENT IN MACHINERY AND
       EQUIPMENT

```
BME9  = BME9R * PME2
```

(C.11) AGRICULTURE AND FISHING INVESTMENT IN MACHINERY AND
       EQUIPMENT IN CONSTANT (1957) DOLLARS

```
AME9R    =AME9 / PME2
```

(C.12) NATIONAL ACCOUNTS INVESTMENT IN MACHINERY AND EQUIPMENT
       RECONCILIATION IN CONSTANT (1957) DOLLARS

```
RME9R  =  RME9 / PME2
```

(C.13) TOTAL INVESTMENT IN MACHINERY AND EQUIPMENT
       IN CONSTANT (1957) DOLLARS

```
SME9R    = BME9R + AME9R + RME9R
```

(C.14) TOTAL INVESTMENT IN MACHINERY AND EQUIPMENT

```
SME9     = BME9 + AME9 + RME9
```

(C.15) BUSINESS NON AGRICULTURE INVESTMENT IN NON RESIDENTIAL
       CONSTRUCTION IN CONSTANT (1957) DOLLARS

```
BNR9R    = -0.118527 * KCB9S + 0.001777 * KCB9S * ALOG (CPG9/
            (4.28)             (.33)
1           (KCB9S + KMB9S)/(PNR2*(LIC*0.01+0.035)))
2         + 0.704390 * BNR9S + 0.146014 * GAP * KCB9S
            (8.40)             (4.35)
          RBSQ=.9666     DW=1.33    SDR=0.1584      PD=28-40,47-66
```

(C.16) BUSINESS NON AGRICULTURE INVESTMENT IN NON RESIDENTIAL
CONSTRUCTION

$$BNR9 = BNR9R * PNR2$$

(C.17) AGRICULTURE AND FISHING INVESTMENT IN NON RESIDENTIAL
CONSTRUCTION IN CONSTANT (1957) DOLLARS

$$ANR9R = ANR9 / PNR2$$

(C.18) NATIONAL ACCOUNTS INVESTMENT IN NON RESIDENTIAL
CONSTRUCTION RECONCILIATION IN CONSTANT (1957) DOLLARS

$$RNR9R = RNR9 / PNR2$$

(C.19) TOTAL INVESTMENT IN NON RESIDENTIAL CONSTRUCTION
IN CONSTANT (1957) DOLLARS

$$SNR9R = BNR9R + ANR9R + RNR9R$$

(C.20) TOTAL INVESTMENT IN NON RESIDENTIAL CONSTRUCTION

$$SNR9 = BNR9 + ANR9 + RNR9$$

(C.21) TOTAL INVESTMENT IN NON RESIDENTIAL CONSTRUCTION AND
MACHINERY AND EQUIPMENT IN CONSTANT (1957) DOLLARS

$$BCF9R = SME9R + SNR9R$$

(C.22) TOTAL INVESTMENT IN NON RESIDENTIAL CONSTRUCTION AND
MACHINERY AND EQUIPMENT

$$BCF9 = SNR9 + SME9$$

(C.23) BUSINESS GROSS FIXED CAPITAL FORMATION
IN CONSTANT (1957) DOLLARS

$$SCF9R = SNR9R + SME9R + RES9R$$

(C.24) BUSINESS GROSS FIXED CAPITAL FORMATION

$$SCF9 = SNR9 + SME9 + RES9$$

(C.25) VALUE OF PHYSICAL CHANGE IN BUSINESS NON FARM INVENTORIES
IN CONSTANT (1957) DOLLARS

DHB9R   = 0.667563 - 0.487167 * IKB9S + 0.586112 *
           (4.35)   (4.65)   (2.80)
1   (DUR9S - DUR9T) + 0.133919 * YGD9R
                              (4.86)
           RBSQ=.7897   DW=1.85   SDR=.1329   PD=28-40,47-66

(C.26) VALUE OF PHYSICAL CHANGE IN TOTAL INVENTORIES
IN CONSTANT (1957) DOLLARS

$$VPC9R = DHB9R + DHA9R$$

(C.27) VALUE OF PHYSICAL CHANGE IN BUSINESS NON FARM
INVENTORIES

DHB9   = -0.2458 + 0.0535 * IVA9 + 0.9782 * DHB9R
           (5.01)   (1.00)   (24.36)
1   + 0.0268 * IKB9S + 0.6596 * (PYB2 - PYB21)/PYB21
           (5.05)   (2.05)
           RBSQ=.9875   DW=1.90   SDR=0.0318   PD=48-66

(C.28) VALUE OF PHYSICAL CHANGE IN TOTAL INVENTORIES

VPC9 = DHB9   +   DHA9

(C.29) CAPITAL STOCK IN BUSINESS NON AGRICULTURE
MACHINERY AND EQUIPMENT IN CONSTANT (1957) DOLLARS

KMB9R = BME9R + (1.0-.12) * KMB9S

(C.30) CAPITAL STOCK IN FARMING AND FISHING MACHINERY AND
EQUIPMENT IN CONSTANT (1957) DOLLARS

KMA9R = AME9R + (1.0-.14) * KMA9S

(C.31) CAPITAL STOCK IN BUSINESS NON AGRICULTURE NON
RESIDENTIAL CONSTRUCTION IN CONSTANT (1957) DOLLARS

KCB9R = BNR9R + (1.0-.035) * KCB9S

(C.32) CAPITAL STOCK IN AGRICULTURE AND FISHING NON RESIDENTIAL
CONSTRUCTION IN CONSTANT (1957) DOLLARS

KCA9R = ANR9R + (1.0-0.035) * KCA9S

(C.33) TOTAL FIXED CAPITAL STOCK IN AGRICULTURE AND FISHING
IN CONSTANT (1957) DOLLARS

KA9R   = KMA9R + KCA9R

(C.34) CAPITAL STOCK IN HOUSING IN CONSTANT (1957) DOLLARS

KRS9R = RES9R + (1.0-0.02) * KRS9S

(C.35) STOCK OF BUSINESS NON FARM INVENTORIES IN
CONSTANT (1957) DOLLARS

IKB9R   = IKB9S + DHB9R

(C.36) CAPITAL STOCK PER MANHOUR IN BUSINESS NON AGRICULTURE
IN CONSTANT (1957) DOLLARS

KBORM = (KMB9S + KCB9S + KRS9S) / EMB9

(C.37) CAPITAL STOCK PER MANHOUR IN AGRICULTURE
IN CONSTANT (1957) DOLLARS

KAORM = (KMA9S + KCA9S) / EMA9

D.   FOREIGN TRADE
_____

(D.0) INDEX OF INDUSTRIAL PRODUCTION FOR THE REST OF THE WORLD

IRW2   = IPW2 - .315 * IPU2 - .052 * IPG2

(D.1) EXPORT OF FARM AND FISH PRODUCTS TO THE U.S.
IN CONSTANT (1957) DOLLARS

XFU9R   = 0.7181 + 0.0435 * GDU2 - 0.4238 * PFU2/(EXC * UPF2)
           (5.80)   (0.79)   (2.98)

           RBSQ = .4097   DW = 1.30   SDR = 0.0291   PD=53-66 O.L.S.

(D.2) EXPORT OF FARM AND FISH PRODUCTS TO THE U.K.
IN CONSTANT (1957) DOLLARS

XFG9R   = XFG9 / PFG2

(D.3) EXPORTS OF FARM AND FISH PRODUCTS TO THE REST OF THE WORLD
IN CONSTANT (1957) DOLLARS

XFW9R   = XFW9 / PFW2

(D.4) REAL EXPORTS OF FOREST PRODUCTS TO THE U.S.
IN CONSTANT (1957) DOLLARS

XPU9R   = 1.4897 + 0.6795 * GDU2   − 0.9259 * PPU2/(EXC * UPP2)
             (5.13)   (9.07)   (4.29)

             RBSQ=.9839   DW=1.99   SDR=.0238   PD=53−66 O.L.S.

(D.5) REAL EXPORTS OF FOREST PRODUCTS TO THE U.K.
IN CONSTANT (1957) DOLLARS

XPG9R   = −0.1695 + 0.3456 * IPG2   − 0.1355 * PPG2/EXC/PPS2/EXS
             (1.28)   (5.69)   (0.38)

             RBSQ = .9047   DW = 1.50   SDR = 0.0165   PD=53−66 O.L.S.

(D.6) REAL EXPORTS OF FOREST PRODUCTS TO REST OF THE WORLD
IN CONSTANT (1957) DOLLARS

XPW9R   = −0.0296 + 0.2591 * IRW2
             (1.39)   (10.11)

             RBSQ = .8861   DW = 0.89   SDR = 0.0233   PD=53−66 O.L.S.

(D.7) REAL EXPORTS OF METALS AND MINERALS TO THE U.S.
IN CONSTANT (1957) DOLLARS

XMU9R   = 2.2946 + 1.0059 * GDU2   − 2.3327 * PMU2/(EXC * UPM2)
             (4.50)   (8.76)   (5.45)

             RBSQ = .9420   DW = 1.66   SDR = 0.0676   PD=53−66 O.L.S.

(D.8) REAL EXPORTS OF METALS AND MINERALS TO THE U.K.
IN CONSTANT (1957) DOLLARS

XMG9R   = 0.0036 + 0.3608 * IPG2   − 0.1865 * PMG2/EXC/GPM2/EXG
             (0.02)   (4.60)   (0.62)

             RBSQ = .7878   DW = 1.66   SDR = 0.0283   PD=53−66 O.L.S.

(C.9) REAL EXPORTS OF METALS AND MINERALS TO REST OF
WORLD IN CONSTANT (1957) DOLLARS

XMW9R   = 0.5321 + 0.5024 * IRW2   − 0.5462 * PMU2/(EXC*UPM2)
             (2.02)   (7.60)   (2.38)

             RBSQ = .9128   DW = 1.72   SDR = 0.0473   PD=53−66 O.L.S.

(D.10) REAL EXPORTS OF OTHER MANUFACTURED GOODS TO THE U.S.
IN CONSTANT (1957) DOLLARS

XIU9R   = −0.3916 + 1.0762 * GDU2 − 0.3703 * PIU2/(EXC * UPI2)
             (2.18)   (17.42)   (2.40)

             RBSQ = .9635   DW = 2.23   SDR = 0.0415   PD=53−66 O.L.S.

(D.11) REAL EXPORTS OF OTHER MANUFACTURED GOODS TO THE U.K.
IN CONSTANT (1957) DOLLARS

$$XIG9R = - 0.054992 + 0.147655 * IPG2 - 0.165288 *$$
$$(0.73) \quad\quad (4.58) \quad\quad\quad\quad (1.37)$$
1   PIG2 / EXC / GPI2 / EXG
RBSQ=.9755   DW=1.68   SDR=0.00437   PD=53-66 O.L.S.

(D.12) EXPORTS OF OTHER MANUFACTURED GOODS TO THE REST OF THE
WORLD IN CONSTANT (1957) DOLLARS

$$XIW9R = 0.369089 + 0.330812 * IRW2 - 0.377537 * (PIW2/EXC/UPI2)$$
$$(2.55) \quad\quad (6.48) \quad\quad\quad\quad (2.59)$$
RBSQ = .7708   DW =1.24   SDR=0.0461   PD=53-66 O.L.S.

(D.13) REAL EXPORTS OF CHEMICALS AND FERTILIZERS TO ALL COUNTRIES
IN CONSTANT (1957) DOLLARS

$$XCT9R = -0.9550 + 1.0198 * PCU2 - 0.1034 * WRB + 0.0248 * TTB$$
$$(2.21) \quad (1.95) \quad\quad\quad (0.54) \quad\quad\quad (1.75)$$
RBSQ=0.9609   DW=1.60   SDR=0.0143   PD=53-66 O.L.S.

(D.14)   EXPORTS OF FARM AND FISH PRODUCTS TO THE U.S.
XFU9   = XFU9R * PFU2
(D.15)   EXPORTS OF FOREST PRODUCTS TO THE U.S.
XPU9   = XPU9R * PPU2
(D.16)   EXPORTS OF FOREST PRODUCTS TO THE U.K.
XPG9   = XPG9R * PPG2
(D.17)   EXPORTS OF FOREST PRODUCTS TO REST OF THE WORLD
XPW9   = XPW9R * PPW2
(D.18)   EXPORTS OF METALS AND MINERALS TO THE U.S.
XMU9   = XMU9R * PMU2
(D.19)   EXPORTS OF METALS AND MINERALS TO THE U.K.
XMG9   = XMG9R * PMG2
(D.20)   EXPORTS OF METALS AND MINERALS TO
REST OF WORLD
XMW9   = XMW9R * PMW2
(D.21)   EXPORTS OF OTHER MANUFACTURED GOODS TO THE U.S.
XIU9   = PIU2 * (XAU9/PAU2 + XIU9R) - XAU9
(D.22)   EXPORTS OF OTHER MANUFACTURED GOODS TO THE U.K.
XIG9   = XIG9R * PIG2
(D.23)   EXPORTS OF OTHER MANUFACTURED GOODS TO
REST OF WORLD
XIW9   = XIW9R * PIW2
(D.24)   EXPORTS OF CHEMICALS AND FERTILIZERS TO ALL COUNTRIES
XCT9   = XCT9R * PCT2
(D.25)   EXPORTS OF GOLD AVAILABLE FOR EXPORT TO ALL COUNTRIES
XG9 = EXC / XXU * XGZ
(D.26)   REAL EXPORTS OF GOLD AVAILABLE FOR EXPORT TO ALL
COUNTRIES
XG9R   = XG9
(D.27)   TOTAL EXPORTS OF GOODS IN CONSTANT (1957) DOLLARS
XE9R   = XFU9R + XFG9R + XFW9R + XPU9R + XPG9R + XPW9R
1   +XMU9R + XMG9R + XMW9R + XIU9R + XIG9R + XIW9R
2   +XCT9R + XAU9/PAU2 + XTT9 /((ND9+SER9)/(ND9R + SER9R))
(D.28)   TOTAL EXPORTS OF GOODS
XE9   = XFU9 + XFG9 + XFW9 + XPU9 + XPG9 + XPW9
1   +XMU9 + XMG9 + XMW9 + XIU9 + XIG9 + XIW9
2   +XCT9 + XAU9 + XTT9
(D.29)   TOTAL REAL EXPORTS OF GOODS AND SERVICES
IN CONSTANT (1957) DOLLARS
X9R   = XE9R + XFS9/PXE2 + XG9R+ IDR9R + XSD9R
(D.30)   TOTAL EXPORTS OF GOODS AND SERVICES
X9   = XE9 + XFS9 + XG9 + IDR9 + XSD9

(C.31) INTEREST AND DIVIDENDS RECEIVED FROM NON RESIDENTS

$$IDR9 = IDR91^{**} 0.961844 * EXP(0.5 * 0.0144)$$
$$(71.09)$$

RBSQ =0.9313   D.W.=1.88   P.D.=47-66 O.L.S.
DEPENDENT VARIABLE FOR REGRESSION WAS LOG(IDR9)
REGRESSION WAS IN LOG-LINEAR FORM

(D.32) INTEREST AND DIVIDENDS RECEIVED FROM NON RESIDENTS
        CONSTANT (1957) DOLLARS

$$IDR9R = IDR9 / PIM2$$

(D.33) INTEREST AND DIVIDENDS PAID TO NON RESIDENTS

$$IDP9 = 0.160413 + 0.022784 * LIC + 0.246920 *DIV9$$
$$(1.583)   (1.309)   (1.473)$$
1    $$+ 0.013327 *DIV9* TTB$$
$$(2.042)$$
RBSQ=.983   DW=1.847   SDR=.0344   PD=48-66

(D.34) INTEREST AND DIVIDENDS PAID TO NON RESIDENTS IN
        CONSTANT (1957) DOLLARS

$$IDP9R = IDP9 / PX2$$

(D.35) IMPORTS OF GOODS AND SERVICES IN CONSTANT (1957) DOLLARS

$$NMP9R = 2.469791 + 0.880530 *(0.285* DUR9R + 0.212 * ND9R$$
$$(.76)   (12.6)$$
1    $$+ 0.120*SER9R +0.088*G9R + 0.123*(RES9R + BNR9R$$
2    $$+ ANR9R) + 0.464*(BME9R +AME9R) + 0.142 * X9R)$$
3    $$+ 0.351975 * VPC9R - 4.885741 * (PIM2/PY2)$$
$$(1.59)   (3.48)$$
4    $$+ 3.119369 * GAP + API9R$$
$$(1.06)$$
RBSQ=.9856   DW=1.71   SDR=0.2148   PD=47-66

(D.36) TOTAL IMPORTS OF GOODS AND SERVICES IN CONSTANT (1957)
        DOLLARS (NATIONAL ACCOUNTS)

$$IMP9R = NMP9R + IDP9R$$

(D.37) TOTAL IMPORTS OF GOODS AND SERVICES

$$IMP9 = IMP9R * PIM2$$

(D.38) BALANCE OF EXPORTS OVER IMPORTS (NATIONAL ACCOUNTS)

$$CRA9 = X9 - IMP9$$

E.   GROSS NATIONAL EXPENDITURE

(E.1) GROSS NATIONAL EXPENDITURE IN CONSTANT (1957) DOLLARS

$$Y9R = C9R + BCF9R + G9R + RES9R + X9R - IMP9R + DHB9R + DHA9R$$
1    $$+ REY9 / PY2$$

(E.2) GROSS NATIONAL EXPENDITURE

$$Y9 = PY2 * Y9R$$

(E.3) DISCREPANCY IN GROSS NATIONAL EXPENDITURE

$$ERA9 = Y9 - (C9 + BCF9 + RES9 + X9 - IMP9 + G9 + DHB9 + DHA9)$$
1    $$- REY9$$

F.   PRODUCTION

   (F.1)   OUTPUT IN AGRICULTURE, FISHING, HUNTING AND TRAPPING

   YA9   = YA9R * PYA2

   (F.2)   OUTPUT PER MANHOUR IN AGRICULTURE IN CONSTANT (1957)
           DOLLARS

   YAORM = YA9R / EMA9

   (F.3)   OUTPUT IN GOVERNMENT AND PERSONAL SECTORS

   YPA9 = WGP9 + MPA9 + IRG9

   (F.4)   OUTPUT IN GOVERNMENT AND PERSONAL SECTORS IN CONSTANT
           (1957) DOLLARS

   YPA9R = (WGP9 + MPA9) / PGW2 + IRG9 / PYI2

   (F.5)   GROSS DOMESTIC PRODUCT AT FACTOR COST

   YGD9 =Y9 - (IT9- SU9) + IDP9 - IDR9 + REY9

   (F.6)   GROSS DOMESTIC PRODUCT AT FACTOR COST
           IN CONSTANT (1957) DOLLARS

   YGD9R = Y9R - (IT9R - SU9R) +IDP9R - IDR9R +REY9/PY2

   (F.7)   OUTPUT IN BUSINESS NON AGRICULTURE AT FACTOR COST IN
           CONSTANT (1957) DOLLARS
   YB9R = YGD9R - YA9R - YPA9R

   (F.8)   OUTPUT IN BUSINESS NON AGRICULTURE AT FACTOR COST

   YB9   = YB9R * PYB2

   (F.9)   OUTPUT PER MANHOUR IN BUSINESS NON AGRICULTURE AT
           FACTOR COST IN CONSTANT (1957) DOLLARS

   YBORM = YB9R / EMB9

   (F.10) POTENTIAL OUTPUT IN BUSINESS NON AGRICULTURE AT FACTOR
           COST IN CONSTANT (1957) DOLLARS

YBP9R   = SMB9 * ((KMB9S + KCB9S + KRS9S)/SMB9) ** 0.517442 *
                                                       (8.86)
1   EXP(-0.489763 + 0.016807 * T -0.033096 * (4.0 * DMB)
              (7.69)   (10.32)   (4.8)
2   +0.007132 * (4.0 * (1.0 -DMB)) +0.000905 * (4.0 * DMB)**2
           (0.24)   (2.34)
3   -0.002322 * (4.0 * (1.0 - DMB)) ** 2 +0.123865 * DMB
           (0.77)   (1.55)
4   +0.5 * 0.00042)
           RBSQ=0.995   D.W.=2.02   P.D.=28-40,47-66
           DEPENDENT VARIABLE FOR REGRESSION WAS LOG(YB9R/EMB9)
           REGRESSION WAS IN LOG-LINEAR FORM

   (F.11) UTILIZATION RATIO IN BUSINESS NON AGRICULTURE

   GAP   = YB9R / YBP9R

(F.12) EXCESS OF UTILIZATION RATIO ABOVE NORMAL CAPACITY (1.01)

```
GAPB     = 0.0
IF(GAP.GT.1.01)GAPB=GAP - 1.01
```

G.   PRICES, WAGES, AND EXCHANGE RATE

(G.1) AVERAGE WAGE RATE PER HOUR IN BUSINESS NON AGRICULTURE

```
WRB       = WRB01 * ( EXP( 0.013195 + C.139554 * (1.0/U )
                          (1.50)        (3.25)
1           +  0.5 * 0.000212 ) * ( PC2 / PC21 )** 0.309225)
                                                    (1.76)
          RBSQ=.6897      DW=1.75                 PD=49-66
          DEPENDENT VARIABLE FOR REGRESSION WAS LOG(WRB/WRB01)
          REGRESSION WAS IN LOG-LINEAR FORM
```

(G.2) CHANGE IN BUSINESS NON AGRICULTURAL WAGE RATE PER HOUR

```
WRB0C1 = WRB - WRB01
```

(G.3) REAL WAGE RATE IN BUSINESS NON AGRICULTURE

```
WRB0R = WRB / PYB2
```

(G.4) PRICE LEVEL OF FINAL EXPENDITURE

```
PYI2   = ( Y9 - X9 + IMP9) / (Y9R - X9R + IMP9R)
```

(G.5) PRICE LEVEL OF OUTPUT IN BUSINESS NON AGRICULTURE

```
PYB2      = PYB21 *    EXP( 0.004307 - 0.043037 * DKW
                          (.956)        (3.21)
1           + 0.5 * 0.000308 ) * ( WRB / WRB01 ) * * 0.488980
                                                        (3.84)
2           * ( YB0RM / YB0SM ) ** ( -0.666731 )
                                        (5.00)
3           * ( PYB21 / PYB22 ) ** 0.282141
                                    (3.36)
4           * ( PIM2 / PIM21 ) ** 0.310505
                                    (3.27)
          RBSQ=.8498      DW=2.695            PD=28-40,47-66
          DEPENDENT VARIABLE FOR REGRESSION WAS LOG(PYB2/PYB21)
          REGRESSION WAS IN LOG-LINEAR FORM
```

(G.6) PRICE LEVEL OF OUTPUT IN GOVERNMENT AND PERSONAL SECTOR

```
PPA2   = YPA9 / YPA9R
```

(G.7) PRICE LEVEL OF GROSS DOMESTIC PRODUCT AT FACTOR COST

```
PYG2   = ( PYB2 * YB9R + PYA2 * YA9R + PPA2 * YPA9R) / YGD9R
```

(G.8) PRICE LEVEL OF GROSS NATIONAL EXPENDITURE BY CANADIANS

```
PY2    = (PYG2 * YGD9R + PSI2 * ( IT9R - SU9R) - PX2 * IDP9R
1           + PIM2 * IDR9R - REY9) / Y9R
```

(G.9) PRICE LEVEL OF CONSUMER EXPENDITURE ON DURABLE GOODS

```
PD2       = PD21 + PD21 * (0.057933 + 1.096281 * ((PY2-PY21)/PY21)
                          (1.62)        (7.25)
1           - 0.002389 * (TTB + 21.0) - 0.049158 * DMB )
              (2.30)                     (1.33)
          RBSQ=.7572      DW=2.25                PD=28-40,47-66
          DEPENDENT VARIABLE FOR REGRESSION WAS (PD2-PD21)/PD21
```

(G.10) PRICE LEVEL OF CONSUMER EXPENDITURE CN NON DURABLE
       GOODS

PND2   = (-0.0083 + (0.8358 * ((PY2 - PY21)/PY21)) + (0.3384 *
            (2.41)   (5.75)   (3.19)
1   ((PIM2 - PIM21)/PIM21)))*PND21 + PND21
            RBSQ=0.9068   DW=1.93   PD=28-40,47-66
            DEPENDENT VARIABLE FOR REGRESSION WAS (PND2-PND21)/PND21

   (G.11) PRICE LEVEL OF CONSUMER EXPENDITURE ON SERVICES

PSR2   = (-0.0766 + (0.2372 * ((PY2 - PY21)/PY21)) + (0.5136 *
            (2.35)   (3.47)   (5.62)
1   ((PSR21 - PSR22)/PSR22)) + 0.0861 * GAP)*PSR21 + PSR21
                                         (2.44)
            RBSQ=0.8714   DW=1.96   PD=28-40,47-66
            DEPENDENT VARIABLE FOR REGRESSION WAS (PSR2-PSR21)/PSR21

     (G.12) PRICE LEVEL OF CONSUMER EXPENDITURE ON GOODS AND
            SERVICES

  PC2   =   C9 / C9R

     (G.13) RESIDENTIAL RENTAL COST INDEX

PRC2= .211107 - 0.1192*(KRS9S/POP61) + 0.9797*PRC21
                 (1.46)   (13.75)
         RBSQ=0.9894 DW=1.64 SDR=0.01449 PD. 1950-1966

     (G.14) PRICE LEVEL OF RESIDENTIAL CONSTRUCTION

PRS2   = ((0.2735 *((PIM2 - PIM21)/PIM21))+ (0.9360 * ((PY2 -
             (2.71)   (6.89)
1   PY21)/PY21)) + 0.0064 * GAP + 0.2881 * GAPB)*PRS21 +
                             (1.76)   (1.72)
2   PRS21
             RBSQ=0.9184   DW=1.95   PD=28-40,47-66
             DEPENDENT VARIABLE FOR REGRESSION WAS (PRS2-PRS21)/PRS21

     (G.15) PRICE LEVEL OF GROSS INVESTMENT IN NON RESIDENTIAL
            CONSTRUCTION

PNR2   = PNR21   + PNR21 * (0.013352 + 0.050329 * (
                               (2.93)   (1.67)
1   (BNR9R-BNR9S)/BNR9S - (YB9R- YB9S)/YB9S)

2   + 0.642510 * (PRS2- PRS21) /PRS21)
              (8.36)
            RBSQ=0.8441   DW=1.73   PD=48-66
            DEPENDENT VARIABLE FOR REGRESSION WAS (PNR2-PNR21)/PNR21

     (G.16) PRICE LEVEL OF GROSS INVESTMENT IN MACHINERY AND
            EQUIPMENT

PME2   = (-0.267491 + 0.283697 * GAPO1
             (1.71)   (1.79)
1   + 0.185664 * (PYB2 - PYB21)/PYB21
             (1.04)
2   + 0.735404 * (PIM2 - PIM21)/PIM21) * PME21 + PME21
             (6.33)
            RBSQ=.8539   DW=1.945   PD=48-66
            DEPENDENT VARIABLE FOR REGRESSION WAS (PME2-PME21)/PME21

     (G.17) PRICE LEVEL OF INVESTMENT IN NON RESIDENTIAL CONSTRUCTION
            AND MACHINERY AND EQUIPMENT

PBC2   = BCF9/BCF9R

(G.18) PRICE LEVEL OF BUSINESS GROSS FIXED CAPITAL FORMATION

PSF2   = SCF9/SCF9R

(G.19) FOREIGN EXCHANGE RATE (CANADIAN DOLLARS PER U.S. DOLLAR)

```
            FIXED EXCHANGE RATE PERIOD
 IF(T.LT.25.0 .OR. T.GT.36.0) EXC= XXU
            FLOATING EXCHANGE RATE PERIOD (1950-1961)
 IF(T.GE.25.0.AND.T.LE.36.0 )
1EXC        = 0.5249  - 0.0278 * (SIC - SIU) + 0.0780 * S9
            (3.87)    (3.19)                   (4.92)
1           + 0.0482 * DR9  + 0.4653 * (EXCO1)
            (2.85)          (3.43)
            RBSQ=.9129      DW=2.11    SDR=0.0117      PD=1950-1961 O.L.S.
```

(G.20) INDEX OF FOREIGN EXCHANGE RATE

PEX2   = EXC/0.9588

(G.21) PRICE LEVEL OF TOTAL EXPORTS OF GOODS AND SERVICES

PX2   = X9/X9R

(G.22) PRICE LEVEL OF TOTAL EXPORTS OF GOODS

PXE2   = XE9 /XE9R

(G.23) PRICE LEVEL OF FARM AND FISH PRODUCTS EXPORTED TO THE U.S.

```
PFU2     = 0.317346 + 0.290503 * UPF2 * EXC + 0.282909 * WRB
           (3.13)     (2.50)                  (13.13)
           RBSQ=0.9597    DW=2.41    SDR=0.0199    PD=53-66 O.L.S.
```

(G.24) PRICE LEVEL OF FARM AND FISH PRODUCTS EXPORTED TO THE U.K.

```
PFG2     = 0.0524  + 0.3198 * PFU2  + 0.6333 * PFG21
           (0.41)    (2.81)           (3.64)
           RBSQ=.8633      DW=1.51         SDR=0.0267       PD=54-66 O.L.S.
```

(G.25) PRICE LEVEL OF FARM AND FISH PRODUCTS EXPORTED TO THE REST
       OF THE WORLD

```
PFW2     = 0.0348  + 0.3940 * PFU2  + 0.5779 * PFW21
           (0.22)    (3.03)           (3.43)
           RBSQ=0.7840    DW=1.57         SDR=0.0377       PD=54-66 O.L.S.
```

(G.26) PRICE LEVEL OF FOREST PRODUCTS EXPORTED TO THE U.S.

```
PPU2     = 0.5143  + 0.3203 * UPP2*EXC + 0.1740 * WRB - 0.0181 *
           (3.15)    (2.21)              (1.97)          (2.63)
1          ( TTB - 6.0 )

           RBSQ = .3274   DW = 0.96      SDR = 0.0114   PD= 53-66 O.L.S.
```

(G.27) PRICE LEVEL OF FOREST PRODUCTS EXPORTED TO THE U.K.

```
PPG2     = -0.6480  + 1.6423 * PPU2  - 0.0160 * TTB
           (1.46)     (4.14)           (10.84)
           RBSQ=0.9217    DW=0.95         SDR=0.0220       PD=53-66 O.L.S.
```

(G.28) PRICE LEVEL OF FOREST PRODUCTS EXPORTED TO THE REST OF
       THE WORLD

```
PPW2     = -0.3284  + 1.3419 * PPU2  - 0.0015 * TTB
           (2.05)     (8.38)           (2.80)
           RBSQ=0.8700    DW=2.13         SDR=0.0079       PD=53-66 O.L.S.
```

(G.29) PRICE LEVEL OF METALS AND MINERALS EXPORTED TO U.S.

PMU2   = -0.1309 + 0.9602 * UPM2*EXC + 0.2072 * WRB - 0.0229 *
            (0.32)   (2.57)   (0.90)   (1.14)
1   (TTB - 6.0)

          RBSQ = .8546   DW = 0.91   SDR = 0.0295   PD= 53-66 O.L.S.

(G.30) PRICE LEVEL OF METALS AND MINERALS EXPORTED TO U.K.

PMG2   = -0.2803 + 1.3070 * PMU2
            (1.95)   (9.12)
          RBSQ=0.8634   DW=1.50   SDR=0.0400   PD=53-66 O.L.S.

(G.31) PRICE LEVEL OF METALS AND MINERALS EXPORTED TO THE
       REST OF WORLD

PMW2   = -0.4550 + 1.1701 * PMU2 + 0.4113 * PMW21 - 0.0094 * TTB
            (1.33)   (2.47)   (1.47)   (1.16)
          RBSQ=0.6717   DW=1.71   SDR=0.0518   PD=54-66 O.L.S.

(G.32) PRICE LEVEL OF OTHER MANUFACTURED GOODS EXPORTED TO U.S.

PIU2   = 0.8863 + 0.0204 * (TTB-6.0)
           (89.21)   (17.45)

          RBSQ = .9589   DW = 0.77   SDR = 0.0176   PD= 53-66 O.L.S.

(G.33) PRICE LEVEL OF OTHER MANUFACTURED GOODS EXPORTED TO U.K.

PIG2   = 0.3206 + 0.6196 * PIU2 + 0.0061 * TTB
            (1.80)   (2.66)   (1.26)
          RBSQ=0.9685   DW=1.69   SDR=0.0142   PD=53-66 O.L.S.

(G.34) PRICE LEVEL OF OTHER MANUFACTURED GOODS EXPORTED TO THE
       REST OF THE WORLD

PIW2   = -0.6214 + 1.6675 * PIU2 + 0.1231 * PIW21 - 0.0145 * TTB
            (6.21)   (9.36)   (1.03)   (5.24)
          RBSQ=0.9929   DW=2.21   SDR=0.0079   PD=54-66 O.L.S.

(G.35) PRICE LEVEL OF TOTAL EXPORTS OF CHEMICALS AND FERTILIZERS

PCT2   = -0.4806 + 0.6416 * PCU2 + 0.8282 * PCT21
            (2.61)   (4.38)   (8.63)
          RBSQ = 0.8758   DW=1.70   SDR=0.0063   PD=54-66 O.L.S.

(G.36) PRICE LEVEL OF IMPORTS OF GOODS AND SERVICES

PIM2 = PFR2 * PEX2

H.   EMPLOYMENT

(H.1) UNEMPLOYMENT AS A PERCENT OF LABOUR FORCE

U   = ((LF6 - E6)/LF6) * 100.

(H.2)   AVERAGE HOURS WORKED PER WEEK IN BUSINESS NON
        AGRICULTURE

HB   =   EXP(3.7555 - 0.00284 * TTB + 0.1389 * DMB
                         (6.14)   (17.53)
1   + 0.00191 * U - 0.00061 * U **2 + 0.5 * 0.C0010)
             (1.C8)   (7.09)
         RBSQ=.9763   DW=2.06   PD=28-40,47-66
         DEPENDENT VARIABLE FOR REGRESSION WAS LOG(HB)
         REGRESSION WAS IN LOG-LINEAR FORM

(H.3)   STANDARD HOURS WORKED PER WEEK IN BUSINESS NON
        AGRICULTURE

SHB   =   EXP(3.7555   -0.00284 * TTB +0.1389 * DMB
                          (6.14)   (17.53)
1   +0.00191 * 4.0 -0.00061 * 16.0 + 0.5 * 0.00010)
              (1.08)   (7.09)
          RBSQ=.9763   DW=2.06   PD=28-40,47-66
          DEPENDENT VARIABLE FOR REGRESSION WAS LOG(HB)
          REGRESSION WAS IN LOG-LINEAR FORM

(H.4)   REALIZED DEMAND FOR LABOUR IN AGRICULTURE AND FISHING
        (NUMBER EMPLOYED)

EA6   = (EXP(.551061 + .007605 * T - .175097 * DMA
                (2.79)   (2.71)   (2.50)
1   - .016535 * TTB + 0.5 * .001018) * KA9S ** (-.169418)
             (2.37)   (2.28)
2   * EMA91 ** .587133
               (4.11)
3   * (YA91/(EMA91*WRB01)) ** .068850) / (.052 * HB)
                                    (1.72)
         RBSQ=.9919   DW=1.106   PD=28-40,47-66
         DEPENDENT VARIABLE FOR REGRESSION WAS LOG(EA6*HB*.052)
         REGRESSION WAS IN LOG-LINEAR FORM

(H.5)   REALIZED DEMAND FOR LABOUR IN BUSINESS NON AGRICULTURE
        (NUMBER EMPLOYED)

EB6   =   YB9R*EXP(-0.085735 -0.014898*T+0.003370*UC1)
                     (.25)   (2.35)   (.46)
1   *(EB61/YB9R)**0.501294*(YB9R/(KMB9S+KCB9S
                            (2.26)
2   +KRS9S))**0.360966
                     (1.69)
          RBSQ=.9962   DW=1.46   SDR=.0109   PD=48-66
          DEPENDENT VARIABLE FOR REGRESSION WAS LOG(EB6/YB9R)
          REGRESSION WAS IN LOG-LINEAR FORM

(H.6)   TOTAL MANHOURS WORKED PER ANNUM IN AGRICULTURE

EMA9   = EA6*HB*52.0*10.0**(-3)

(H.7)   TOTAL MANHOURS WORKED PER ANNUM IN BUSINESS NON
        AGRICULTURE

EMB9   = EB6*HB*52.0*10.C**(-3)

(H.8)   STANDARD TOTAL MANHOURS WORKED PER ANNUM IN BUSINESS
        NON AGRICULTURE

SMB9   = SMBZ
  IF(T.GE.45.0)SMB9=EB6/(1.0-(U-4.0)/100.0)*SHB*.052

(H.9)   TOTAL REALIZED DEMAND FOR LABOUR (NUMBER EMPLOYED)

E6   = EB6 + EA6 + EG6

I.   INCOME

       (I.1) WAGE BILL IN GOVERNMENT AND PERSONAL SECTORS

   WGP9   = WSG9 + WSP9

       (I.2) WAGE BILL IN BUSINESS NON AGRICULTURE

   WSB9   = WRB * EMB9

       (I.3) TOTAL WAGE BILL

   WSS9   = WSB9 + WSA9 + WGP9

       (I.4) GROSS CORPORATE PROFITS

   CPG9   = -1.6587 + 0.4499* (YB9 - WSB9)   + 1.6065 * GAP
               (4.17)   (22.5)   (3.54)
1   +0.0229*T
               (2.65)
             RBSQ= .9955   DW=1.00   SDR = 0.1788   PD=28-40,47-66

       (I.5) NET CORPORATE PROFITS

   CPN9   = CPG9 - CAB9

       (I.6) DIVIDENDS

   DIV9   = -0.003689 + 0.130465 *(CPN9 - CT9) + 0.811068*DIV91
               (0.22)   (3.11)   (8.49)
             RBSQ = 0.986   SDR =   0.0497   PD=28-40, 47-66

       (I.7) UNDISTRIBUTED CORPORATE PROFITS

   UCP9   = CPN9 - DIV9 - CT9 - CCD9

       (I.8) OTHER NATIONAL INCOME

   MIN9   = NFC9 - WSS9 - MPA9 - CPN9

       (I.9) NET NATIONAL INCOME AT FACTOR COST

      NFC9   = Y9 - IT9 + SU9 - CCA9 + REY9

       (I.10) INTEREST ON THE PUBLIC DEBT

   IPD9   = -0.031784 +1.104535 * IPD91 +0.008697 * (GDF9*LIC)
               (1.45)   (45.85)   (2.52)
             RBSQ=0.9921   D.W.=2.326   SDR=0.0365   P.D.=47-66

       (I.11) EMPLOYER AND EMPLOYEE CONTRIBUTIONS TO SOCIAL INSURANCE
              AND GOVERNMENT PENSION FUNDS EXCLUDING CANADA AND
              QUEBEC PENSION PLANS

   ECS9   = E6 * (+0.007127 + 0.988777 * (ECS91/E61))
                     (2.65)   (35.73)
             RBSQ=0.9853   D.W.=2.17   SDR=0.00433   P.D.=47-66

       (I.12) TOTAL EMPLOYER AND EMPLOYEE CONTRIBUTIONS TO SOCIAL
              INSURANCE AND GOVERNMENT PENSION FUNDS.

   SIP9   = ECS9 + CCP9 + QCP9

(I.13) PERSONAL INCOME

PI9   = NFC9 + TR9 + IPD9 - UCP9 - CT9 - WT9 - GI9 - AGT9 - IVA9
1   - SIP9

(I.14) PERSONAL DISPOSABLE INCOME

PDI9   = PI9 - PT9

(I.15) PERSONAL DISPOSABLE INCOME IN CONSTANT (1957) DOLLARS
        PER PERSON

PDI3RC = PDI9/(POP6 * PC2)

(I.16) CHANGE IN PERSONAL DISPOSABLE INCOME IN CONSTANT (1957)
        DOLLARS   PER PERSON

PDI3RD = PDI3RC - PDI3SC

(I.17) PERSONAL SAVING

PS9   = PDI9 - C9

J.   TAXES

(J.1) PERSONAL INCOME TAXES

PIT9   = ((PI9/E6 - EL3) ** 1.189221) * ((RPT*100.0)** 0.743994)
                            (8.7)   (3.72)
1   * EXP(-4.531474 + 0.191292 * E6 + 0.426333 * GAP
                  (6.48)   (2.80)   (0.62)
2   + 0.5 * 0.0036)
          RBSQ=0.9879 D.W.=1.94   P.D.=47-66
          DEPENDENT VARIABLE FOR REGRESSION WAS LOG(PIT9)

(J.2) TOTAL PERSONAL DIRECT TAXES

PT9   = PIT9 + POT9

(J.3) CORPORATE INCOME TAXES

CT9   = HS2 * CPN9 + (HR2-HS2) * (4.962559 - 3.589086 * GAP
                                     (2.24)   (1.65)
1   + 0.685288 * CPN9 - 0.041341 * L3 + 0.002008 * L3 * CPN9)
            (3.22)   (2.69)   (.41)
          RBSQ=.8586   DW=1.54   PD=47-66
          DEPENDENT VARIABLE FOR REGRESSION WAS
          (CT9 - HS2 * CPN9) / (HR2 - HS2)

(J.4) TOTAL INDIRECT TAXES

IT9   = -0.116710 + 1.087943* (BME9 + AME9) * RIT01
            (1.24)   (1.93)
1   +1.044156 * (DUR9 + ND9)* RIT01
              (10.09)
1   + 0.819683* DMI * (RES9 + BNR9 + ANR9)* RIT01
              (4.29)
3   - 0.793868 * (DMI -DMI01) * (RES9 + BNR9 + ANR9)* RIT01
              (1.83)
          RBSQ = .9963   DW= 2.51   SDR= 0.1161   PD= 47-66

(J.5) INDIRECT TAXES LESS SUBSIDIES

ITS9   = IT9 - SU9

(J.6) INDIRECT TAXES IN CONSTANT 1957 DOLLARS

IT9R   = IT9 / PSI2

(J.7) SUBSIDIES IN CONSTANT 1957 DOLLARS

SU9R   = SU9 / PSI2

K.   INTEREST RATES

(K.1) TREASURY BILL RATE

SIC_1 = 4.429849 + 0.963229 * SIU + 8.439313 * (EXC - EXCO1)
                (2.26)   (5.91)   (2.17)
               -10.703708 * (M9 / Y9)
                (2.59)
            RBSQ= 0.9012   DW=1.63   SDR=0.47551   PD=48-66

(K.2) LONG-TERM INTEREST RATE

LIC   = 1.017071 + 0.303535 * SIC + 0.592041 * LICO1
          (3.50)   (4.14)   (5.42)
         RBSQ = 0.950   SDR = 0.231   DW =1.697 PD = 47-66

L.   INTERNATIONAL CAPITAL FLOWS

(L.1) U.S. DIRECT INVESTMENT IN CANADA

$LDU9_1$ = - 0.434705 + 0.073321 * BCF9R - 0.180586 * DMF
$_2$ (1.36)   (5.06)   (2.41)
               + 0.480294 * (PY2/PYU2/EXC)
                (1.38)
               - 0.784577 * ((M9 - M91)/M91)
                (1.69)
            RBSQ=0.7861   DW=1.60   SDR=0.06398   PD=48-66

(L.2) NET MOVEMENT OF LONG-TERM CANADIAN SECURITIES TO THE U.S

$CIF9_1$ = 1.290166   + 0.057514 * BCF9 + 0.138184 * (LIC-LIU)
$_2$ (1.88)   (1.80)   (.78)
               - 1.197821 * PY2 / PYU2 / EXC + 0.144289 *
                (1.93)   (1.80)
               (SIC - SIU) - 0.144613 * (LIU - SIU)
                               (1.32)
            RBSQ = 0.7492 DW=2.133   SDR = 0.1325   PD = 48-66

(L.3) NET MOVEMENT OF SHORT-TERM SECURITIES

S9   = IMP9 -X9 -LDU9 - CIF9 -LN9 -F9 + DR9

(L.4) TOTAL NET CAPITAL INFLOW

$$CAP9 = LDU9 + CIF9 + S9 + LN9$$

(L.5) CURRENT ACCOUNT BALANCE

$$CR9 = X9 - IMP9 + F9$$

M.   GOVERNMENT REVENUE AND EXPENDITURE ACCOUNT

(M.1) GOVERNMENT EXPENDITURE

$$GEX9 = G9 + TR9 + IPD9 + SU9 + CAS9$$

(M.2) GOVERNMENT REVENUE

$$GRV9 = PT9 + CT9 + IT9 + WT9 + GI9 + SIP9$$

(M.3) GOVERNMENT DEFICIT

$$GCF9 = GEX9 - GRV9$$

N.   CAPTIAL FORMATION AND SAVING ACCOUNT

(N.1) TOTAL CAPITAL FORMATION
       (DISPOSITION OF NATIONAL SAVING)

$$CF9 = BCF9 + RES9 + VPC9 + CRA9 + REY9$$

(N.2) SOURCE OF NATIONAL SAVING

$$SAV9 = PS9 + UCP9 + CCA9 + AGT9 + CAS9 + IVA9 - GDF9 - REY9$$

(N.3) DISCREPANCY IN NATIONAL SAVING ACCOUNT

$$ERB9 = CF9 - SAV9$$

3 Ex post forecasts:
a test of the model

In order to quantify the dynamic characteristics of our model, we performed a variety of *ex post* forecasts and simulation experiments. In this section we discuss the results of four different *ex post* forecasting experiments presented in Table 1. It is only against this background of forecasting performance that the subsequent simulation results can be adequately assessed. Unless a model forecasts reasonably well using actual values of exogenous variables, there is no point in computing multiplier effects of changes in the values of exogenous variables by comparing the difference between solutions using augmented values of specific exogenous variables and the *ex post* forecast solution (the control situation).[1]

The first experiment consisted of a series of year-by-year *ex post* forecasts. For each year the model was solved using actual values of exogenous and lagged endogenous variables relevant to that particular year. The resulting percentage forecast errors are reported in row 2 of Table 1. Such a solution or forecast in any one year is independent of solutions for all other years. The set of these results gives the most realistic indication of the forecasting capability of the model in that an actual forecasting context would place primary emphasis upon the outlook one year ahead, using all the relevant information available.

There is, in addition considerable interest in medium-term forecasts, say of up to five years, for which an annual model may be more suitable than a quarterly model. In such a forecast, the model must run consecutively forward on its own, using its own generated solutions for lagged endogenous values as required. In an actual forecasting context, independently derived forecasts of exogenous variables would also be required. In our *ex post* forecasts we were able to use the actual values of exogenous variables. The results therefore in effect relate to the longer-range forecasting capability of the model in the absence of forecast error in relation to any of the exogenous variables. It would be very useful to have additional information on the success rate of forecasts of these exogenous variables. Of course, if we had succeeded in *ex post* forecasts of these ourselves we would have made them endogenous.[2] When confronted with an actual forecast stituation we resorted to a variety of techniques, enlisting whenever possible the specialist opinions of business analysts. Only an extended period of such actual forecasting experience would reveal the degree of success of our approach to forecasting exogenous variables.

In the tests of longer-range forecasting ability which we performed, alternative base years were selected in an attempt to capture the influence of cyclical position and

---

1 The nonlinear nature of the model makes it impossible to compute a matrix of multipliers which holds regardless of the position of the economy.
2 In some cases exogenous variables may be forecast by autoregressive functions or adaptive forecasting techniques without becoming truly endogenous variables.

TABLE 1

Actual values and percentage 'forecast' errors (solution values minus actual values as percentages of actual values) for subsets of the sample period. The values for each variable are:

(1) actual values; (2) percentage forecast errors for independent year-by-year solutions; (3) percentage forecast errors for consecutive solutions, with model generating its own lagged values from 1957 on; (4) percentage forecast errors for consecutive solutions, with model generating its own lagged values from 1960 on; (5) percentage forecast errors for consecutive solutions, with model generating its own lagged values from 1964 on.

Variable		1957	1958	1959	1960	1961	1962	1963	1964	1965	1966
DUR9R	(1)	2.430	2.464	2.592	2.582	2.686	2.935	3.208	3.585	4.005	4.173
	(2)	4.56	4.22	−1.40	2.55	2.82	3.52	1.21	−2.92	−2.32	1.61
	(3)	4.56	8.59	7.27	12.07	14.97	16.68	14.64	8.36	4.48	6.46
	(4)				2.55	5.38	7.20	5.83	0.67	−2.14	0.35
	(5)								−2.92	−4.45	−1.41
DUR9	(1)	2.430	2.499	2.678	2.664	2.716	2.960	3.246	3.592	4.001	4.169
	(2)	1.12	4.33	−2.43	1.04	2.14	2.75	−0.36	−2.45	−2.28	3.25
	(3)	1.12	4.63	2.87	6.47	8.40	9.06	6.32	0.99	3.55	−1.63
	(4)				1.04	3.40	5.63	3.87	−0.65	−4.33	−1.71
	(5)								−2.45	−4.17	−0.20
ND9R	(1)	10.402	10.642	11.091	11.460	11.723	12.332	12.641	13.234	13.913	14.647
	(2)	−0.71	1.22	−0.82	−0.75	0.12	0.14	1.27	−0.25	0.91	0.26
	(3)	−0.71	1.03	0.68	0.21	0.93	1.38	2.74	1.33	0.87	0.00
	(4)				−0.75	−0.12	0.15	1.38	0.03	−0.34	−1.07
	(5)								−0.25	0.23	−0.01
ND9	(1)	10.402	10.878	11.373	11.813	12.178	12.965	13.518	14.389	15.434	16.913
	(2)	−1.40	2.64	0.87	−0.99	−0.93	0.97	1.22	−0.10	0.89	0.22
	(3)	−1.40	1.44	3.15	2.49	1.91	2.42	4.40	3.20	1.97	−0.06
	(4)				−0.99	−1.15	1.38	3.53	2.40	1.29	−0.53
	(5)								−0.10	0.21	−0.54
SER9R	(1)	7.240	7.601	8.028	8.360	8.696	8.906	9.411	10.027	10.544	11.072
	(2)	0.27	0.47	−1.58	−1.07	−1.18	3.29	−1.02	−2.08	0.96	0.35
	(3)	0.27	0.85	0.13	−0.64	−1.04	3.13	1.60	−1.12	−0.85	−0.96
	(4)				−1.07	−1.68	2.17	0.43	−2.34	−2.07	−2.13
	(5)								−2.08	−1.21	−0.90

Continued

TABLE 1 (Continued)

Actual values and percentage 'forecast' errors (solution values minus actual values as percentages of actual values) for subsets of the sample period.

Variable		1957	1958	1959	1960	1961	1962	1963	1964	1965	1966
SER9	(1)	7.240	7.868	8.540	9.063	9.572	10.001	10.723	11.685	12.628	13.758
	(2)	-0.95	0.74	-0.89	-0.73	-1.11	3.50	-0.20	-2.09	0.88	0.38
	(3)	-0.95	-0.81	-0.87	-0.68	-0.39	4.44	4.28	2.12	2.44	1.67
	(4)				-0.73	-1.00	3.52	3.16	0.92	1.21	0.50
	(5)								-2.09	-1.15	-1.09
C9R	(1)	20.072	20.707	21.711	22.402	23.105	24.173	25.260	26.846	28.462	29.892
	(2)	0.28	1.30	-1.17	-0.49	-0.05	1.71	0.41	-1.29	0.47	0.48
	(3)	0.28	1.86	1.26	1.26	1.82	3.88	3.82	1.35	0.74	0.55
	(4)				-0.49	-0.07	1.75	1.59	-0.77	-1.24	-1.27
	(5)								-1.29	-0.96	-0.53
C9	(1)	20.072	21.245	22.591	23.540	24.466	25.926	27.487	29.666	32.063	34.840
	(2)	-0.93	2.14	-0.19	-0.66	-0.66	2.15	0.48	-1.17	0.48	0.65
	(3)	-0.93	0.98	1.60	1.72	1.73	3.96	4.58	2.51	1.47	0.43
	(4)				-0.66	-0.59	2.69	3.43	1.45	0.55	-0.26
	(5)								-1.17	-0.87	-0.72
G9R	(1)	5.722	6.113	6.205	6.268	6.562	6.811	6.848	7.113	7.571	8.250
	(2)	0.28	-0.86	-0.14	0.42	0.53	-0.15	0.01	-0.16	-0.21	-0.22
	(3)	0.28	-0.33	-0.83	-0.62	-0.10	-0.18	-0.56	-0.74	-0.46	0.04
	(4)				0.42	0.71	-0.18	-0.75	-0.97	-0.76	-0.30
	(5)								-0.16	-0.24	-0.11
RES9R	(1)	1.409	1.722	1.633	1.323	1.328	1.396	1.461	1.640	1.644	1.605
	(2)	6.96	-5.87	-1.45	6.18	11.24	-0.10	5.33	-0.51	-0.52	-1.92
	(3)	6.96	-3.78	-4.74	3.53	9.28	0.17	-0.11	-3.62	-0.26	-0.98
	(4)				6.18	12.64	2.09	0.60	-2.85	0.38	-0.71
	(5)								-0.51	0.80	-2.00
RES9	(1)	1.409	1.763	1.734	1.443	1.458	1.577	1.707	2.021	2.124	2.178
	(2)	7.80	-3.35	-1.54	5.19	11.73	0.51	5.08	-2.38	-1.48	-1.06
	(3)	7.80	-0.78	-1.32	6.43	12.62	3.78	3.36	-2.10	-0.53	-1.64
	(4)				5.19	12.38	3.85	3.09	-2.23	-0.81	-2.20
	(5)								-2.38	-2.27	-4.69

Continued

TABLE 1 (Continued)

Actual values and percentage 'forecast' errors (solution values minus actual values as percentages of actual values) for subsets of the sample period.

Variable		1957	1958	1959	1960	1961	1962	1963	1964	1965	1966
BME9R	(1)	2.477	1.967	2.020	2.052	1.886	1.987	2.113	2.541	3.048	3.518
	(2)	-5.67	24.20	9.11	4.67	14.15	14.19	6.97	-5.07	-8.44	-11.29
	(3)	-5.67	20.24	25.68	25.00	37.63	43.03	38.30	17.29	0.10	-11.03
	(4)				4.67	18.60	26.02	23.10	5.49	-9.09	-18.32
	(5)								-5.07	-12.95	-19.04
BME9	(1)	2.477	2.022	2.115	2.190	2.043	2.217	2.419	3.019	3.715	4.380
	(2)	-4.66	28.25	9.06	4.50	14.08	14.82	7.77	-6.47	-8.47	-9.52
	(3)	-4.66	25.07	31.37	30.90	44.39	49.32	47.16	23.24	4.27	-6.83
	(4)				4.50	18.78	28.91	28.15	8.22	-7.67	-16.64
	(5)								-6.47	-14.51	-19.43
BNR9R	(1)	2.798	2.385	2.068	2.005	2.065	1.960	2.062	2.384	2.709	3.112
	(2)	-19.14	9.20	15.37	4.35	-1.29	17.23	5.19	-3.00	-1.93	-7.17
	(3)	-19.14	-6.68	12.47	15.99	12.90	28.81	26.24	11.46	0.26	-10.49
	(4)				4.35	2.76	19.49	18.11	5.22	-4.51	-13.91
	(5)								-3.00	-6.12	-11.77
BNR9	(1)	2.798	2.423	2.165	2.149	2.222	2.156	2.344	2.830	3.411	4.127
	(2)	-18.84	12.00	15.60	4.37	0.28	18.88	5.47	-3.50	-3.84	-7.28
	(3)	-18.84	-3.96	16.66	20.48	18.88	36.85	34.75	17.86	2.98	-9.13
	(4)				4.37	4.58	24.36	23.80	9.34	-3.59	-14.00
	(5)								-3.50	-8.61	-14.50
VPC9R	(1)	0.231	-0.314	0.338	0.397	0.029	0.508	0.510	0.354	0.938	0.942
	(2)	-0.123	0.230	-0.006	-0.005	-0.268	0.122	0.249	0.148	-0.041	-0.037
	(3)	-0.123	0.351	-0.004	-0.064	-0.182	0.277	0.287	-0.063	-0.395	-0.159
	(4)				-0.005	-0.202	0.294	0.280	-0.056	-0.385	-0.148
	(5)								0.148	-0.238	-0.080
VPC9	(1)	0.231	-0.322	0.357	0.410	0.030	0.532	0.535	0.386	0.948	0.995
	(2)	-0.112	0.254	-0.027	-0.009	-0.268	0.125	0.268	0.147	0.322	-0.023
	(3)	-0.112	0.365	-0.014	-0.056	-0.180	0.274	0.318	-0.044	-0.020	-0.151
	(4)				-0.009	-0.201	0.296	0.310	-0.041	-0.014	-0.143
	(5)								0.147	0.131	-0.072

Continued.

TABLE 1 (Continued)

Actual values and percentage 'forecast' errors (solution values minus actual values as percentages of actual values) for subsets of the sample period.

Variable		1957	1958	1959	1960	1961	1962	1963	1964	1965	1966
X9R	(1)	6.391	6.365	6.683	6.884	7.379	7.747	8.445	9.550	10.023	11.179
	(2)	-1.64	-2.64	-0.39	-0.98	-2.28	2.51	0.95	-2.08	0.18	0.17
	(3)	-1.64	-2.16	0.73	-0.38	-1.59	2.12	0.77	-2.91	-1.16	-0.74
	(4)				-0.98	-1.82	2.56	1.24	-2.40	-0.64	-0.24
	(5)								-2.08	-0.31	-0.09
X9	(1)	6.391	6.340	6.683	7.008	7.631	8.259	9.111	10.507	11.156	12.869
	(2)	-2.46	-0.15	1.59	-0.06	-1.69	2.76	1.36	-2.78	-0.35	0.53
	(3)	-2.46	0.13	4.18	3.00	1.26	2.99	1.77	-2.51	-0.75	0.21
	(4)				-0.06	-1.13	2.86	1.74	-2.53	-0.78	0.15
	(5)								-2.78	-0.99	-0.01
IMP9R	(1)	7.813	7.313	8.058	8.020	8.132	8.306	8.550	9.589	10.750	11.991
	(2)	-6.09	2.22	-2.13	0.06	-2.10	5.31	4.80	-1.42	-0.37	-1.78
	(3)	-6.09	1.60	0.17	2.57	1.55	11.50	11.92	2.52	-0.80	-2.96
	(4)				0.06	-1.09	7.67	8.39	-0.25	-3.02	-4.63
	(5)								-1.42	-2.74	-3.83
IMP9	(1)	7.813	7.423	8.131	8.172	8.542	9.082	9.618	10.919	12.297	13.970
	(2)	-6.12	5.86	-0.25	0.14	-3.84	5.27	4.79	-1.44	-0.31	-1.77
	(3)	-6.12	5.35	5.63	7.16	3.73	11.45	11.92	2.50	-0.75	-2.95
	(4)				0.14	-2.55	7.62	8.39	-0.27	-2.96	-4.62
	(5)								-1.44	-2.69	-3.82
Y9R	(1)	31.909	32.284	33.398	34.200	35.081	37.429	39.352	41.886	44.773	47.430
	(2)	-0.82	2.14	1.06	0.31	0.41	2.38	0.89	-1.13	-0.39	-0.71
	(3)	-0.82	1.89	2.75	2.32	2.99	4.80	3.93	0.78	-0.63	-1.02
	(4)				0.31	1.00	3.12	2.14	-0.85	-2.11	-2.36
	(5)								-1.13	-1.76	-1.78
Y9	(1)	31.909	32.894	34.915	36.287	37.471	40.575	43.424	47.403	52.109	57.781
	(2)	-1.52	3.55	1.25	-0.32	-0.15	2.75	0.93	-0.99	-0.11	-0.21
	(3)	-1.52	2.15	3.79	3.24	3.29	5.38	5.31	2.33	0.37	-0.92
	(4)				-0.32	0.07	3.61	3.78	1.00	-0.80	-1.85
	(5)								-0.99	-1.49	-1.65

Continued

TABLE 1 (Continued)

Actual values and percentage 'forecast' errors (solution values minus actual values as percentages of actual values) for subsets of the sample period.

Variable		1957	1958	1959	1960	1961	1962	1963	1964	1965	1966
YB9R	(1)	23.507	23.452	24.916	25.419	25.999	27.713	29.127	31.463	33.946	36.153
	(2)	-1.21	1.76	1.61	0.42	0.36	3.01	0.37	-1.01	-0.47	-0.93
	(3)	-1.21	1.62	3.24	2.30	2.98	5.47	3.20	0.54	-0.99	-1.15
	(4)				0.42	1.06	3.66	1.25	-1.25	-2.60	-2.61
	(5)								-1.01	-1.88	-1.82
YB9	(1)	23.507	23.867	25.493	26.206	26.921	28.817	30.736	33.532	36.782	40.313
	(2)	-2.17	3.65	1.95	-0.45	-0.37	3.70	0.32	-0.86	-0.11	-0.18
	(3)	-2.17	1.92	4.64	3.46	3.40	6.39	5.00	2.51	0.29	-0.86
	(4)				-0.45	-0.18	4.47	3.38	1.14	-0.95	-1.79
	(5)								-0.86	-1.55	-1.46
GAP	(1)	1.003	0.967	0.978	0.964	0.956	0.970	0.983	1.007	1.018	1.015
	(2)	-0.01	0.02	0.02	0.00	0.00	0.03	0.00	-0.01	-0.01	-0.01
	(3)	-0.01	0.02	0.03	0.02	0.02	0.04	0.01	-0.02	-0.04	-0.04
	(4)				0.00	0.01	0.03	0.00	0.03	-0.04	-0.04
	(5)								-0.01	-0.02	-0.01
PYB2	(1)	1.00	1.018	1.023	1.031	1.035	1.040	1.055	1.066	1.084	1.115
	(2)	-0.97	1.82	0.34	-0.85	-0.67	0.64	-0.04	0.04	0.32	0.77
	(3)	-0.97	0.27	1.37	1.14	0.43	0.85	1.76	1.95	1.20	0.30
	(4)				-0.85	-1.21	0.76	2.12	2.40	1.65	0.86
	(5)								0.14	0.29	0.39
PY2	(1)	1.000	1.019	1.045	1.061	1.068	1.084	1.103	1.131	1.164	1.218
	(2)	-0.70	1.38	0.23	-0.62	-0.53	0.37	0.08	0.20	0.27	0.46
	(3)	-0.70	0.25	1.05	0.90	0.30	0.55	1.38	1.60	0.99	0.12
	(4)				-0.62	-0.92	0.48	1.65	1.92	1.32	0.54
	(5)								0.20	0.27	0.15
PC2	(1)	1.00	1.026	1.041	1.051	1.059	1.073	1.088	1.105	1.127	1.166
	(2)	-1.21	0.82	0.95	-0.20	-0.62	0.39	0.08	0.13	-0.04	0.12
	(3)	-1.21	-0.87	0.28	0.43	-0.10	0.03	0.75	1.14	0.68	-0.15
	(4)				-0.20	-0.53	0.88	1.82	2.24	1.77	0.97
	(5)								0.13	0.05	-0.22

Continued

TABLE 1 (Continued)

Actual values and percentage 'forecast' errors (solution values minus actual values as percentages of actual values) for subsets of the sample period.

Variable		1957	1958	1959	1960	1961	1962	1963	1964	1965	1966
PBC2	(1)	1.000	1.022	1.047	1.070	1.080	1.108	1.141	1.188	1.239	1.286
	(2)	0.73	2.89	0.08	-0.12	0.72	0.97	0.51	-1.05	-1.04	0.76
	(3)	0.73	3.50	4.14	4.26	5.08	5.29	6.56	5.35	3.35	2.93
	(4)				-0.12	0.91	3.16	4.44	3.19	1.19	0.80
	(5)								-1.05	-2.28	-1.93
PRS2	(1)	1.000	1.024	1.062	1.091	1.098	1.130	1.168	1.232	1.292	1.357
	(2)	0.79	2.66	-0.10	-0.95	0.43	0.59	-0.21	-1.84	-0.96	0.87
	(3)	0.79	3.12	3.58	2.77	3.03	3.01	3.51	1.60	-0.28	-0.67
	(4)				-0.95	-0.25	1.70	2.50	0.67	-1.19	-1.50
	(5)								-1.84	-3.05	-2.75
WRB	(1)	1.500	1.593	1.641	1.719	1.769	1.830	1.887	1.962	2.090	2.249
	(2)	-1.76	-1.12	1.80	-1.04	0.37	1.32	1.17	0.67	-0.95	-1.50
	(3)	-1.76	-3.01	-0.14	-0.51	0.32	2.22	4.18	4.88	2.71	-0.15
	(4)				-1.04	-0.50	1.13	2.69	3.09	0.75	-2.16
	(5)								0.67	-0.88	-2.87
U	(1)	4.60	7.00	6.00	7.00	7.20	5.90	5.50	4.70	3.90	3.60
	(2)	0.70	-1.43	-0.80	-0.16	0.29	-1.00	0.21	0.43	0.16	0.51
	(3)	0.70	-1.44	-2.28	-1.62	-1.11	-1.90	-0.83	0.60	1.86	2.22
	(4)				-0.15	0.01	-1.00	-0.03	1.25	2.37	2.57
	(5)								0.43	1.00	1.04
E6	(1)	5.731	5.706	5.870	5.965	6.055	6.225	6.375	6.609	6.862	7.152
	(2)	-0.72	1.56	0.81	0.13	-0.36	1.05	-0.20	-0.47	-0.16	-0.51
	(3)	-0.72	1.57	2.38	1.69	1.13	2.02	0.90	-0.66	-1.95	-2.30
	(4)				0.13	-0.07	1.05	0.05	-1.33	-2.45	-2.64
	(5)								-0.47	-1.03	-1.05
CPG9	(1)	5.298	5.166	5.807	5.764	5.874	6.499	7.035	7.902	8.614	8.902
	(2)	-1.24	10.03	1.36	4.01	4.90	6.23	1.21	-2.97	-2.89	0.08
	(3)	-1.24	8.94	6.34	8.21	9.44	8.49	4.61	-0.98	-3.07	0.66
	(4)				4.01	5.61	7.66	4.65	-0.47	-2.43	1.74
	(5)								-2.97	-4.33	0.19

Continued

TABLE 1 (Continued)

Actual values and percentage 'forecast' errors (solution values minus actual values as percentages of actual values) for subsets of the sample period.

Variable		1957	1958	1959	1960	1961	1962	1963	1964	1965	1966
PDI9	(1)	21.274	22.880	23.948	25.075	26.011	28.243	30.018	31.725	34.990	38.278
	(2)	−0.96	1.29	0.94	−1.08	−1.01	1.71	−0.43	−0.11	0.37	−0.08
	(3)	−0.96	0.04	2.72	1.45	1.34	3.39	2.52	1.76	−0.24	−1.91
	(4)				−1.08	−0.80	2.32	1.69	1.14	−0.62	−2.04
	(5)								−0.11	−0.72	−1.35
CT9	(1)	1.337	1.315	1.581	1.544	1.612	1.710	1.827	1.996	2.164	2.190
	(2)	0.27	17.09	2.59	6.38	6.25	4.46	−0.02	−2.32	−3.45	0.55
	(3)	0.27	15.12	9.09	11.97	12.19	7.63	5.35	1.78	−2.12	2.86
	(4)				6.38	7.06	6.78	5.85	2.91	−0.90	4.79
	(5)								−2.32	−5.32	0.91
PT9	(1)	1.917	1.795	2.088	2.360	2.511	2.729	2.916	3.428	3.912	4.434
	(2)	−10.07	6.47	4.92	−0.97	−2.70	5.08	3.10	−1.55	1.15	−0.58
	(3)	−10.07	4.79	7.59	2.46	0.52	7.46	7.01	0.31	−0.80	−3.87
	(4)				−0.97	−2.34	5.91	5.75	−0.56	−1.32	−4.03
	(5)								−1.55	−0.64	−2.30
GDF9	(1)	−0.100	1.007	0.556	0.717	1.005	0.854	0.690	0.021	−0.246	−0.280
	(2)	0.206	−0.671	−0.220	−0.079	−0.004	−0.317	−0.425	0.282	0.063	0.202
	(3)	0.206	−0.525	−0.591	−0.716	−0.686	−0.956	−1.446	−0.732	−0.499	−0.127
	(4)				−0.079	−0.048	−0.471	−0.946	−0.210	0.058	0.449
	(5)								0.282	0.356	0.589
SIC	(1)	3.780	2.310	4.820	3.340	2.830	4.010	3.570	3.740	3.970	5.000
	(2)	−0.37	0.16	−0.96	−0.02	−0.08	−0.32	0.04	0.14	0.34	0.32
	(3)	−0.37	0.12	−0.88	0.04	0.03	−0.41	0.21	0.27	0.36	0.30
	(4)				−0.02	−0.05	−0.17	0.15	0.22	0.31	0.26
	(5)								0.14	0.28	0.27
LIC	(1)	4.190	4.520	5.000	5.110	5.070	5.090	5.020	5.120	5.140	5.760
	(2)	−0.01	−0.27	−0.14	−0.12	−0.19	0.05	0.11	0.05	0.22	−0.08
	(3)	−0.01	−0.29	−0.28	−0.28	−0.32	−0.17	0.06	0.12	0.29	0.08
	(4)				−0.12	−0.26	−0.06	0.11	0.13	0.29	0.07
	(5)								0.05	0.23	0.03

Continued

TABLE 1 (Continued)

Actual values and percentage 'forecast' errors (solution values minus actual values as percentages of actual values) for subsets of the sample period.

Variable		1957	1958	1959	1960	1961	1962	1963	1964	1965	1966
LDU9	(1)	0.403	0.304	0.428	0.461	0.366	0.328	0.220	0.188	0.421	0.644
	(2)	8.84	26.71	11.80	-11.88	-2.86	21.72	-15.36	13.35	-38.48	-47.07
	(3)	8.84	13.59	12.93	-5.09	7.12	39.03	22.04	49.88	-32.96	-48.70
	(4)				-11.88	-0.46	27.70	6.92	34.01	-39.31	-52.23
	(5)								13.35	-42.59	-51.67
CIF9	(1)	0.558	0.539	0.505	0.215	0.465	0.516	0.551	0.726	0.696	0.785
	(2)	-26.38	-29.06	-14.21	75.76	-24.28	19.28	9.30	-13.66	8.88	7.75
	(3)	-26.38	-32.61	-3.98	110.59	-3.91	23.38	26.74	-0.06	15.41	11.03
	(4)				75.76	-21.08	25.37	18.50	-6.82	8.28	4.86
	(5)								-13.66	4.77	3.97
EXC	(1)	0.959	0.971	0.959	0.970	1.013	1.069	1.078	1.079	1.078	1.077
	(2)	-0.03	3.54	1.91	0.04	-1.73	0.00	0.00	0.00	0.00	0.00
	(3)	-0.03	3.67	5.43	4.43	2.19	0.00	0.00	0.00	0.00	0.00
	(4)				0.04	-1.44	0.00	0.00	0.00	0.00	0.00
	(5)								0.00	0.00	0.00
BCF9R	(1)	5.926	5.103	4.929	4.908	4.797	4.859	5.157	5.965	6.890	7.825
	(2)	-11.49	13.20	10.18	3.74	4.87	12.60	4.84	-3.19	-4.34	-7.98
	(3)	-11.49	4.18	15.08	16.26	19.48	28.30	25.02	11.04	-0.41	-9.51
	(4)				3.74	8.33	17.96	15.90	3.88	-6.00	13.83
	(5)								-3.19	-7.76	-12.88
BCF9	(1)	5.926	5.212	5.160	5.249	5.177	5.383	5.884	7.082	8.527	10.036
	(2)	-10.84	16.54	10.28	3.67	5.70	13.70	5.37	-4.14	-5.23	-7.03
	(3)	-10.84	7.89	19.87	21.27	25.64	35.11	33.23	17.06	3.05	-6.61
	(4)				3.67	9.40	21.70	21.05	7.25	-4.78	-12.90
	(5)								-4.14	-9.76	-14.32

*All values shown in rows numbered (2), (3), (4), and (5) are percentage differences between solution values and actual values except for GAP, U, LIC, SIC, VPC9, VPC 9R, and GDF9, which are shown as arithmetic differences between solution and actual values.

structural change. For the first run we selected as base 1957, a year of low unemployment and a flexible exchange rate. These percentage forecast errors are reported in row 3 of Table 1. For the second run we selected as base 1960, a year of high unemployment under the same flexible exchange rate regime. The percentage forecast errors were those reported in row 4 of Table 1. The final run was based on 1964, a year of approximately the same low unemployment rate as that of 1957, but with the exchange rate fixed. Canada returned to a pegged exchange rate in 1962, thereby ending a floating rate system that was adopted in 1950 in response to considerable accumulation of reserves of foreign exchange, fed, in large part, by speculation of appreciation of the Canadian dollar. In response to a similar situation in 1970, the Canadian dollar was freed again. This latter development of course has no bearing on our *ex post* forecasts or simulation results, which do not extend beyond 1966. We did, however, make an actual forecast for 1970 on the assumption that the exchange rate would remain fixed at its 1969 level. We have not re-run that forecast with the benefit of this particular hindsight. We have instead concentrated upon the comparative *ex post* forecasting performance for the alternative exchange rate regimes. Our percentage forecast errors for the run based on 1964, with the exchange rate fixed, are reported in row 5 of Table 1.

Our choice of the base years 1957, 1960 and 1964 reflects our concern not only that the actual economy be captured at different cyclical points and under varying exchange rate structures, but also that the model be initiated in correspondingly different situations. Conformity between the model solution and the real world is reasonably close in each of the selected base years. The base years are therefore appropriate to an investigation of the properties of the model as evidenced by behaviour consequent upon different initial sets of circumstances.

To facilitate interpretation, actual values for each forecasted variable are shown in row 1 of Table 1. The percentage forecast errors for each experiment are calculated as solution values minus actual values as percentages of actual values. In some cases we have reported arithmetic rather than percentage forecast errors. The latter give a decidedly exaggerated picture of forecasting error for series such as VPC9R, VPC9, and GDF9 which can change from positive to negative in sign and have a base near zero for the percentage calculation. In the case of the employment rate, U, the arithmetic error is shown since this variable is residually determined and is a small number and therefore also characterized by the appearance of exaggerated errors when these are presented in percentage form. The relatively small size of the base was also the reason for reporting arithmetic errors for GAP, LIC and SIC.

In discussing our results we focus upon the variables of most direct interest; U, PY2, and Y9R. We trace the performance of Y9R back through its components C9R, RES9R, BCF9R, VPC9R, X9R and IMP9R.[3] We then relate this performance to the structure of the model and the exogenous shocks to which the system was subjected.

The year-by-year *ex post* forecasts of Y9R are generally quite accurate. The years 1958 and 1962 were farthest off; in each case Y9R was over-predicted by between 2

---

3 One component of VPC9R, DHA9R, is exogenous. All service exports, except interest and dividends received from abroad, are exogenous and exports of motor vehicles and parts were exogenous. Government expenditure on goods and services, G9, was exogenous in nominal dollars. The residual error of estimate in the National Accounts was set at its actual value.

and 2½ percent. We failed to capture the slow-down in the rate of growth of real output in 1958, and to a lesser extent, in 1959. The 1958-9 inventory recession in the United States was much less pronounced in Canada. It is somewhat surprising that the exogenous role of the US activity level did not cause us to underpredict rather than overpredict Y9R. The conversion loan of 1958 created financial uncertainty and an increased demand for liquidity. The monetary-real linkages in our model are weak and this, possibly, could account for our difficulty. This presumption is somewhat reinforced by the fact that in 1962 and 1963, characterized by another financial crisis and associated period of austerity, our errors were similar for Y9R to those in 1958 and 1959.

Weakness of monetary-real linkages contributes slightly to the price-inelasticity of the aggregate demand curve in the model and its failure to shift enough in response to monetary disturbances. Given the nominal money supply, increases in the general price level reduce real cash balances and interest rate increases follow, but these do not contribute much to a reduction in aggregate demand because interest effects are relatively weak in the model. This same weakness of interest rate effects means that the aggregate demand curve does not shift much in response to changes in the nominal money supply for a given price level. When exchange rates are fixed (so that the aggregate supply curve does not shift via changes in the exchange rate influencing price levels) and unemployment is relatively high (so that the aggregate supply curve is fairly horizontal), the elasticity of the aggregate demand curve is of little or no consequence in that the results of a shift in aggregate demand are the same whatever the elasticity of this curve. On the other hand, if unemployment is low, or the exchange rate is flexible, the outcome of shifts in aggregate demand will depend upon the elasticity of the aggregate demand curve. Therefore, when unemployment is low, or when the exchange rate is flexible, the weakness of monetary-real linkages could have an important bearing upon the performance of the model. In 1958 the unemployment rate was high (7 per cent) but the exchange rate was flexible, (the Canadian dollar depreciated over the year, returning to its 1957 value in 1959). In 1962 the unemployment rate was declining but still high (5.9 per cent) while the exchange rate remained flexible until mid-year (and the Canadian dollar again depreciated for the year as a whole). However, there was also depreciation during 1960 and substantial depreciation during 1961 (both years of high (7 per cent) unemployment), while our forecasts were quite accurate in both years. It would therefore seem that our difficulties in 1958 and 1962 resulted in part from the special factors generating uncertainty referred to above and from the fact that the aggregate demand curve did not shift enough in response to the financial disturbances of the time, because of weak monetary-real linkages in the model.

In 1957 the solution values (ex post forecasts) are very close to actual for U, PY2 and Y9R. Nevertheless, the good performance apparent for Y9R results from substantial but offsetting errors in major components. Thus we under-predicted BCF9R by 11.5 per cent, IMP9R by 6 per cent and overpredicted RES9R by 7 per cent. The unemployment rate in 1957 was only 4.6 per cent. We evidently failed to capture in our investment or import equations the effect of boom conditions on these variables, even though the unemployment rate and real output were forecast quite well. A similar failure is apparent in the result for residential construction which has displayed a contracyclical pattern over much of the postwar period.

In 1958 we over-predicted Y9R by about 2 per cent. Associated with this was an understatement of the unemployment rate of 1.4 percentage points and an overestimate of the price level of 1.4 per cent. Between 1957 and 1958 the unemployment rate rose sharply from 4.6 per cent to 7.0 per cent. Our model did not capture this turn-about in the rate of activity very well. Consequently we underestimated RES9R by about 6 per cent and X9R by 2.6 per cent and overestimated BCF9R by 13.2 per cent, C9R by 1.3 per cent, and IMP9R by 2.2 per cent. We underestimated inventory investment in both 1957 and 1958, which might suggest that the inventory recession in Canada got underway somewhat earlier than in the United States. (We did not underestimate inventory investment by much in 1959.)

In 1959 our overprediction of Y9R was only about 1 per cent, or half of the relative error of the preceding year. Similarly, the errors in U and PY2 were substantially reduced. We again had a substantial (10.2 per cent) overestimate of BCF9R, but without such great offsets in components, indicating that forecasts of Y9R are very sensitive to forecast errors in BCF9R.

In 1960 our forecasts of Y9R, U and PY2 were again all very close. Actual unemployment had returned to 7 per cent from 6 per cent in 1959. Our overprediction of BCF9R was only 3.7 per cent, but RES9R was overpredicted by 6.2 per cent. 1961 was another year of relative accuracy. Forecasts of Y9R, U and PY2 were very close. BCF9R was overpredicted by almost 5 per cent and RES9R by 11 per cent. Underpredictions of X9R and IMP9R were about 2 per cent but very great for VPC9R.

In 1962 our forecast of PY2 was accurate but we over-estimated Y9R by more than 2 per cent and under-estimated U by one percentage point. The trouble was primarily in BCF9R, which was overpredicted by 12.6 per cent, although there were also overestimates of C9R, X9R and IMP9R. Actual unemployment had declined from 7.2 per cent to 5.9 per cent.

Actual unemployment declined further in 1963, to 5.5 per cent, and our forecast was accurate for U as well as for PY2. We over-predicted X9R by about one per cent. RES9R, BCF9R and IMP9R were all overestimated by about 5 per cent.

Actual unemployment continued to decline, reaching 4.7 per cent for 1964. Forecasts of U and PY2 were quite close but we underpredicted Y9R by a little more than one per cent. For the first time since 1957 we underpredicted BCF9R (by 3 per cent). We also underpredicted C9R, X9R, and IMP9R, but overpredicted VPC9R.

By 1965 actual unemployment had declined to 4.7 per cent. Our forecasts of Y9R, U and PY2 were all very accurate. We underpredicted BCF9R for the second year in a row, this time by 4 per cent. Since forecasts of all other components were very accurate, this essentially accounted for the error in Y9R.

By 1966 actual unemployment had declined to 3.6 per cent. We overestimated it by half a percentage point but were quite close on Y9R and PY2. For the third consecutive year we underpredicted BCF9R (by 8 per cent). We also underestimated RES9R and IMP9R by about 2 per cent.

A very crude indication of the impact of the errors in BCF9R on Y9R is presented in Table 2. The percentage forecast errors in BCF9R are scaled by the ratio of BCF9R

TABLE 2

Forecast errors in Y9R adjusted for forecast errors in BCF9R

	BCF9R/Y9R	Adjusted % forecast errors Y9R	Actual forecast errors Y9R
1957	0.19	1.36	−0.82
1958	0.16	0.03	2.14
1959	0.15	−0.47	1.06
1960	0.14	−0.21	0.31
1961	0.14	−0.27	0.41
1962	0.13	0.74	2.38
1963	0.13	0.32	0.95
1964	0.14	−0.68	−1.13
1965	0.15	0.26	−0.39
1966	0.16	0.57	−0.71

to Y9R in each year and subtracted from the percentage forecast errors in Y9R to yield an "adjusted" percentage forecast error in Y9R.

With the exception of 1957, the errors in BCF9R are in such a direction in relation to the average of other errors as to account (in this purely arithmetic sense) for much of the error in Y9R. Such arithmetic is, of course, inadequate. The simultaneity of the model is such that errors are interdependent. A single equation is best judged by its performance on its own with actual values of the independent variables. Within the simultaneous solution of the model, even on a year-by-year forecast basis where actual values of variables which are exogenous to the whole model or lagged are employed an individual equation can do better or worse than in isolation, depending on the errors in the contemporaneous endogenous variables appearing as independent in that equation. The job of tracing the source of errors is therefore as complicated as the structure of the model itself.

There is, nevertheless, reason to believe that the equations (C.9 and C.12) underlying BCF9R are especially sensitive to errors in the rest of the model and in turn, are such as to augment them. This is because the investment demand functions are very sensitive to simultaneous values of endogenous variables and yet slow to adjust to the corrective mechanism operating through changes in the level of capital stock. The actual yield on capital (real profits per unit of capital) and the implicit real rental of capital services (the real price of a unit of capital goods multiplied by the rate of interest plus the depreciation rate) entering into these functions are current values of endogenous variables. The utilization ratio (of which expected output is an exponential function) is, of course, also a simultaneous endogenous variable. Errors in these endogenous variables lead to errors in the difference between desired capital stock and actual capital stock. Because of lags in the adjustment of actual to desired capital stock, such errors in desired investment carry over into subsequent years. There are no exogenous variables to help keep actual investment on track or to restore it to its actual path once it has diverged. The only lagged values are lagged investment and lagged capital stock. In year-by-year forecasts, these variables are set at their actual values, so that errors from this source cannot arise. In a free run, lagged values of these endogenous variables reflect solutions in the preceding period and therefore whatever errors were made in the preceding period. Errors in investment carry over directly to contribute to errors in the same direction in the current period and indirectly, through changes in lagged capital stock, to constitute a corrective mechanism for such past errors. But the lags in investment and the coefficients of lagged capital stock are such that the corrective role is slow and weak. For example, if investment is too high, although the excessive rate of growth of the stock of capital will exaggerate the level of potential output, the long lag in investment will dominate the demand side via the influence of the utilization rate so that the rate of growth of capital and potential output will not be great enough to offset the lagged influence of investment on actual output.

If a particular equation performs badly in isolation in a given year, there may be scope for "fine tuning," adjustment of the constant term in that year by the benefit of hindsight. Because of the simultaneity of the system, such adjustment should ordinarily not correspond to complete elimination of the error term in the regression equation. The change in the constant in any one equation would have spillover effects throughout the system such that complete elimination of error in the regression equation might make things worse rather than better.

It would be an interesting exercise to assess the performance of the model in the event that the constant in every equation be adjusted in advance to eliminate the error in the regression equation. We have not done this nor, indeed, have we made any adjustments to any equations for purposes of our ex post forecasts and simulation experiments. In an actual forecasting context such adjustments can be useful in putting the system closer to track in order to project several periods ahead. In this sense, our forecasting ability as represented in the tables presented here is perhaps understated. If instead of making our year-by-year forecasts in a mechanical way, we had carried out fine tuning on the basis of a given year's results before forecasting the next, we could have done better.

Turning now to the forecasts based on free-runs of the model initiated in each of the years 1957, 1960, and 1964, we can see the forecasting performance of the model in a longer-run context. These results are presented in rows 3, 4, and 5 respectively of Table 1. As can be seen from row 3, when a free-running forecast for a ten-year period is made, the model stays reasonably well on track. The forecast error of -1.02 per cent in 1966 for Y9R compares very well with the -0.71 per cent error made in the forecast shown in row 2 using actual values of the lagged variables. The free-running forecast was, in fact, further off track in the middle years of the period and tended to come back to the actual in later years. This reflects the fact that the years 1958-61 were years of relatively slow growth following a period of rapid expansion in 1955-6. By 1962 the economy had again begun a period of more rapid and steady growth. The free-running forecasts begun in 1960 (row 4) and 1964 (row 5) show somewhat similar tendencies. (Forecast errors from these two experiments are not shown after 1966, the end of the sample period for estimation, because, of revisions to National Accounts data which are not incorporated into the data used for estimation.)

Some indication of the model's ability to catch turning points is shown in Table 3, a tabulation of direction of change data for real residential construction and the unemployment rate, two variables which exhibited cyclical behaviour over the sample period. For residential construction the three turning points in 1959, 1961 and 1966 are forecast correctly in all three experiments but one false turning point was indicated

TABLE 3

Directions of change and turning points*

RES9R	57–58	58–59	59–60	60–61	61–62	62–63	63–64	64–65	65–66	Score
Actual	+	–	–	+	+	+	+	+	–	
Year-by-year forecast	+	–	–	+	–	+	+	+	–	8/9
1957 forecast	+	–	–	+	–	+	+	+	–	8/9
1960 forecast				+	–	+	+	+	–	5/6
1964 forecast								+	–	2/2
U										
Actual	+	–	+	+	–	–	–	–	–	
Year-by-year forecast	+	–	+	+	–	+	–	–	=	7/9
1957 forecast	+	–	+	+	–	+	+	+	=	5/9
1960 forecast				+	–	+	+	+	=	3/6
1964 forecast								–	–	2/2

*An equals sign means no change in the value of the variable.

TABLE 4

Income shares, actual and ex post forecast values

	Actual	Year-by-year	1957 free-run	1960 free-run	1964 free-run
CPG9/WSB9					
1957	0.401	0.407	0.407		
1958	0.385	0.417	0.422		
1959	0.413	0.405	0.422		
1960	0.398	0.418	0.419	0.418	
1961	0.396	0.419	0.423	0.422	
1962	0.412	0.422	0.419	0.428	
1963	0.421	0.424	0.415	0.428	
1964	0.435	0.424	0.416	0.431	0.424
1965	0.424	0.415	0.413	0.429	0.415
1966	0.388	0.397	0.408	0.424	0.407
CPG9/PI9					
1957	0.228	0.229	0.229		
1958	0.209	0.226	0.227		
1959	0.223	0.223	0.230		
1960	0.210	0.220	0.223	0.220	
1961	0.205	0.218	0.222	0.219	
1962	0.209	0.218	0.219	0.220	
1963	0.213	0.216	0.217	0.219	
1964	0.224	0.218	0.219	0.221	0.218
1965	0.221	0.214	0.215	0.217	0.213
1966	0.208	0.208	0.214	0.216	0.211

TABLE 5

Actual and ex post forecast values of yield on capital and ratio to real implicit rental price of capital services.

	Actual	Year-by-year	1957 free-run	1960 free-run	1964 free-run
CPG9/[(KCB9S + KMB9S) PY2]					
1957	0.154	0.153	0.153		
1958	0.135	0.147	0.150		
1959	0.142	0.143	0.151		
1960	0.133	0.139	0.141	0.139	
1961	0.130	0.137	0.138	0.138	
1962	0.137	0.145	0.142	0.145	
1963	0.143	0.144	0.137	0.142	
1964	0.151	0.147	0.135	0.141	0.147
1965	0.153	0.148	0.134	0.142	0.147
1966	0.143	0.143	0.134	0.140	0.146
CPG9/[(KCB9S + KMB9S) PME2 (0.01 LIC + 0.12)]					
1957	0.950	0.926	0.926		
1958	0.811	0.878	0.884		
1959	0.831	0.847	0.868		
1960	0.774	0.812	0.803	0.834	
1961	0.751	0.797	0.774	0.802	
1962	0.780	0.822	0.786	0.814	
1963	0.810	0.807	0.735	0.779	
1964	0.842	0.830	0.720	0.772	0.825
1965	0.855	0.827	0.714	0.776	0.826
1966	0.783	0.791	0.702	0.761	0.805
CPG9/[(KCB9S + KMB9S) PNR2 (0.01 LIC + 0.035)]					
1957	2.000	1.974	1.974		
1958	1.703	1.876	1.888		
1959	1.662	1.704	1.786		
1960	1.532	1.615	1.641	1.659	
1961	1.494	1.586	1.574	1.604	
1962	1.568	1.645	1.581	1.628	
1963	1.628	1.622	1.471	1.543	
1964	1.676	1.611	1.422	1.495	1.611
1965	1.648	1.572	1.373	1.477	1.577
1966	1.414	1.434	1.304	1.398	1.483

in 1962. The unemployment series had turning points in 1959, 1960, and 1962. All three were correctly forecast but the model signalled a false turning point in 1963. It is apparent that the model does not explain well the situation around 1962. This is not surprising in view of the peculiarity of economic policy in this period which was impossible to quantify in the specification of exogenous variables.

In Table 4 we present information on relative income shares, measured by the ratio of gross corporate profits, CPG9, to non-agricultural business wage income, WSB9, and to personal income, PI9, to permit a comparison of actual values with the results of the various ex post forecasts. In the year-by-year forecasts the share of profits is overestimated in 1958, 1960, 1961, and 1962, the years of relatively high actual unemployment in our sample period. In 1958 and 1962 we also substantially underestimated unemployment in the year-by-year forecasts; for the other years our forecasts were reasonably close. In 1964 and 1965 we were under in our forecast of profit-share, while in 1959 we were close although unemployment was high.

In the 1957 free-run, profit-share is overestimated for the years 1958 through 1962, as well as 1966, and underestimated for 1964 and 1965. A similar pattern appears in the 1964 free-run.

The errors in forecasting income shares, measured in this way, are evidently related to the cyclical position of the economy but the choice of base-year is not the critical factor. These shares are fairly well predicted on the average considering that they are estimated indirectly, as a function of non-wage income, which is a residual.

From the point of view of the investment functions in our model, the yield in capital and implicit rental value of capital services are relevant variables. In Table 5 we present actual and ex post forecast values of the real yield on capital and the ratio of yield to implicit real rental value for machinery and equipment and non-residential construction. In the year-by-year forecast, we tend to overpredict the yield in years of high unemployment, just as we overpredicted capital's share of income. In the free-runs there is a tendency to overpredict between 1958 and 1962 and underpredict subsequently.

The last two sets of values in Table 5 are those which enter directly into the equations for investment in machinery and equipment and non-residential construction, respectively. The pattern exhibited by these values is dominated by the behaviour of the yield on capital outlined above and evidently established in the first place by our forecasting performance with respect to gross corporate profits CPG9.

4 Policy multipliers under fixed and flexible exchange rates

We report in this chapter on a few experiments involving changes in policy variables in order to illuminate the major structural characteristics of the Canadian economy, as implied by our model, and to provide some evidence on the differing effects of monetary and fiscal policy under fixed and flexible exchange rate regimes.[1] The results of three simulation experiments designed to show the effect of fiscal and monetary policy instruments in periods of high and medium unemployment and in periods of flexible and fixed exchange rates are shown in Tables 6, 7, and 8 which relate respectively to the base years 1957, 1960, and 1964. (The Canadian exchange rate floated from mid-1950 to mid-1962.) The first row for each variable is the control solution, the ex post forecast of Chapter 3, generated by a free run on each base year. The rows numbered 1, 2, and 3 relate to the three experiments. Experiment 1: The first simulation investigated the balanced budget multiplier associated with an increase in government non-wage expenditure accompanied by an increase in the rate of personal income tax such as to leave the government deficit or surplus in the initial year virtually identical to its value in the control solution for that year.[2] The supply of money was held constant in this experiment. Experiment 2: The second multiplier to be considered was also related to an increase in government non-wage expenditure but without any variation in tax rates. It was implicitly assumed for this second experiment that the increase in government expenditure was financed by central bank open market operations such that the money supply remained unchanged after the increase in government expenditure had taken place.[3] This method of financing results in higher interest rates. Experiment 3: The final multiplier was defined with respect to an increase in the money supply. Effects of the policy instruments were assessed in relation to control values which were the solution value for the free-run ex post forecasts for corresponding time periods. To facilitate comparisons among years, we augmented

---

1 A preliminary report on the findings of this chapter was given in a paper "Some Simulation Results from the TRACE Econometric Model of the Canadian Economy" presented by Choudhry, Kotowitz, Sawyer and Winder to the Second World Congress of the Econometric Society, Cambridge, England, September, 1970.
    Some simulations involving the effects of changes in income tax rates have been performed by Jutlah (1970) using the TRACE model.
    The seminal article dealing with the behaviour of the Canadian economy under a fluctuating exchange rate is Rhomberg (1964). Further evidence has been contributed by Officer (1968) and Caves and Reuber (1969). The complete study by Caves and Reuber (1971), of which the 1969 study was a summary, has not been published at the time we write. The theory of the differing effects of monetary and fiscal policies under fixed and flexible exchange rates has been discussed by Mundell (1962), (1963), and (1964), Sohmen (1969), Johnson (1966), Jones (1968), Takayama (1969), and Dernberg (1970).
2 For a discussion of the balanced budget multiplier, see Evans (1969a).
3 Carl Christ (1968) points out the need to incorporate the government budget constraint explicitly into the model.

TABLE 6

Simulation results based on 1957 experiments*. (In 1957 only, the following changes were introduced: (1) government non-wage expenditure was increased by two per cent of the control value of GNP, while personal income tax rates were adjusted to prevent the government surplus or deficit from changing in the initial year; (2) government non-wage expenditure was increased by two per cent of the control value of GNP and the government deficit was free to vary accordingly; and (3) the money supply was increased by five per cent of its actual value.)

Variable		1957	1958	1959	1960	1961	1962	1963	1964	1965	1966
DUR9R	Control solution	2.541	2.676	2.781	2.894	3.088	3.425	3.678	3.885	4.184	4.443
	(1)	-0.81	-0.75	-0.55	-0.36	-0.21	-0.16	-0.12	-0.10	-0.07	-0.07
	(2)	1.64	0.30	-0.26	-0.32	-0.24	-0.16	-0.12	-0.10	-0.07	-0.07
	(3)	0.18	0.20	0.14	0.08	0.06	0.02	0.00	-0.01	0.00	-0.02
DUR9		2.457	2.615	2.755	2.836	2.944	3.228	3.451	3.628	3.859	4.101
	(1)	-0.15	0.17	-0.03	-0.08	-0.08	-0.06	-0.07	-0.09	-0.06	-0.05
	(2)	2.67	1.90	0.89	0.41	0.24	0.18	0.14	0.09	0.10	0.10
	(3)	0.45	0.38	0.26	0.17	0.08	0.02	-0.01	-0.05	-0.04	-0.05
ND9R		10.328	10.751	11.166	11.484	11.832	12.502	12.987	13.411	14.034	14.647
	(1)	-0.26	-0.16	-0.14	-0.12	-0.10	-0.08	-0.08	-0.07	-0.06	-0.05
	(2)	1.08	0.46	0.17	0.05	0.00	-0.02	-0.02	-0.03	-0.02	-0.02
	(3)	-0.02	-0.02	-0.03	-0.03	-0.03	-0.03	-0.03	-0.03	-0.02	-0.02
ND9		10.257	11.034	11.731	12.107	12.410	13.279	14.113	14.849	15.739	16.902
	(1)	0.46	0.62	0.29	0.08	-0.01	-0.03	-0.04	-0.05	-0.05	-0.04
	(2)	2.24	1.94	1.19	0.67	0.41	0.23	0.16	0.12	0.10	0.10
	(3)	0.44	0.19	0.11	0.04	-0.01	-0.05	-0.05	-0.05	-0.05	-0.05
SER9R		7.259	7.666	8.039	8.307	8.605	9.185	9.562	9.915	10.454	10.966
	(1)	-0.30	-0.13	-0.16	-0.16	-0.13	-0.12	-0.11	-0.10	-0.08	-0.07
	(2)	1.39	0.43	0.19	0.10	0.07	0.04	0.01	0.00	0.00	0.00
	(3)	0.00	-0.01	-0.03	-0.04	-0.03	-0.03	-0.03	-0.04	-0.03	-0.03
SER9		7.171	7.805	8.465	9.001	9.535	10.445	11.182	11.933	12.937	13.988
	(1)	0.01	0.35	0.30	0.21	0.31	0.07	0.03	-0.01	-0.03	-0.04
	(2)	1.85	1.21	1.01	0.81	0.63	0.49	0.37	0.27	0.20	0.16
	(3)	0.06	0.06	0.04	0.02	-0.01	-0.03	-0.04	-0.05	-0.06	-0.06

Continued

TABLE 6 (Continued)

Simulation results based on 1957 experiments.

Variable		1957	1958	1959	1960	1961	1962	1963	1964	1965	1966
C9R	Control solution	20.128	21.093	21.985	22.685	23.525	25.111	26.226	27.210	28.673	30.055
	(1)	-0.35	-0.22	-0.19	-0.16	-0.12	-0.10	-0.09	-0.08	-0.07	-0.06
	(2)	1.26	0.43	0.13	0.02	-0.01	-0.01	-0.02	-0.03	-0.03	-0.02
	(3)	0.01	0.01	0.00	-0.02	-0.02	-0.02	-0.02	-0.02	-0.03	-0.02
C9		19.885	21.454	22.952	23.944	24.889	26.952	28.747	30.410	32.534	34.991
	(1)	0.22	0.46	0.25	0.11	0.03	0.01	-0.02	-0.04	-0.04	-0.04
	(2)	2.15	1.67	1.08	0.69	0.47	0.32	0.23	0.18	0.14	0.12
	(3)	0.31	0.17	0.10	0.05	0.00	-0.03	-0.04	-0.05	-0.05	-0.05
RES9R		1.507	1.657	1.556	1.370	1.451	1.406	1.459	1.581	1.640	1.589
	(1)	-3.35	-1.81	0.71	1.04	0.97	0.86	0.72	0.48	0.36	0.31
	(2)	-4.83	-3.45	0.09	1.15	1.24	1.28	1.13	0.81	0.63	0.54
	(3)	0.30	0.39	0.24	0.14	0.10	0.03	0.02	-0.07	-0.08	-0.04
RES9		1.519	1.749	1.711	1.536	1.642	1.637	1.764	1.979	2.113	2.142
	(1)	-2.59	-0.91	1.20	1.26	1.03	0.84	0.68	0.44	0.31	0.24
	(2)	-3.45	-1.65	1.43	2.06	1.89	1.69	1.47	1.13	0.92	0.81
	(3)	0.72	0.63	0.40	0.21	0.10	-0.02	-0.03	-0.11	-0.11	-0.09
BME9R		2.337	2.365	2.539	2.565	2.596	2.842	2.922	2.980	3.051	3.130
	(1)	3.49	0.94	0.11	-0.22	-0.44	-0.46	-0.50	-0.51	-0.51	-0.49
	(2)	4.84	2.07	0.57	-0.05	-0.44	-0.55	-0.66	-0.74	-0.79	-0.80
	(3)	0.12	0.13	0.06	0.01	-0.05	-0.05	-0.04	-0.04	-0.05	-0.05
BME9		2.362	2.529	2.778	2.867	2.950	3.310	3.560	3.720	3.874	4.081
	(1)	4.15	1.91	0.72	0.12	-0.21	-0.29	-0.41	-0.46	-0.51	-0.49
	(2)	5.94	3.84	1.84	0.79	0.18	-0.15	-0.39	-0.54	-0.67	-0.72
	(3)	0.75	0.35	0.23	0.08	-0.01	-0.06	-0.09	-0.08	-0.11	-0.10
BNR9R		2.263	2.226	2.326	2.326	2.331	2.525	2.603	2.657	2.716	2.786
	(1)	3.11	1.20	0.35	-0.10	-0.34	-0.46	-0.51	-0.53	-0.51	-0.49
	(2)	4.33	2.39	0.96	0.20	-0.25	-0.51	-0.65	-0.74	-0.78	-0.79
	(3)	0.10	0.09	0.04	-0.03	-0.06	-0.10	-0.10	-0.09	-0.09	-0.11

Continued

TABLE 6 (Continued)

Simulation results based on 1957 experiments.

Variable		1957	1958	1959	1960	1961	1962	1963	1964	1965	1966
BNR9	Control solution	2.271	2.327	2.526	2.589	2.642	2.951	3.158	3.336	3.513	3.750
	(1)	3.69	1.89	0.066	0.06	-0.33	-0.48	-0.54	-0.60	-0.59	-0.52
	(2)	5.38	3.76	1.86	0.81	0.13	-0.26	-0.44	-0.60	-0.65	-0.63
	(3)	0.40	0.25	0.11	0.02	-0.08	-0.13	-0.11	-0.15	-0.14	-0.12
VPC9R		0.108	0.037	0.334	0.333	-0.153	0.785	0.797	0.291	0.543	0.783
	(1)	0.068	-0.065	-0.011	0.001	0.001	0.001	-0.001	-0.001	-0.001	0.000
	(2)	0.095	-0.035	-0.062	-0.016	0.001	0.003	0.002	0.000	-0.001	-0.001
	(3)	0.002	0.002	-0.002	-0.002	-0.002	0.000	0.000	0.000	0.000	0.000
VPC9		0.119	0.043	0.343	0.354	-0.150	0.806	0.853	0.342	0.928	0.844
	(1)	0.072	-0.059	-0.013	-0.002	0.000	0.000	-0.001	-0.001	0.000	0.000
	(2)	0.101	-0.026	-0.062	-0.019	-0.001	0.002	0.001	-0.001	-0.001	-0.001
	(3)	0.004	0.001	-0.002	-0.003	-0.001	0.000	0.000	0.000	0.000	0.000
X9R		6.286	6.228	6.659	6.858	7.262	7.911	8.510	9.272	9.907	11.906
	(1)	-0.10	-0.27	-0.22	-0.19	-0.17	-0.11	-0.08	-0.06	-0.05	-0.04
	(2)	-0.14	-0.38	-0.38	-0.36	-0.35	-0.28	-0.23	-0.20	-0.16	-0.14
	(3)	0.18	0.02	0.00	0.00	0.00	0.00	0.01	0.01	0.01	0.01
X9		6.234	6.348	6.963	7.218	7.727	8.506	9.273	10.243	11.073	12.896
	(1)	0.39	0.11	0.05	0.01	-0.02	0.00	0.00	0.01	0.00	0.01
	(2)	0.67	0.43	0.25	0.15	0.08	0.01	0.00	0.02	0.02	0.02
	(3)	0.53	0.17	0.11	0.07	0.03	0.00	0.00	0.00	0.00	0.00
IMP9R		7.338	7.430	8.072	8.226	8.258	9.261	9.570	9.831	10.664	11.636
	(1)	2.15	-0.27	-0.05	-0.08	-0.11	-0.13	-0.16	-0.16	-0.14	-0.11
	(2)	3.45	0.43	-0.01	0.00	-0.03	-0.02	-0.09	-0.13	-0.13	-0.12
	(3)	-0.34	-0.02	-0.03	-0.04	-0.05	-0.02	-0.03	-0.04	-0.03	-0.02
IMP9		7.336	7.820	8.589	8.758	8.861	10.122	10.764	11.192	12.205	13.558
	(1)	2.86	-0.01	0.06	-0.06	-0.14	-0.13	-0.15	-0.16	-0.13	-0.11
	(2)	4.66	1.24	0.43	0.25	0.11	-0.02	-0.08	-0.13	-0.13	-0.12
	(3)	0.46	0.23	0.12	0.04	0.00	-0.02	-0.03	-0.04	-0.03	-0.03

Continued

TABLE 6 (Continued)

Simulation results based on 1957 experiments.

Variable		1957	1958	1959	1960	1961	1962	1963	1964	1965	1966
Y9R	Control solution	31.646	32.894	34.316	34.992	36.128	39.226	40.898	42.212	44.489	46.945
	(1)	1.71	-0.36	-0.17	-0.12	-0.11	-0.09	-0.09	-0.09	-0.08	-0.07
	(2)	2.57	-0.03	-0.17	-0.11	-0.11	-0.11	-0.11	-0.12	-0.11	-0.11
	(3)	0.12	0.04	0.01	-0.01	-0.01	-0.01	-0.01	-0.01	-0.01	-0.01
Y9		31.426	33.600	36.239	37.462	38.703	42.757	45.732	48.507	52.303	57.249
	(1)	2.30	0.46	0.29	0.10	0.00	-0.02	-0.05	-0.06	-0.06	-0.05
	(2)	3.49	1.40	0.86	0.52	0.32	0.19	0.12	0.07	0.05	0.04
	(3)	0.35	0.19	0.11	0.04	0.00	-0.03	-0.04	-0.04	-0.04	-0.04
YB9R		23.223	23.831	25.723	26.003	26.774	29.228	30.060	31.632	33.610	35.739
	(1)	2.19	-0.61	-0.26	-0.17	-0.14	-0.11	-0.10	-0.10	-0.08	-0.07
	(2)	3.04	-0.39	-0.38	-0.24	-0.19	-0.16	-0.15	-0.16	-0.15	-0.14
	(3)	0.07	0.01	0.00	-0.02	-0.02	-0.01	-0.01	-0.01	-0.01	-0.01
YB9		22.998	24.325	26.675	27.114	27.837	30.658	32.274	34.372	36.888	39.965
	(1)	3.01	0.51	0.35	0.15	0.02	-0.01	-0.04	-0.06	-0.06	-0.05
	(2)	4.32	1.56	0.99	0.63	0.40	0.26	0.16	0.11	0.08	0.07
	(3)	0.39	0.22	0.12	0.05	0.00	-0.03	-0.04	-0.05	-0.05	-0.05
GAP		0.990	0.987	1.012	0.984	0.976	1.013	0.991	0.983	0.979	0.978
	(1)	0.022	-0.007	-0.003	-0.003	-0.002	-0.002	-0.002	-0.002	-0.001	-0.001
	(2)	0.030	-0.005	-0.005	-0.004	-0.003	-0.003	-0.003	-0.003	-0.002	-0.002
	(3)	0.001	0.000	0.000	-0.001	0.000	0.000	0.000	-0.001	0.000	0.000
PYB2		0.990	1.021	1.037	1.043	1.039	1.049	1.074	1.087	1.097	1.118
	(1)	0.82	1.12	0.61	0.32	0.16	0.10	0.06	0.04	0.02	0.02
	(2)	1.28	1.95	1.37	0.87	0.59	0.42	0.31	0.27	0.23	0.21
	(3)	0.32	0.21	0.12	0.07	0.02	-0.02	-0.03	-0.04	-0.04	-0.04
PY2		0.993	1.022	1.056	1.071	1.071	1.090	1.118	1.149	1.176	1.219
	(1)	0.59	0.82	0.46	0.22	0.11	0.07	0.04	0.03	0.02	0.02
	(2)	0.92	1.43	1.03	0.63	0.43	0.30	0.23	0.19	0.16	0.15
	(3)	0.23	0.15	0.10	0.05	0.01	-0.02	-0.03	-0.03	-0.03	-0.03

Continued

TABLE 6 (Continued)

Simulation results based on 1957 experiments.

Variable		1957	1958	1959	1960	1961	1962	1963	1964	1965	1966
PC2	Control solution	0.988	1.017	1.044	1.056	1.058	1.073	1.096	1.118	1.135	1.164
	(1)	0.57	0.68	0.44	0.27	0.15	0.11	0.07	0.04	0.03	0.02
	(2)	0.89	1.24	0.95	0.67	0.48	0.33	0.25	0.21	0.17	0.14
	(3)	0.30	0.16	0.10	0.07	0.02	-0.01	-0.02	-0.03	-0.02	-0.03
PBC2		1.007	1.058	1.090	1.116	1.135	1.167	1.216	1.252	1.281	1.324
	(1)	0.63	0.79	0.49	0.21	0.12	0.05	0.03	-0.03	-0.05	-0.06
	(2)	1.05	1.51	1.10	0.69	0.51	0.29	0.24	0.15	0.11	0.08
	(3)	0.49	0.16	0.15	0.02	0.01	-0.05	-0.04	-0.07	-0.07	-0.07
PRS2		1.008	1.056	1.100	1.121	1.131	1.164	1.209	1.252	1.288	1.348
	(1)	0.76	0.90	0.49	0.22	0.06	-0.02	-0.04	-0.04	-0.05	-0.07
	(2)	1.38	1.80	1.34	0.91	0.65	0.41	0.34	0.32	0.29	0.27
	(3)	0.42	0.24	0.16	0.07	0.00	-0.05	-0.05	-0.04	-0.03	-0.05
WRB		1.474	1.545	1.639	1.710	1.775	1.871	1.966	2.058	2.147	2.246
	(1)	0.94	0.99	0.69	0.57	0.44	0.31	0.24	0.17	0.13	0.11
	(2)	1.50	1.73	1.40	1.22	1.04	0.82	0.70	0.59	0.52	0.47
	(3)	0.08	0.08	0.04	0.04	-0.01	-0.04	-0.03	-0.05	-0.06	-0.06
U		5.301	5.557	3.722	5.382	6.086	3.997	4.668	5.304	5.764	5.831
	(1)	-1.217	0.050	0.210	0.184	0.159	0.141	0.117	0.098	0.079	0.063
	(2)	-1.698	-0.174	0.226	0.251	0.228	0.212	0.183	0.163	0.143	0.123
	(3)	-0.041	-0.014	0.007	0.018	0.021	0.019	0.014	0.013	0.010	0.009
E6		5.690	5.796	6.010	6.066	6.124	6.351	6.432	6.566	6.728	6.988
	(1)	1.28	-0.06	-0.22	-0.19	-0.17	-0.15	-0.12	-0.11	-0.08	-0.07
	(2)	1.78	0.18	-0.25	-0.27	-0.25	-0.23	-0.18	-0.18	-0.15	-0.13
	(3)	0.04	0.01	-0.01	-0.02	-0.03	-0.03	-0.01	-0.02	-0.01	-0.01
CPG9		5.232	5.628	6.175	6.237	6.429	7.051	7.360	7.825	8.349	8.961
	(1)	2.93	-0.15	0.24	0.04	-0.13	-0.13	-0.14	-0.13	-0.11	-0.10
	(2)	4.16	0.64	0.72	0.41	0.10	-0.04	-0.10	-0.13	-0.12	-0.12
	(3)	0.58	0.32	0.20	0.11	0.03	-0.02	-0.03	-0.04	-0.03	-0.03

Continued

TABLE 6 (Continued)
Simulation results based on 1957 experiments.

Variable		1957	1958	1959	1960	1961	1962	1963	1964	1965	1966
PD19	Control solution	21.070	22.889	24.599	25.437	26.358	29.202	30.776	32.284	34.906	37.545
	(1)	-0.03	0.56	0.31	0.14	0.05	0.02	-0.02	-0.04	-0.04	-0.03
	(2)	3.31	1.45	0.87	0.57	0.41	0.29	0.21	0.16	0.13	0.12
	(3)	0.25	0.14	0.07	0.02	-0.02	-0.04	-0.05	-0.06	-0.06	-0.06
CT9		1.341	1.514	1.725	1.729	1.808	1.840	1.925	2.031	2.118	2.253
	(1)	2.94	0.21	0.56	0.19	-0.04	-0.08	-0.15	-0.12	-0.14	-0.15
	(2)	4.23	1.27	1.39	0.84	0.38	0.13	-0.04	-0.06	-0.11	-0.14
	(3)	0.82	0.47	0.29	0.16	0.09	0.02	-0.05	-0.02	-0.04	-0.06
PT9		1.724	1.881	2.246	2.418	2.524	2.933	3.120	3.439	3.881	4.262
	(1)	31.54	0.51	0.37	0.15	0.04	-0.03	-0.05	-0.09	-0.09	-0.06
	(2)	5.19	1.73	1.05	0.69	0.48	0.30	0.22	0.13	0.09	0.11
	(3)	0.37	0.19	0.11	0.02	-0.03	-0.07	-0.06	-0.09	-0.09	-0.07
GDF9		0.106	0.482	-0.035	0.001	0.319	-0.102	-0.756	-0.711	-0.745	-0.407
	(1)	-0.001	-0.047	-0.034	-0.012	0.000	0.003	0.008	0.011	0.013	0.013
	(2)	0.369	-0.140	-0.097	-0.056	-0.030	-0.014	-0.004	0.004	0.010	0.012
	(3)	-0.039	-0.025	-0.018	-0.011	-0.006	-0.002	-0.001	0.001	0.001	0.001
SIC		3.408	2.429	3.939	3.377	2.864	3.596	3.775	4.011	4.326	5.298
	(1)	0.145	-0.016	0.000	-0.003	-0.005	0.002	-0.002	-0.002	-0.003	-0.002
	(2)	0.228	0.029	0.003	0.005	0.003	-0.005	0.004	0.003	0.002	0.002
	(3)	-0.116	-0.036	-0.003	-0.003	-0.004	-0.005	-0.002	-0.001	-0.002	-0.001
LIC		4.183	4.231	4.718	4.835	4.749	4.920	5.076	5.240	5.432	5.841
	(1)	0.044	0.021	0.012	0.007	0.002	0.002	0.000	0.000	0.000	0.000
	(2)	0.069	0.049	0.030	0.020	0.012	0.006	0.005	0.003	0.003	0.003
	(3)	-0.035	-0.032	-0.020	-0.013	-0.009	-0.006	-0.005	-0.003	-0.002	-0.001
LDU9		0.439	0.345	0.483	0.438	0.392	0.456	0.268	0.282	0.282	0.330
	(1)	2.27	1.82	0.55	-0.05	-0.19	-0.33	-0.53	-0.82	-0.66	-0.48
	(2)	3.03	2.91	1.10	0.28	-0.03	-0.19	-0.49	-0.92	-0.87	-0.72
	(3)	-9.88	12.23	0.04	-0.17	-0.08	-0.07	0.03	-0.23	-0.07	0.00

Continued

TABLE 6 (Continued)

Simulation results based on 1957 experiments.

Variable		1957	1958	1959	1960	1961	1962	1963	1964	1965	1966
CIF9	Control solution	0.411	0.363	0.485	0.453	0.447	0.637	0.698	0.726	0.803	0.872
	(1)	9.40	-0.24	-0.14	-0.43	-0.69	-0.33	-0.31	-0.45	-0.33	-0.39
	(2)	14.79	3.94	0.62	0.20	-0.21	-0.71	-0.37	-0.56	-0.47	-0.55
	(3)	-3.19	-2.08	-0.41	-0.41	-0.37	-0.34	-0.09	-0.17	-0.05	-0.12
EXC		0.959	1.006	1.011	1.013	1.035	1.069	1.078	1.079	1.078	1.077
	(1)	0.65	0.27	0.12	-0.01	0.01	0.000	0.000	0.000	0.000	0.000
	(2)	1.13	0.82	0.46	0.22	0.18	0.000	0.000	0.000	0.000	0.000
	(3)	0.75	0.27	0.16	0.05	0.08	0.000	0.000	0.000	0.000	0.000
BCF9R		5.245	5.316	5.672	5.706	5.732	6.234	6.447	6.624	6.862	7.081
	(1)	2.84	0.82	0.15	-0.16	-0.36	-0.40	-0.44	-0.46	-0.43	-0.40
	(2)	3.92	1.72	0.52	-0.03	-0.38	-0.49	-0.60	-0.67	-0.69	-0.68
	(3)	0.06	0.08	0.04	-0.01	-0.06	-0.05	-0.06	-0.07	-0.06	-0.06
BCF9		5.284	5.623	6.185	6.366	6.504	7.273	7.839	8.290	8.787	9.372
	(1)	3.44	1.64	0.59	0.08	-0.21	-0.33	-0.40	-0.45	-0.45	-0.42
	(2)	4.97	3.28	1.59	0.68	0.15	-0.17	-0.36	-0.48	-0.55	-0.56
	(3)	0.50	0.26	0.15	0.05	-0.02	-0.08	-0.09	-0.10	-0.10	-0.09

	GNW9	RPT	M9
(1)	0.629	0.075	0.000
(2)	0.629	0.000	0.000
(3)	0.000	0.000	0.575

*All values shown in rows numbered (1), (2) and (3) are percentage differences between simulation and control solutions, except for GAP, U, LIC, SIC, VPC9, VPC9R, and GDF9, which are shown as arithmetic differences between simulation and control solutions. The differences between simulation and control values which were introduced in these experiments were the following:

TABLE 7

Simulation results based on 1960 experiments*. (In 1960 only, the following changes were introduced: (1) government non-wage expenditure was increased by two per cent of the control value of GNP, while personal income tax rates were adjusted to prevent the government surplus or deficit from changing in the initial year. (2) government non-wage expenditure was increased by two per cent of the control value of GNP and the government deficit was free to vary accordingly; and (3) the money supply was increased by five per cent of its actual value.)

Variable		1960	1961	1962	1963	1964	1965	1966
DUR9R	Control solution	2.647	2.830	3.146	3.395	3.609	3.919	4.187
	(1)	−0.70	−0.69	−0.44	−0.26	−0.16	−0.10	−0.07
	(2)	1.71	0.39	−0.03	−0.05	−0.03	−0.01	0.00
	(3)	0.20	0.24	0.21	0.14	0.09	0.05	0.03
DUR9		2.692	2.808	3.127	3.372	3.569	3.828	4.098
	(1)	−0.14	0.20	−0.08	−0.15	−0.15	−0.15	−0.14
	(2)	2.63	1.81	0.69	0.27	0.15	0.09	0.05
	(3)	0.41	0.39	0.22	0.13	0.06	0.01	−0.02
ND9R		11.374	11.709	12.351	12.816	13.237	13.865	14.490
	(1)	−0.21	−0.14	−0.13	−0.12	−0.11	−0.09	−0.09
	(2)	1.04	0.45	0.17	0.08	0.03	0.00	−0.02
	(3)	−0.02	−0.02	−0.01	−0.01	−0.01	−0.01	−0.02
ND9		11.698	12.038	13.144	13.995	14.735	15.632	16.824
	(1)	0.49	0.63	0.15	−0.02	−0.09	−0.11	−0.13
	(2)	2.19	1.80	0.72	0.33	0.16	0.08	0.02
	(3)	0.42	0.19	0.01	−0.01	−0.03	−0.04	−0.05
SER9R		8.270	8.550	9.100	9.452	9.793	10.325	10.836
	(1)	−0.22	−0.12	−0.15	−0.15	−0.15	−0.13	−0.12
	(2)	1.29	0.40	0.16	0.10	0.06	0.04	0.01
	(3)	0.00	−0.01	−0.01	−0.01	−0.02	−0.01	−0.02
SER9		8.996	9.476	10.353	11.062	11.793	12.780	13.827
	(1)	0.09	0.38	0.31	0.21	0.12	0.07	0.02
	(2)	1.75	1.18	0.92	0.75	0.59	0.47	0.37
	(3)	0.05	0.07	0.05	0.02	0.00	−0.01	−0.02
C9R		22.291	23.089	24.597	25.663	26.639	28.110	29.514
	(1)	−0.27	−0.20	−0.18	−0.15	−0.13	−0.11	−0.10
	(2)	1.21	0.42	0.14	0.07	0.03	0.01	−0.01
	(3)	0.01	0.02	0.02	0.01	−0.00	−0.01	−0.01
C9		23.386	24.322	26.624	28.429	30.096	32.240	34.748
	(1)	0.26	0.48	0.19	0.06	−0.01	−0.05	−0.07
	(2)	2.07	1.56	0.80	0.48	0.33	0.23	0.17
	(3)	0.28	0.16	0.05	0.02	0.00	−0.02	−0.03
RES9R		1.404	1.496	1.425	1.470	1.593	1.650	1.594
	(1)	−3.53	−2.25	0.67	0.95	0.87	0.78	0.67
	(2)	−5.00	−3.88	0.32	1.16	1.07	1.01	0.94
	(3)	0.44	0.46	0.37	0.17	0.05	0.00	−0.08
RES9		1.518	1.639	1.638	1.760	1.976	2.107	2.130
	(1)	−2.89	−1.46	0.97	1.06	0.88	0.74	0.67
	(2)	−3.96	−2.53	0.92	1.45	1.23	1.09	1.04
	(3)	0.80	0.65	0.38	0.16	0.02	−0.05	−0.08
BME9R		2.148	2.237	2.504	2.601	2.680	2.771	2.873
	(1)	4.65	1.58	0.52	0.10	−0.15	−0.33	−0.41
	(2)	6.34	3.03	1.17	0.54	0.17	−0.12	−0.32
	(3)	0.12	0.15	0.11	0.07	0.04	−0.01	−0.02

Continued

TABLE 7 (Continued)

Simulation results based on 1960 experiments*.

Variable		1960	1961	1962	1963	1964	1965	1966
BME9	Control solution	2.289	2.427	2.858	3.100	3.267	3.430	3.651
	(1)	5.39	2.65	1.08	0.52	0.18	−0.05	−0.21
	(2)	7.58	4.89	2.12	1.29	0.80	0.44	0.14
	(3)	0.76	0.38	0.13	0.08	0.04	−0.01	−0.04
BNR9R		2.092	2.122	2.342	2.435	2.509	2.587	2.679
	(1)	4.36	2.01	0.84	0.32	−0.08	−0.28	−0.40
	(2)	5.95	3.62	1.70	0.93	0.38	0.04	−0.21
	(3)	0.13	0.15	0.10	0.07	−0.01	−0.04	−0.05
BNR9		2.243	2.324	2.681	2.902	3.094	3.289	3.549
	(1)	4.94	2.66	1.10	0.38	−0.03	−0.31	−0.44
	(2)	6.86	4.74	2.20	1.14	0.53	0.09	−0.19
	(3)	0.39	0.27	0.12	0.05	0.01	−0.06	−0.07
VPC9R		0.392	−0.173	0.802	0.790	0.298	0.553	0.794
	(1)	0.081	−0.068	−0.015	0.001	0.001	−0.001	−0.001
	(2)	0.111	−0.035	−0.068	−0.012	0.001	0.001	0.000
	(3)	0.002	0.003	−0.002	−0.001	−0.001	−0.001	0.000
VPC9		0.401	−0.171	0.828	0.845	0.345	0.934	0.852
	(1)	0.085	−0.063	−0.019	−0.002	−0.001	−0.001	−0.002
	(2)	0.116	−0.027	−0.070	−0.015	−0.001	0.000	−0.001
	(3)	0.004	0.002	−0.003	−0.001	−0.002	−0.001	−0.001
X9R		6.817	7.245	7.945	8.550	9.320	9.958	11.152
	(1)	−0.02	−0.19	−0.17	−0.12	−0.09	−0.07	−0.05
	(2)	−0.01	−0.23	−0.30	−0.24	−0.21	−0.17	−0.14
	(3)	0.15	0.02	−0.01	−0.01	0.00	0.00	0.00
X9		7.005	7.545	8.495	9.270	10.242	11.069	12.889
	(1)	0.48	0.19	0.02	0.01	0.01	0.01	0.01
	(2)	0.80	0.51	0.03	0.02	0.01	0.02	0.02
	(3)	0.52	0.18	0.02	0.00	0.00	0.00	0.00
IMP9R		8.024	8.043	8.943	9.268	9.565	10.426	11.435
	(1)	2.22	−0.17	0.02	−0.04	−0.12	−0.15	−0.16
	(2)	3.44	0.52	0.18	0.17	0.08	−0.02	−0.08
	(3)	−0.32	−0.01	0.05	0.02	0.00	−0.02	−0.02
IMP9		8.184	8.324	9.774	10.425	10.889	11.933	13.324
	(1)	3.01	0.14	0.03	−0.04	−0.11	−0.15	−0.16
	(2)	4.78	1.36	0.18	0.17	0.08	−0.02	−0.08
	(3)	0.48	0.25	0.05	0.02	−0.00	−0.02	−0.02
Y9R		34.302	35.433	38.597	40.196	41.532	43.829	46.312
	(1)	1.88	−0.29	−0.12	−0.07	−0.07	−0.06	−0.06
	(2)	2.73	0.10	−0.08	0.02	0.01	−0.01	−0.03
	(3)	0.11	0.05	0.02	0.01	0.00	0.00	−0.01
Y9		36.175	37.496	42.038	45.065	47.875	51.693	56.714
	(1)	2.40	0.51	0.22	0.05	−0.04	−0.09	−0.11
	(2)	3.57	1.37	0.58	0.32	0.18	0.09	0.03
	(3)	0.31	0.19	0.05	0.01	0.01	−0.03	−0.03
YB9R		25.520	26.275	28.727	29.492	31.071	33.064	35.209
	(1)	2.39	−0.50	−0.19	−0.09	−0.08	−0.07	−0.07
	(2)	3.27	−0.17	−0.24	−0.03	−0.02	−0.02	−0.04
	(3)	0.08	0.03	0.01	0.01	0.00	0.00	0.00
Continued								

TABLE 7 (Continued)

Simulation results based on 1960 experiments.

Variable		1960	1961	1962	1963	1964	1965	1966
YB9	Control solution	26.095	26.873	30.104	31.775	33.913	36.433	39.591
	(1)	3.15	0.59	0.27	0.08	−0.04	−0.10	−0.12
	(2)	4.43	1.52	0.64	0.39	0.22	0.11	0.04
	(3)	0.33	0.23	0.06	0.02	−0.01	−0.03	−0.04
GAP		0.968	0.965	1.005	0.983	0.977	0.976	0.977
	(1)	0.023	−0.006	−0.003	−0.002	−0.002	−0.002	−0.002
	(2)	0.032	−0.003	−0.004	−0.002	−0.002	−0.002	−0.002
	(3)	0.001	0.000	0.000	0.000	0.000	0.000	0.000
PYB2		1.022	1.022	1.048	1.077	1.092	1.102	1.125
	(1)	0.76	1.09	0.46	0.17	0.04	−0.03	−0.05
	(2)	1.16	1.69	0.88	0.42	0.24	0.13	0.08
	(3)	0.25	0.20	0.05	0.01	−0.01	−0.03	−0.04
PY2		1.055	1.058	1.089	1.121	1.153	1.179	1.225
	(1)	0.52	0.80	0.34	0.12	0.03	−0.03	−0.05
	(2)	0.84	1.27	0.64	0.30	0.17	0.10	0.06
	(3)	0.20	0.14	0.03	0.00	−0.01	−0.03	−0.02
PC2		1.049	1.053	1.082	1.108	1.130	1.147	1.177
	(1)	0.53	0.68	0.37	0.21	0.12	0.06	0.03
	(2)	0.86	1.14	0.66	0.41	0.30	0.22	0.18
	(3)	0.27	0.14	0.03	0.01	0.00	−0.01	−0.02
PBC2		1.069	1.090	1.143	1.192	1.226	1.254	1.296
	(1)	0.61	0.85	0.41	0.24	0.17	0.10	0.11
	(2)	1.00	1.44	0.72	0.47	0.38	0.29	0.29
	(3)	0.44	0.17	0.02	−0.02	−0.02	−0.04	0.01
PRS2		1.081	1.095	1.149	1.197	1.240	1.277	1.337
	(1)	0.64	0.79	0.30	0.11	0.01	−0.04	0.00
	(2)	1.04	1.35	0.60	0.29	0.16	0.08	0.10
	(3)	0.36	0.19	0.01	−0.01	−0.03	−0.05	0.00
WRB		1.701	1.760	1.851	1.938	2.023	2.106	2.200
	(1)	0.62	0.67	0.46	0.35	0.26	0.21	0.19
	(2)	0.93	1.09	0.85	0.71	0.61	0.54	0.51
	(3)	0.11	0.06	0.00	0.00	−0.02	−0.02	0.01
U		6.847	7.209	4.898	5.473	5.946	6.267	6.166
	(1)	−1.206	−0.067	0.139	0.142	0.139	0.126	0.116
	(2)	−1.647	−0.325	0.111	0.133	0.140	0.142	0.145
	(3)	−0.037	−0.026	−0.005	0.001	0.008	0.012	0.012
E6		5.972	6.050	6.291	6.378	6.521	6.694	6.963
	(1)	1.30	0.07	−0.15	−0.15	−0.14	−0.14	−0.12
	(2)	1.78	0.37	−0.10	−0.13	−0.15	−0.15	−0.16
	(3)	0.04	0.03	0.00	0.00	−0.01	−0.01	−0.01
CPG9		5.998	6.204	6.997	7.362	7.865	8.404	9.057
	(1)	3.18	0.12	0.23	0.04	−0.11	−0.15	−0.18
	(2)	4.51	0.87	0.43	0.24	0.03	−0.07	−0.14
	(3)	0.49	0.33	0.07	0.02	−0.02	−0.02	−0.04
PDI9		24.803	25.803	28.899	30.527	32.087	34.773	37.496
	(1)	0.08	0.54	0.22	0.07	−0.01	−0.05	−0.08
	(2)	3.20	1.34	0.61	0.37	0.26	0.17	0.12
	(3)	0.22	0.13	0.03	0.00	−0.02	−0.03	−0.04

Continued

TABLE 7 (Continued)

Simulation results based on 1960 experiments.

Variable		1960	1961	1962	1963	1964	1965	1966
CT9	Control solution	1.644	1.726	1.826	1.934	2.054	2.145	2.295
	(1)	3.44	0.52	0.57	0.18	−0.07	−0.20	−0.23
	(2)	4.95	1.49	0.95	0.51	0.17	−0.04	−0.13
	(3)	0.70	0.48	0.12	0.04	−0.01	−0.06	−0.06
PT9		2.337	2.452	2.890	3.084	3.409	3.860	4.255
	(1)	26.27	0.47	0.20	0.03	−0.07	−0.11	−0.16
	(2)	4.91	1.53	0.65	0.41	0.26	0.15	0.07
	(3)	0.31	0.19	0.05	−0.01	−0.04	−0.04	−0.06
GDF9		0.635	0.957	0.383	−0.256	−0.189	−0.188	0.169
	(1)	−0.007	−0.066	−0.034	−0.012	0.002	0.011	0.017
	(2)	0.390	−0.165	−0.078	−0.042	−0.021	−0.004	0.009
	(3)	−0.042	−0.029	−0.012	−0.008	−0.004	−0.002	0.000
SIC		3.322	2.783	3.842	3.719	3.961	4.280	5.262
	(1)	0.157	−0.018	−0.018	0.002	−0.002	−0.004	−0.004
	(2)	0.243	0.022	−0.050	0.012	0.007	0.003	0.002
	(3)	−0.119	−0.037	−0.021	0.000	−0.001	−0.001	−0.001
LIC		4.986	4.813	5.033	5.126	5.254	5.427	5.827
	(1)	0.047	0.023	0.008	0.005	0.003	0.000	−0.001
	(2)	0.073	0.051	0.015	0.012	0.009	0.006	0.005
	(3)	−0.036	−0.032	−0.025	−0.015	−0.009	−0.006	−0.004
LDU9		0.406	0.364	0.419	0.235	0.252	0.256	0.308
	(1)	3.10	2.17	0.85	0.55	−0.22	−0.73	−0.75
	(2)	4.02	3.34	1.79	1.69	0.58	−0.18	−0.47
	(3)	−10.77	11.20	0.09	0.20	−0.02	−0.25	−0.21
CIF9		0.378	0.367	0.647	0.653	0.677	0.754	0.823
	(1)	12.15	0.55	−0.32	0.18	−0.05	−0.16	−0.17
	(2)	18.53	4.93	−0.93	0.62	0.34	0.13	0.01·
	(3)	−3.49	−2.03	−1.02	−0.29	−0.24	−0.15	−0.06
EXC		0.970	0.999	1.069	1.078	1.079	1.078	1.077
	(1)	0.80	0.27	0.000	0.000	0.000	0.000	0.000
	(2)	1.31	0.81	0.000	0.000	0.000	0.000	0.000
	(3)	0.83	0.22	0.000	0.000	0.000	0.000	0.000
BCF9R		5.091	5.197	5.732	5.977	6.196	6.477	6.743
	(1)	3.66	1.36	0.49	0.12	−0.13	−0.28	−0.36
	(2)	4.96	2.55	1.08	0.53	0.16	−0.10	−0.28
	(3)	0.04	0.09	0.08	0.05	0.02	−0.02	−0.03
BCF9		5.442	5.663	6.551	7.123	7.596	8.120	8.741
	(1)	4.30	2.25	0.92	0.38	0.05	−0.15	−0.27
	(2)	6.02	4.06	1.83	1.02	0.55	0.22	−0.02
	(3)	0.48	0.30	0.10	0.06	0.01	−0.03	−0.05

*All values shown in rows numbered (1), (2) and (3) are percentage differences between simulation and control solutions, except for GAP, U, LIC, SIC, VPC9, VPC9R and GDF9, which are shown as arithmetic differences between simulation and control solution. The differences between simulation and control values which were introduced in these experiments were the following:

		GNW9	RPT	M9
	(1)	0.723	0.065	0.000
	(2)	0.723	0.000	0.000
	(3)	0.000	0.000	0.670

TABLE 8

Simulation results based on 1964 experiments*. (In 1964 only, the following changes were introduced: (1) government non-wage expenditure was increased by two per cent of the control value of GNP, while personal income tax rates were adjusted to prevent the government surplus or deficit from changing in the initial year; (2) government non-wage expenditure was increased by two per cent of the control value of GNP and the government deficit was free to vary accordingly; and (3) the money supply was increased by five per cent of its actual value.)

Variable		1964	1965	1966
DUR9R	Control solution	3.480	3.827	4.114
	(1)	−0.52	−0.48	−0.41
	(2)	1.94	0.70	0.03
	(3)	0.30	0.30	0.21
DUR9		3.504	3.834	4.161
	(1)	−0.19	0.44	0.16
	(2)	2.52	2.19	1.17
	(3)	0.31	0.34	0.24
ND9R		13.200	13.945	14.646
	(1)	−0.20	−0.08	−0.10
	(2)	1.21	0.64	0.30
	(3)	0.02	0.04	0.03
ND9		14.375	15.466	16.821
	(1)	0.05	0.61	0.33
	(2)	1.65	1.75	1.16
	(3)	0.04	0.07	0.06
SER9R		9.819	10.416	10.972
	(1)	−0.24	−0.04	−0.11
	(2)	1.42	0.58	0.29
	(3)	0.02	0.05	0.03
SER9		11.441	12.483	13.608
	(1)	0.03	0.43	0.36
	(2)	1.83	1.34	1.13
	(3)	0.03	0.06	0.06
C9R		26.499	28.188	29.732
	(1)	−0.26	−0.12	−0.15
	(2)	1.39	0.63	0.26
	(3)	0.06	0.08	0.05
C9		29.320	31.783	34.590
	(1)	0.01	0.52	0.32
	(2)	1.82	1.64	1.15
	(3)	0.07	0.10	0.08
RES9R		1.631	1.657	1.573
	(1)	−2.84	−1.93	0.45
	(2)	−4.07	−3.47	−0.18
	(3)	0.68	0.58	0.19
RES9		1.973	2.076	2.076
	(1)	−2.33	−0.93	1.20
	(2)	−3.13	−1.80	1.31
	(3)	0.66	0.58	0.22
BME9R		2.412	2.653	2.848
	(1)	4.57	1.48	0.30
	(2)	6.38	3.04	1.04
	(3)	0.19	0.28	0.18

Continued

TABLE 8 (Continued)

Simulation results based on 1964 experiments.

Variable		1964	1965	1966
BME9	Control solution	2.824	3.176	3.529
	(1)	4.65	2.33	0.91
	(2)	6.53	4.29	2.12
	(3)	0.17	0.29	0.22
BNR9R		2.313	2.543	2.746
	(1)	4.58	1.94	0.62
	(2)	6.42	3.70	1.59
	(3)	0.12	0.25	0.15
BNR9		2.731	3.117	3.529
	(1)	5.12	2.75	1.17
	(2)	7.33	5.09	2.68
	(3)	0.16	0.28	0.19
VPC9R		0.502	0.700	0.862
	(1)	0.097	−0.080	−0.023
	(2)	0.137	−0.034	−0.091
	(3)	0.002	0.009	−0.004
VPC9		0.533	1.079	0.923
	(1)	0.099	−0.072	−0.024
	(2)	0.139	−0.023	−0.088
	(3)	0.003	0.009	−0.003
X9R		9.352	9.992	11.169
	(1)	−0.25	−0.30	−0.24
	(2)	−0.40	−0.52	−0.47
	(3)	−0.01	−0.02	−0.01
X9		10.215	11.046	12.868
	(1)	0.00	0.02	0.04
	(2)	0.01	0.04	0.07
	(3)	0.00	0.00	0.01
IMP9R		9.453	10.455	11.531
	(1)	2.40	−0.03	−0.03
	(2)	3.95	0.94	0.15
	(3)	0.10	0.15	0.05
IMP9		10.762	11.967	13.436
	(1)	2.40	−0.03	−0.04
	(2)	3.95	0.94	0.15
	(3)	0.09	0.14	0.05
Y9R		41.412	43.983	46.588
	(1)	1.83	−0.28	−0.18
	(2)	2.73	0.11	−0.14
	(3)	0.06	0.08	0.03
Y9		46.933	51.333	56.828
	(1)	2.13	0.53	0.33
	(2)	3.25	1.41	0.88
	(3)	0.08	0.11	0.07
YB9R		31.144	33.306	35.496
	(1)	2.34	−0.48	−0.29
	(2)	3.29	−0.15	−0.35
	(3)	0.06	0.08	0.02

Continued

TABLE 8 (Continued)

Simulation results based on 1964 experiments.

Variable		1964	1965	1966
YB9	Control solution	33.245	36.210	39.723
	(1)	2.90	0.60	0.39
	(2)	4.13	1.60	1.01
	(3)	0.08	0.13	0.07
GAP		0.996	1.001	1.002
	(1)	0.024	−0.006	−0.005
	(2)	0.033	−0.003	−0.006
	(3)	0.001	0.000	0.000
PYB2		1.068	1.087	1.119
	(1)	0.56	1.08	0.68
	(2)	0.84	1.75	1.36
	(3)	0.02	0.05	0.05
PY2		1.133	1.167	1.220
	(1)	0.30	0.81	0.51
	(2)	0.52	1.30	1.02
	(3)	0.02	0.03	0.04
PC2	(	1.106	1.128	1.163
	(1)	0.27	0.64	0.47
	(2)	0.43	1.01	0.89
	(3)	0.01	0.02	0.03
PBC2		1.176	1.211	1.261
	(1)	0.25	0.81	0.60
	(2)	0.44	1.27	1.10
	(3)	−0.03	0.01	0.06
PRS2		1.209	1.253	1.320
	(1)	0.51	1.00	0.75
	(2)	0.94	1.67	1.49
	(3)	−0.02	0.00	0.03
WRB		1.975	2.072	2.184
	(1)	0.95	1.07	0.93
	(2)	1.53	1.90	1.79
	(3)	0.03	0.04	0.09
U		5.128	4.896	4.635
	(1)	−1.223	−0.053	0.202
	(2)	−1.718	−0.353	0.185
	(3)	−0.032	−0.050	−0.015
E6		6.578	6.791	7.077
	(1)	1.29	0.06	−0.22
	(2)	1.81	0.37	−0.20
	(3)	0.03	0.06	0.01
CPG9		7.668	8.241	8.919
	(1)	2.51	−0.23	0.14
	(2)	3.48	0.25	0.36
	(3)	0.08	0.11	0.03
PDI9		31.690	34.738	37.761
	(1)	−0.16	0.62	0.34
	(2)	3.02	1.48	0.92
	(3)	0.06	0.09	0.05

Continued

TABLE 8 (Continued)

Simulation results based on 1964 experiments.

Variable		1964	1965	1966
CT9	Control solution	1.950	2.049	2.210
	(1)	2.99	−0.10	0.45
	(2)	4.13	0.57	0.89
	(3)	0.11	0.14	0.07
PT9		3.375	3.887	4.332
	(1)	24.25	0.52	0.27
	(2)	5.02	1.70	0.94
	(3)	0.09	0.13	0.06
GDF9		0.303	0.110	0.306
	(1)	0.003	−0.085	−0.065
	(2)	0.535	−0.223	−0.158
	(3)	−0.014	−0.022	−0.018
SIC		3.883	4.252	5.270
	(1)	0.083	0.021	0.013
	(2)	0.124	0.055	0.033
	(3)	−0.195	0.004	0.003
LIC		5.168	5.367	5.794
	(1)	0.025	0.021	0.017
	(2)	0.037	0.039	0.034
	(3)	−0.059	−0.033	−0.019
LDU9		0.213	0.242	0.311
	(1)	8.05	3.83	1.31
	(2)	11.40	7.23	3.06
	(3)	−19.47	17.31	0.35
CIF9		0.627	0.729	0.816
	(1)	4.36	0.80	0.30
	(2)	6.27	2.10	0.89
	(3)	−5.75	−0.43	−0.20
EXC		1.079	1.078	1.077
	(1)	0.000	0.000	0.000
	(2)	0.000	0.000	0.000
	(3)	0.000	0.000	0.000
BCF9R		5.775	6.355	6.817
	(1)	3.70	1.24	0.29
	(2)	5.16	2.51	0.89
	(3)	0.13	0.20	0.14
BCF9		6.789	7.694	8.598
	(1)	3.99	2.08	0.86
	(2)	5.67	3.84	1.98
	(3)	0.14	0.23	0.18

*All values shown in rows numbered (1), (2) and (3) are percentage differences between simulation and control solutions, except for GAP, U, LIC, SIC, VPC9, VPC9R, and GDF9, which are shown as arithmetic differences between simulation and control solutions. The differences between simulation and control values which were introduced in these experiments were the following:

		GNW9	RPT	M9
	(1)	0.939	0.060	0.000
	(2)	0.939	0.000	0.000
	(3)	0.000	0.000	0.868

government non-wage expenditure in each of the base years by two per cent of the control solution value of nominal GNP in the same base year and augmented the money supply by five per cent of its value in the base year.

Multipliers should be calculated in terms of pure numbers in order to compare different years. For example, the multiplier of nominal GNP with respect to nominal government non-wage expenditure, dY9/dGNW9, is such a number in that the numerator and denominator of the expression are measured in the same units. It is possible to re-write this multiplier in a form which reflects our procedure of augmenting government non-wage expenditure in each base year by a fixed percentage of nominal GNP and decompose it into expressions involving the multipliers for real GNP and the price level.

$$
\begin{aligned}
dY9/dGNW9 \ &= \ PY2\,(dY9R/dGNW9) \ + \ Y9R\,(dPY2/dGNW9) \\
&= \ (dY9R/dGNW9)\,(Y9/Y9R) \ + \ (dPY2/dGNW9)\,(Y9/PY2) \\
&= \ (dY9R/Y9R)\,/\,(dGNW9/Y9) \ + \ (dPY2/PY2)\,/\,(dGNW9/Y9).
\end{aligned}
$$

This illustrates that comparisons among multipliers for real values of the form dY9R/dGNW9, for example, would be inappropriate since such multipliers are of dimension $1/PY2$. We have, in effect, adjusted for this when we take dGNW9/Y9 as base, provided we make our comparisons in terms of proportional changes in Y9R. This multiplier is a special case, however, in that

$$
dY9/dGNW9 \ = \ (dY9/Y9)/(dGNW9/Y9).
$$

In the case of multipliers for components of GNP, such as RES9 (residential construction in nominal dollars), the result is somewhat different.

$$
\begin{aligned}
dRES9/dGNW9 \ &= \ RES9R\,(dPRS2/dGNW9) \ + \ PRS2\,(dRES9R/dGNW9) \\
&= \ (RES9/Y9)\,(dPRS2/PRS2)\,/\,(dGNW9/Y9) \\
&\quad + \ (RES9/Y9)\,(dRES9R/RES9R)\,/\,(dGNW9/Y9)
\end{aligned}
$$

i.e., $(dRES9/RES9)/(dGNW9/Y9) \ = \ (dPRS2/PRS2)/(dGNW9/Y9)$
$$
+ \ (dRES9R/RES9R)/(dGNW9/Y9).
$$

The proportional changes in price and constant dollar expenditure sum to the proportional change in nominal dollar expenditure. This is still a pure number, in the sense that the numerator and denominator are measured in the same units. We have, in effect, standardized the multiplier for the share (in nominal terms) of RES9 in Y9.

In the case of the unemployment rate, or interest rates, which are already measured as proportions, the appropriate numerator would be the change in the proportion since the denominator is a change in the proportion GNW9/Y9. For example, we want to compare values of dU/(dGNW9/Y9); it would be inappropriate to make comparisons in terms of either of dU/dGNW9 or (dU/U)/(dGNW9/Y9).

The experiments involving changes in the money supply (M9) require a somewhat different approach. Simplifying the notation for convenience of exposition, we have the following, where V is velocity, $M = M9$, and $Y = Y9$.

$$Y = MV \tag{1}$$

$$dY/dM = M(dV/dM) + V \tag{2}$$

$$(dY/Y) / (dM/Y) = dY/dM = V[1 + (dV/V)/(dM/M)] \tag{3}$$

$$(dY/Y) / (dM/M) = (dY/dM)(M/Y) = [\![1 + [(dV/V)/(dM/M)]]\!] $$
$$= (1/V)(dY/Y)/(dM/Y). \tag{4}$$

Thus comparisons of money supply multipliers constructed on the same basis as government expenditure multipliers would be inappropriate in that they would be of dimension V. We have, instead, calculated the elasticity of GNP with respect to the money supply, thereby effectively dividing the inappropriate multiplier by V.

Comparisons between 1957 and 1960 are between years in which the control value of the unemployment rate was 5.3 per cent and 6.8 per cent. In the latter year, a year of greater slack in the economy, we note that both the increased government expenditure as well as the increased money supply have a greater impact on real output than in 1957 and a smaller inpact on prices. The difference in impact on business capital formation is also quite noticeable.

The linkages between the real and monetary sectors of the model are not entirely satisfactory. This may account for some of the results shown by the increase in the money supply (Experiment 3). The expected result does occur, however, for prices, in that the increase in the money supply has a greater impact on prices in 1957 than in 1960.

In 1964 the control value of the unemployment rate was 5.1 per cent, i.e., close to the level in 1957. In 1964, in contrast to 1957, Canada had, however, a fixed exchange rate. Comparisons between these two years reveal the differing effects of policy instruments under the two exchange rate regimes. The government expenditure multipliers for the nominal increase in GNP are larger under the flexible exchange rate regime: the increases in Y9 are 3.49 and 3.25 in 1957 and 1964, respectively. [4] This is because expansionary fiscal policy leads to increased demand for imports and the resulting devaluation reinforces the expansionary fiscal policy effect by increasing exports and decreasing imports. The higher rate of interest resulting from the expansionary fiscal policy, which raises capital imports and therefore increases the demand for Canadian dollars, is clearly insufficient to offset the impact of increased imports. This is because the demand for money is more responsive to the interest rate and less responsive to income change than capital imports and commodity imports respectively within the period of one year.

We find a difference in the distribution of the impact of expansionary fiscal policy (Experiment 2) between increases in real output (Y9R) and in prices (PY2). In 1957, a year of flexible exchange rates, the increase in Y9R is 2.57 and the increase in PY2 is 0.92, whereas in 1964, a year of fixed rates, the increase in Y9R is 2.73 and the in-

---

4 In comparing the two experiments, it should be noted that the model does not incorporate any reaction by the Exchange Fund Account under the fixed exchange rate regime to changes in foreign exchange reserves. The money supply is exogenous.

crease in PY2 is 0.52. Thus, in the flexible exchange rate year, 26 per cent of the impact effect on nominal GNP is a price effect, while in the fixed rate year only 16 per cent of the effect is a price effect.

Expansionary fiscal policy appears to be much more inflationary under flexible than under fixed exchange rates. This occurs in our model due to the influence of import prices which enter the supply side in two ways. First, import prices affect domestic prices directly through the price equation for the business non-agricultural sector (PYB2) and, secondly, they affect wages through their effect on the price of consumer expenditure (PC2). Thus, the distribution of the effect of a given shift in aggregate demand is affected by changes on the supply side. This effect, which is usually ignored in analyses of open economy macroeconomic models, has important implications with respect to price stabilization. While inflationary pressures from outside will be neutralized by a flexible exchange rate, the trade-off curve between unemployment and price changes becomes steeper when fiscal policy is implemented. It is thus more difficult to achieve full employment and price stability by way of fiscal policy under flexible exchange rates.

Caves and Reuber (1969, p. 63) have concluded that, in the short-run at least, the monetary effects of fiscal policy outweigh the expenditure effects, so that the reserve position would improve under a fixed rate, while a flexible rate would appreciate. Rhomberg (1964) had similar findings. Caves and Reuber do observe, further, that in the longer term (approximately six quarters later) the expenditure effects come to dominate. But the initial appreciation is estimated to have reduced the impact effect of changes in fiscal policy by about 30 per cent and the longer term effect by about 15 per cent (p. 78). Although they repeatedly refer to GNP without specifying whether they mean real or nominal, they presumably mean nominal GNP, since this is the relevant magnitude in assessing expenditure effects. Their conclusion that the effect of fiscal policy is greater with a fixed exchange rate, on the assumption that they are measuring effects in terms of nominal GNP, would be contrary to our own, whereas we would be in agreement if they meant real GNP. They do seem to have used Officer's multipliers for real GNP in their calculations (cf. Caves and Reuber, 1969, p. 40 and p. 62) but this would have led to an underestimate of expenditure effects.

It is, of course, not generally possible to pick up the timing of effects as precisely with annual as with quarterly data, and this may help to explain the difference between our conclusions. If this were all there were to it, the interpretation of the discrepancy would remain largely a matter of judgment; for example, the importance of short-lived appreciation may be over-stated in a quarterly model.

It is not easy to track down the source of such disagreement, particularly when the conclusions of Caves and Reuber are drawn from selected empirical results rather than an internally consistent model. It is a well known econometric fact that successful integration within a complete model imposes a severe test of equations which might otherwise appear robust in isolation, and also, of course, forces complete specification of all relevant relationships. The Caves and Reuber result for fiscal expansion with a flexible exchange rate would seem to imply a very small short-run import propensity and a low interest-elasticity of demand for money.

So far as we can tell, Caves and Reuber regard US direct investment as essentially autonomous so that the capital inflow in effect drives business capital formation in

Canada, with a spillover (p. 34). That is to say, the capital inflow (which is virtually independent of such things as Canadian-U.S. interest differentials) leads dollar-for-dollar to business capital formation undertaken by the subsidiary, and this investment in turn spurs investment by other firms. In our formulation, on the other hand, the real investment prospects of the Canadian economy are conceived to be the driving force behind business capital formation, in which US subsidiaries will typically share, and typically finance in part, by importing capital from the parent firms. Thus, although all decisions are, in principle, interrelated, we view the analysis of real investment prospects as primary and the financing decision as secondary; the fact that there is typically some capital inflow and that this typically precedes actual expenditure is incidental. At any rate, for Caves and Reuber, a large segment of business capital formation in Canada is virtually independent of Canadian economic variables and policies. It is not clear how we are to reconcile this view with the interest-elasticity of investment which they draw from another study.

In the Caves and Reuber formulation, interest differentials are quite important for short-term capital flows, but these are not related to real investment decisions. Interest differentials are also important for long-term portfolio capital flows, however, and these are related to real investment. Autonomous portfolio capital inflows do not lead directly to new business capital formation, according to Caves and Reuber. They do so only to the extent that they force down Canadian interest rates (pp. 35-6). By the same token, portfolio capital inflows induced by rising Canadian interest rates simply prevent the differential from becoming as great as it would without such inflows. Portfolio capital inflows thus prevent business capital formation from falling as far as it otherwise would (had interest rates risen more), in the case of fiscal expansion. In our model the effect of integrated capital markets shows up in the interest responsiveness of portfolio flows and in the interdependence of Canadian and US interest rates; in this we are in essential agreement with Caves and Reuber. Short-term capital movements are residually determined by our model whereas their interest differential sensitivity is explicitly considered by Caves and Reuber. In effect, the same basic forces are reflected in our equation for determination of the flexible exchange rate.

The difference between flexible and fixed exchange rates is even greater for monetary policy. The increases in Y9 are 0.35 and 0.08 for flexible and fixed exchange rates. This occurs because the movement of the exchange rate reinforces the other effects of monetary policy. As the interest rate falls due to the expansionary monetary policy, capital imports are curtailed, depreciating the Canadian exchange rate which reinforces the impact of the lower interest rate on investment. The differential effects on real income and prices are also considerably stronger than for fiscal policy. About 25 per cent of the impact effect is on prices in 1964 relative to about 65 per cent of the impact in 1957. Again the reason is that the exchange rate devaluation affects the aggregate supply side. Because the impact of the devaluation is large relative to the other effects of monetary policy, the impact on the supply side is large relative to the demand side. The slope of the trade-off curve thus appears to be quite different for fiscal and monetary policy. It appears that monetary policy may be a relatively effective anti-inflationary tool in the short-run under flexible exchange rates.

In the Caves-Reuber formulation, monetary expansion reduces the Canadian interest rate and this leads to a reduction in portfolio capital inflows. As mentioned above, the effect of this reduction is simply to cushion the fall in domestic interest rates - given the increased investment (if any) induced by the lower rates, there is just that much more investment to be financed internally. With a flexible exchange rate, we and they agree, the resulting depreciation would enhance the effectiveness of monetary policy.

It may be worth noting that a combination of expansionary fiscal policy and contractionary monetary policy appears to be an effective way to fight inflation, particularly in the case of flexible exchange rates. This policy will, however, cause severe contraction in the investment sector in general and in the construction industry in particular. This seems to have been the case in 1970. In general one might note that the different tradeoffs between prices and employment for monetary and fiscal policy enable the government to obtain a wider range of possible employment-price configurations by an appropriate choice of fiscal and monetary policy. This is particularly true with flexible exchange rates.

Thus, in 1957 if government non-wage expenditure were increased by 1 per cent of GNP, the unemployment rate would have dropped by about 0.85 points while the price of GNP would have risen by about 0.46 per cent, but a restrictive monetary policy of 5 per cent decrease in the money supply would have decreased prices by about 0.23 per cent while raising the unemployment rate by only 0.04 points. The combined effect would have been, therefore, a reduction in the unemployment rate of about 0.80 points at a cost of only 0.23 per cent increase in price.[5] This combined policy will, however, have caused the short-term interest rate to rise by about 0.23 points and a reduction of real residential construction by about 2.7 per cent. The net result of this policy on the balance of payments would be a small appreciation in the exchange rate of about 0.2 per cent and a considerably higher volume of both direct US investment (about 11.5 per cent) and net movement of long term Canadian securities to the US (about 10.5 per cent). Thus, the increased employment is obtained at the cost of higher borrowing from abroad rather than at the cost of a higher level of prices.

Some special differences in the effect of the experiments on components of gross national product stand out. In particular, the negative impact of fiscal expansion on real investment in residential construction is notable. This occurs because the higher interest rate dominates this relation. This also causes residential construction to respond more strongly than other GNP components to monetary policy.

The response of real exports to an expansionary fiscal policy is also noteworthy. The supply price of exports is a function of the Canadian wage rate, the exchange rate, and foreign prices. The expansionary policy raises wage rates and also leads to a devaluation of the exchange rate. Hence, the supply price rises. The demand for exports is also a function of the exchange rate and the devaluation shifts the demand curve to the right. Where the demand curve shift is less than the rise in the supply price, the quantity of real exports falls. This is the case both in 1957 and 1960, years of flexible exchange rates. Monetary expansion, on the other hand, causes a relatively smaller increase in wage rates so that the shift in the demand schedule outweighs the effect of

5 The reader is reminded that the links between the monetary and real sector of our model are weak and this calculation (which amounts to a 0.85 per cent gain in employment) is undoubtedly an overstatement.

TABLE 9

Convergence in 1957 simulations: ratios of percentage or arithmetic differences in each year to corresponding differences (impact multipliers) in 1957.

		1958	1959	1960	1961	1962	1963	1964	1965	1966
C9R	(1)	0.63	0.54	0.46	0.34	0.29	0.26	0.23	0.20	0.17
	(2)	0.34	0.10	0.01	−0.01	−0.01	−0.01	−0.02	−0.02	−0.01
	(3)	1.00	0.00	−2.00	−2.00	−2.00	−2.00	−2.00	−3.00	−2.00
RES9R	(1)	0.54	−0.21	−0.31	−0.29	−0.26	−0.21	−0.14	−0.11	−0.09
	(2)	0.71	−0.02	−0.24	−0.26	−0.27	−0.23	−0.17	−0.13	−0.11
	(3)	1.30	0.80	0.47	0.33	0.10	0.07	−0.23	−0.27	−0.13
BCF9R	(1)	0.29	0.05	−0.05	−0.13	−0.14	−0.15	−0.16	−0.15	−0.14
	(2)	0.44	0.13	−0.01	−0.10	−0.13	−0.15	−0.17	−0.18	−0.17
	(3)	1.33	0.66	−0.17	−1.00	−0.83	−1.00	−1.17	−1.00	−1.00
VPC9R	(1)	−0.96	−0.16	0.01	0.01	0.01	−0.01	−0.01	−0.01	0.00
	(2)	−0.37	−0.65	−0.17	0.01	0.03	0.02	0.00	−0.01	−0.01
	(3)	1.00	−1.00	−1.00	−1.00	0.00	0.00	0.00	0.00	0.00
X9R	(1)	2.70	2.20	1.90	1.70	1.10	0.80	0.60	0.50	0.40
	(2)	2.71	2.71	2.57	2.50	2.00	1.64	1.43	1.14	1.00
	(3)	0.11	0.00	0.00	0.00	0.00	0.05	0.05	0.05	0.05
IMP9R	(1)	−0.13	−0.02	−0.04	−0.05	−0.06	−0.07	−0.07	−0.07	−0.05
	(2)	0.12	0.00	0.00	0.00	0.00	−0.03	−0.04	−0.04	−0.04
	(3)	0.06	0.09	0.12	0.15	0.06	0.09	0.12	0.09	0.06
Y9R	(1)	−0.21	−0.10	−0.07	−0.06	−0.05	−0.05	−0.05	−0.05	−0.04
	(2)	−0.01	−0.07	−0.04	−0.04	−0.04	−0.04	−0.05	−0.04	−0.04
	(3)	0.33	0.08	−0.08	−0.08	−0.08	−0.08	−0.08	−0.08	−0.08
PY2	(1)	1.39	0.78	0.37	0.19	0.12	0.07	0.05	0.03	0.03
	(2)	1.55	1.12	0.68	0.47	0.33	0.25	0.21	0.17	0.16
	(3)	0.65	0.43	0.22	0.04	−0.09	−0.13	−0.13	−0.13	−0.13
U	(1)	−0.04	−0.17	−0.15	−0.13	−0.12	−0.10	−0.08	−0.06	−0.05
	(2)	0.10	−0.13	−0.15	−0.13	−0.12	−0.11	−0.10	−0.08	−0.07
	(3)	0.34	−0.17	−0.44	−0.51	−0.46	−0.34	−0.32	−0.24	−0.22

the increase in the wage rate on the supply prices and real exports increase. In 1964, the expansionary fiscal policy has a greater negative impact on real exports because the cushioning effect of the exchange rate devaluation is absent.

The above discussion related to the impact multipliers of alternative policies, i.e., the effect within the same year as the action was taken. The extent to which such impacts carry over into subsequent years may be indicated by calculating the difference between solution and control values (in arithmetic or percentage form) for each of the subsequent years, and expressing these successive differences relative to the corresponding difference in the impact year as base. In the case of once-for-all shifts in policy variables, such as characterized our simulation experiments, such ratios will approach zero as the system returns to its control solution. In the interim, however, these ratios could rise before falling off, approach zero uniformly, or oscillate about zero. In the following Tables 9, 10 and 11 such ratios are presented for some variables of major interest for the set of simulation experiments based on the years 1957, 1960 and 1964.

In the case of consumption, C9R, the effect of a balanced budget (Experiment 1)

TABLE 10

Convergence in 1960 simulations: ratios of percentage or arithmetic differences in each year to corresponding differences (impact multipliers) in 1960.

		1961	1962	1963	1964	1965	1966
C9R	(1)	0.74	0.67	0.56	0.48	0.41	0.37
	(2)	0.35	0.12	0.06	0.02	0.01	−0.01
	(3)	2.00	2.00	1.00	0.00	−1.00	−1.00
RES9R	(1)	0.64	−0.19	−0.27	−0.25	−0.22	−0.19
	(2)	0.78	−0.06	−0.23	−0.21	−0.20	−0.19
	(3)	1.05	0.84	0.39	0.11	0.00	−0.18
BCF9R	(1)	0.52	0.21	0.09	0.01	−0.03	−0.06
	(2)	0.67	0.30	0.17	0.09	0.04	0.00
	(3)	0.06	0.21	0.13	0.02	−0.06	−0.10
VPC9R	(1)	−0.84	−0.19	0.01	0.01	−0.01	−0.01
	(2)	−0.32	−0.61	−0.11	0.01	0.01	0.00
	(3)	1.50	−1.00	−0.50	−0.50	−0.50	0.00
X9R	(1)	9.50	8.50	6.10	4.50	3.50	2.50
	(2)	23.00	30.00	24.00	21.00	17.00	14.00
	(3)	0.13	−0.07	−0.07	0.00	0.00	0.00
IMP9R	(1)	−0.08	0.01	−0.02	−0.05	−0.07	−0.07
	(2)	0.15	0.05	0.05	0.02	−0.01	−0.02
	(3)	0.03	−0.16	−0.06	0.00	0.06	0.06
Y9R	(1)	−0.15	−0.06	−0.04	−0.04	−0.03	−0.03
	(2)	0.04	−0.03	0.01	0.00	0.00	−0.01
	(3)	0.45	0.18	0.09	0.00	0.00	−0.09
PY2	(1)	1.54	0.65	0.23	0.06	−0.06	−0.10
	(2)	1.51	0.76	0.36	0.20	0.12	0.71
	(3)	0.70	0.15	0.00	−0.05	−0.15	−0.10
U	(1)	0.06	−0.12	−0.12	−0.12	−0.10	−0.10
	(2)	0.20	−0.07	−0.08	−0.09	−0.09	−0.09
	(3)	0.70	0.14	0.03	−0.22	−0.32	−0.32

increase tapers off quite gradually whereas the effect of increasing only government expenditure without a tax increase (Experiment 2) disappears more rapidly. However, for the balanced budget increase, C9R declines, primarily because personal disposable income, PDI9, declines (except for 1960, when it remained virtually unchanged). In subsequent years, PDI9 is above its control value for a while, gradually returning to it. The ratios for the experiment in which the money supply was increased are not very reliable because the initial impact on C9R was so small.

The impact on residential construction, RES9R, was negative for the first two experiments and positive for the third in each of the base years. This reflects the typically contra-cyclical behaviour of RES9R over the sample period, primarily because of the influence of interest rates. Rates rose in each of the first two experiments and declined in the third. This effect is quickly offset by the expansion in income associated with the first two experiments, but the effect takes longer to subside in the third.

Investment, BCF9R, increases for all three experiments in the initial year, but to a negligible extent for an expansion in the money supply. The ratios for the third experiment are consequently not very informative in this case. The effects of increased

TABLE 11

Convergence in 1964 simulations: ratios of percentage or arithmetic differences in each year to corresponding differences (impact multipliers) in 1964.

		1965	1966
C9R	(1)	0.46	0.58
	(2)	0.45	0.19
	(3)	1.33	0.83
RES9R	(1)	0.68	−0.16
	(2)	0.85	0.04
	(3)	0.85	0.28
BCF9R	(1)	0.34	0.08
	(2)	0.49	0.17
	(3)	1.53	1.08
VPC9R	(1)	−0.82	−0.24
	(2)	−0.25	−0.66
	(3)	4.50	−2.00
X9R	(1)	1.20	0.96
	(2)	1.30	1.18
	(3)	2.00	1.00
IMP9R	(1)	−0.01	−0.01
	(2)	0.24	0.04
	(3)	1.50	0.50
Y9R	(1)	−0.15	−0.10
	(2)	0.04	−0.05
	(3)	1.33	0.50
PY2	(1)	2.70	1.70
	(2)	2.50	1.96
	(3)	1.50	2.00
U	(1)	0.04	−0.17
	(2)	0.21	−0.11
	(3)	1.56	0.47

government expenditure, balanced by tax increases or not, subside quite quickly. The effects persisted somewhat longer in the run based on 1960, a year of high unemployment and flexible exchange rates. In part, this may be attributed to the fact that the impact on prices (PME2 and PNR2) was greater in 1957 than in 1960, but there was virtually no impact on these prices in the 1964 run. The percentage changes in GAP were also almost the same in all three base-years, although this change was reversed more substantially for the first experiment in the 1957 run. Corporate profits, CPG9, remained relatively higher in 1961, the second year of the run, than in 1958 or 1965. There was little difference between the third year, 1962, and 1966, in this respect, but 1959 was relatively higher. The slower rate of tapering off in the 1960 run is therefore, in effect, attributable to the absence of a price effect as substantial as that which characterized the 1957 run and a more sustained increase in corporate profits than that which characterized the 1964 run.

The impact on inventory investment, VPC9R, was positive for all three experiments but negligible in the case of monetary expansion (so that in this case also, the ratios for Experiment 3 may be ignored). For the first two experiments, the impact

TABLE 12

Impact-year solution values for income shares, real capital yield, and ratio of capital
yield to implicit rental price of capital services.

	1957	1960	1964
CPG9/WSB9			
(1)	0.405	0.418	0.420
(2)	0.404	0.418	0.418
(3)	0.408	0.420	0.424
CPG9/PI9			
(1)	0.230	0.222	0.219
(2)	0.231	0.223	0.219
(3)	0.230	0.221	0.218
CPG9/[(KCB9S + KMB9S) PY2]			
(1)	0.157	0.142	0.150
(2)	0.159	0.144	0.151
(3)	0.155	0.139	0.147
CPG9/[(KCB9S + KMB9S) PME2 (0.01 LIC + 0.12)]			
(1)	0.951	0.829	0.841
(2)	0.957	0.831	0.851
(3)	0.933	0.807	0.830
CPG9/[(KCB9S + KMB9S) PNR2 (0.01 LIC + 0.035)]			
(1)	2.012	1.641	1.650
(2)	2.012	1.645	1.653
(3)	2.000	1.615	1.627

effect was reversed in the subsequent year in all three runs. The rate of approach to
zero of this oscillatory path seems about the same in all runs. The impact effect is due
to the positive impact multiplier for gross domestic product. In the subsequent year
there is some tendency for inventory investment to be sustained by the lagged effect
of the positive impact multiplier on consumer durables, DUR9R, in the second experiment (otherwise the impact on DUR9R was negligible), but this is evidently outweighed by the effect of the augmented lagged value of inventories. This latter effect also
persists for a while whereas the influence through DUR9R is for one year only.

The impact of increased government expenditure, (balanced or not) on exports,
X9R, was negative but small (negligible in 1960) while that of monetary expansion
was small but positive (except for 1964 for which the impact was negative but negligible). In all runs, the effects of increased government expenditure were greater in the
second than the impact year, gradually tapering off.

The impact multiplier on imports was positive for increased government expenditure (balanced or not) and negligible for monetary expansion. For all practical purposes, there was no effect beyond the initial year.

Real gross national product, Y9R, of course, reflects all the components discussed
above. The net result on Y9R was a negligible impact multiplier for monetary expansion and positive multipliers for fiscal expansion. Fiscal effects were eliminated or
slightly reversed after the impact year but monetary effects, small though they were,
tended to persist for another year or two.

All impact multipliers on the implicit deflator for gross national expenditure, PY 2, were positive although smaller for monetary than for fiscal expansion as they were in the case of real output. There was a decided tendency for the effect to be greater in the year following the initial impact and then to taper off rather slowly. This of course reflects the lags in the rate of adjustment of prices and the influence of past rates of price change on subsequent price changes.

All impact multipliers on the unemployment rate were negative but, of course, small for monetary expansion. As with real output, the effects were mainly limited to the impact year.

Finally, in Table 12 we present impact-year solution values for income shares, the real yield on capital, and the ratio of the real yield on capital to the real implicit rental value of capital services.[6] Table 12 is directly comparable with Tables 4 and 5. Control solution values are those shown as free-run solutions in Tables 4 and 5 for the initiating years 1957, 1960 and 1964. It is clear that the changes in policy variables which we introduced in the three simulation experiments have a negligible impact on income shares measured either as CPG9/WSB9 or CPG9/PI9. The yield on capital is increased, however, with the exception of experiments for monetary expansion in 1960 and 1964.

As far as the ratios of yield to rental value are concerned, there is an increase for all experiments, with the exception of those based on 1960. The year 1960 was, of course, chosen as one base for the set of three experiments because it was characterized by relatively high unemployment. Our simulation results imply, therefore, that monetary or fiscal expansion tend to lower the yield relative to the implicit rental when unemployment is high, which would tend to discourage rather than encourage investment at such times. This effect on investment is also in the wrong direction when unemployment is low. These results should perhaps be viewed with skepticism, however, since the implicit ratios of yields to rental values may be distorted by a high unemployment rate.

6   This is the variable which appears in the equations for BME9R and BNR9R.

5 Forecasts for 1970:
the methodology of ex ante forecasting

The three conditional forecasts for 1970 shown in Table 13 were publicly released on December 12, 1969 by Kotowitz, Sawyer and Winder (1969) in Policy Paper No. 6 of the Institute for the Quantitative Analysis of Social and Economic Policy. Our conclusion was: "Our basic forecast for 1970 is that gross national product at market prices in constant dollars will increase by about 3.4 per cent, while the GNP deflator will increase by approximately 3.0 per cent. With these lower rates of increase in both real output and prices, we anticipate unemployment for the year as a whole will rise to approximately 5.9 per cent of the labour force.." In this chapter we shall try to explain the methodology by which the forecast was made.

Because of difficulties in forecasting the values of the exogenous variables in the export demand and export price equations, equations D.1 to D.30 and equations G.21 to G.35 were suppressed. Total exports of goods and services in nominal dollars and the implicit price index of exports of goods and services were made exogenous variables. Because of difficulties encountered with forecasting the residential construction sector beyond the end of sample period, equations C.1 to C.4 were suppressed and multiple housing starts (MHS3) and single housing starts (SHS3) were made exogenous variables. A final change in the model that was made for the forecast exercise was that equation J.1 was replaced by the following equation:

$$PIT9 = PIT91 + RPT2 * (PI9 - PI91).$$

The making of the forecast was complicated by two sets of revisions to the *National Accounts, Income and Expenditure* published by the Dominion Bureau of Statistics which formed the principal data source for estimating the parameters of the model. In the first place the estimates of the parameters were based on data appearing in the 1966 edition of the National Accounts (published in the summer of 1967). The 1967 edition (published in the summer of 1968) revised the 1965 and 1966 estimates so that a discontinuity existed when the model was used for projections past 1966. In the autumn of 1969, a major revision was made to the National Accounts in order to incorporate data from the 1961 census of merchandising and service establishments. At the same time some major changes were made in the National Accounts to conform to the revised standardized system of National Accounts adopted by the United Nations. Revisions were also made to the deflators used for investment expenditure and a number of other definitional and conceptual changes were made. As a result a completely revised set of National Accounts which changed the estimates for many series all the way back to 1926 came into existence. Beginning with the second quarter of 1969, the new Accounts were published on a quarterly basis in abbreviated form in accordance with the revised estimates although the preliminary complete set of new National Ac-

TABLE 13

Estimated 1969 and forecasts for 1970 from the TRACE model, percentage change over previous year.

	Current Dollars					Constant Dollars				
	Esti-mated Actual 1969	Basic Fore-cast 1970	Alter-native Fore-cast No. 1 1970	Alter-native Fore-cast No. 2 1970	Esti-mated Actual 1970	Esti-mated Actual 1969	Basic Fore-cast 1970	Alter-native Fore-cast No. 1 1970	Alter-native Fore-cast No. 2 1970	Esti-mated Actual 1970
Personal expenditure on consumer goods and services	8.8	6.5	7.1	6.2	5.3	4.8	3.4	3.8	3.1	1.6
Government expenditure on goods and services	10.9	6.5q	8.5	5.8	12.7	3.4	3.2	5.4	2.5	6.0
Business gross fixed capital formation	11.9	5.4	6.7	4.6	-2.4	5.8	1.0	2.2	0.4	-6.0
Exports of goods and services	9.5	6.7	7.7	5.7	11.7	7.4	3.8	4.8	2.8	10.2
Imports of goods and services	13.1	4.6	5.6	3.9	2.4	9.6	1.3	2.2	0.8	-0.2
Gross national product at market prices	9.1	6.5	7.6	5.8	6.2	4.6	3.4	4.3	2.8	2.4
Per cent unemployment rate	4.7	5.9	5.4	6.2	6.1					
Utilization rate (GAP x 100.)	98.5	96.3	97.3	95.8	95.3					

TABLE 13 Continued

Estimated 1969 and forecasts for 1970 from the TRACE model, percentage change over previous year.

	Implicit Price Index				
	Estimated Actual 1969	Basic Forecast 1970	Alternative Forecast No. 1 1970	Alternative Forecast No. 2 1970	Estimated Actual 1970
Personal expenditure on consumer goods and services	3.8	3.1	3.2	3.0	3.7
Government expenditure on goods and services	7.4	3.3	3.1	3.4	6.4
Business gross fixed capital formation	5.8	4.3	4.4	4.2	3.7
Exports of goods and services	2.0	2.8	2.8	2.8	1.4
Imports of goods and services	3.2	3.2	3.3	3.1	2.5
Gross national product at market prices	4.3	3.0	3.1	2.9	3.7
Per cent unemployment rate					
Utilization rate (GAP x 100.)					

Note: Estimated "actual 1969" are estimates as of December 1969, when the forecast was made. Estimated "actual 1970" are estimates as of December 1970

TABLE 14

Constant adjustments.

Period	1968	1969	1970
DUR3RC	0.0	0.005	0.002
ND3RC	−0.004	0.006	0.002
SER3RC	0.0	0.0	0.0
DHB9R	−0.111	−0.480	−0.383
BME9R	−0.080	0.300	0.300
BNR9R	−0.300	−0.200	0.0
RES9R	0.070	0.151	0.151
NMP9R	0.370	0.670	0.520
EB6	0.0	0.025	0.0
IT9	0.060	0.100	0.080
PYB2	−0.005	0.0	0.0
SIC	0.900	0.165	0.165
LIC	0.360	0.263	0.226
IPD9	0.150	0.150	0.150
PD2	0.020	0.012	0.020
PME2	−0.052	−0.016	−0.016
WRB	0.020	0.035	0.035
HB	−0.800	−0.800	−0.800
PND2	0.010	−0.005	0.0
PSR2	0.006	0.010	0.003
ECS9	0.128	0.020	0.0
PRS2	0.027	0.027	0.022
PNR	−0.012	0.018	0.006
CPG9	0.150	−0.150	0.0
DHB9	−0.072	−0.023	−0.023
CT9	−0.090	−0.150	−0.120

counts were not made available until mid-1970.[1] Accounts for 1968 and 1969 prepared on the old basis were also available.

The first step in preparing for the forecast for 1970 was to make an *ex post* forecast for 1968. For this forecast the "old" National Accounts were used and actual values of the lagged variables in 1966 and 1967 (from the 1967 edition of the National Accounts) and the actual values of the exogenous variables for 1968 were used. Thus, differences between the solution values for 1968 obtained from the model and the actual values in the National Accounts resulted from two sources. The first was the revisions made to the National Accounts in the 1967 edition which were not reflected in the parameter estimates of the model. The second source of error was, of course, the model itself. Forecast errors could result from mis-specification of the equations or small sample biases in the estimation procedures. It was decided to compensate for these errors by bringing the forecast for 1968 right on target for key variables by making additive adjustments to the constant terms in a number of equations. These constant adjustments are shown in Table 14.

At the time the forecast was made the National Accounts data for the first three quarters of 1969 were available. On the basis of current economic indicators and trends apparent in the data, figures for the fourth quarter of 1969 were "guessed" by

---

1   At the time of writing the final set of revised Accounts has still not been published.

TABLE 15

Assumptions for alternative forecasts

| | Percentage increase over 1969 | | |
	Basic Forecast	Alternative No. 1	Alternative No. 2
Implicit price of imports of goods and services into Canada (PFR2)	3.2	3.3	3.1
Value of exports of goods and services by Canada (X9)	6.7	7.7	5.7
Value of government expenditure on goods and services excluding wages and salaries (GNW9)	3.9	8.1	2.6
Implicit price of gross national product in the United States (PYU2)	4.6	4.8	4.3

members of the project staff. Using the same constant adjustments as were used for 1968, the model was then used to forecast these "guestimates" for 1969. The year 1969 was featured by an unusually large number of man-days lost through strikes and lock-outs. This affected both the levels and pattern of real output. Business non-farm inventories appear to have been drawn down as a result of strike activities so that the increase in inventories was smaller than would otherwise have occurred. It also appears that some of the increase in imports may have been attributable to strikes. Since the employment figures do not reflect strike activity, the usual relationship between output and employment in the business sector was also affected. Modifications were therefore made to the constant adjustment terms in the relevant equations to reflect this feature of 1969. It was expected that 1970 would not have quite as abnormal an amount of strikes and lock-outs. Hence the constant adjustment terms which were used for 1969 to reflect this activity were modified somewhat for 1970.

For variables such as interest rates, where by the time that the forecast was made the average value for 1969 was known almost with certainty, a constant adjustment was made to put the forecast for 1969 right on target. Apart from the adjustment for strikes and lock-outs, the same constant adjustments were used in 1970 as in 1969 with any modification that was required because of the lag structure of the model. Because of the lag structure, a portion of any adjustment made to 1968 was carried into 1969 and similarly a portion of the adjustment made in 1969 was carried into 1970. Depending on the lag coefficient in the equation the values of the constant adjustments for 1969 and 1970 were adjusted accordingly (see table 14).

TABLE 16

Values of exogenous variables for the basic forecast.

	1968	1969	1970
POP6	20.774	21.061	21.414
PGW2	1.786	1.962	2.022
DMI	1.000	1.000	1.000
DHA9R	0.090	0.470	0.300
ANR9	0.254	0.239	0.220
RNR9R	0.333	0.353	0.350
DHA9	0.181	0.429	0.300
RIT2	0.273	0.275	0.262
SHS3	75.300	81.149	71.683
MHS3	121.600	135.751	119.917
POT9	0.738	0.918	0.940
PX2	1.186	1.210	1.244
AME9	0.765	0.724	0.680
YA9R	2.122	2.196	2.196
PYA2	1.386	1.308	1.308
T	43.000	44.000	45.000
DMB	0.0	0.0	0.0
WSP9	2.015	2.265	2.500
MPA9	0.696	0.680	0.700
IRG9	0.379	0.400	0.420
SU9	0.500	0.513	0.520
WSG9	6.004	6.815	7.260
PFR2	1.075	1.109	1.145
DMA	1.000	1.000	1.000
TTB	22.000	23.000	24.000
TTA	0.0	0.0	0.0
EG6	2.052	2.135	2.200
CAB9	4.117	4.270	4.450
CCD9	0.048	0.048	0.050
CCA9	7.260	7.535	7.785
WT9	0.209	0.220	0.260

Continued

The crucial input into the forecast for 1970 was the forecast of the exogenous variables. In general the forecasts were made on the basis of the judgement of the three principal investigators who participated in the making of the forecast. A small panel of business economists was consulted during November with respect to forecasts for government expenditure on goods and services, exports of goods and services, the implicit price index for these two categories of expenditure, the money supply, and population. Forecasts of the United States variables which appear as exogenous variables in the TRACE model were based on forecasts made by the econometric model of the Wharton Econometric Forecasting Unit. (See Evans and Klein (1968).)

Because of the sensitivity of the Canadian economy to foreign developments, it was decided to make three alternative forecasts based on different assumptions concerning foreign variables. These alternative assumptions are shown in Table 15. We do not have a crystal ball with which to forecast exogenous variables, especially foreign variables. All the TRACE model can do is make *conditional* forecasts, for alternative sets of values for policy instruments and alternative forecasts of exogenous variables. The pre-

TABLE 16 (Continued)

Values of exogenous variables for the basic forecast.

	1968	1969	1970
GI9	2.374	2.754	2.950
AGT9	−0.266	0.042	0.0
IVA9	−0.305	−0.517	−0.300
CCP9	0.686	0.752	0.800
QCP9	0.239	0.280	0.300
EL3	1.000	1.000	1.000
RPT2	0.230	0.270	0.250
L3	35.000	35.000	35.000
HR2	0.530	0.530	0.530
HS2	0.240	0.240	0.240
LIU	5.250	6.060	6.180
LN9	0.286	0.286	0.286
F9	0.151	0.151	0.151
DR9	0.353	−0.264	−0.200
SIU	5.330	6.560	6.090
XXU	1.078	1.078	1.078
TR9	7.194	8.044	9.100
CAS9	0.070	0.070	0.070
M9	26.716	27.900	29.000
PYU2	1.223	1.283	1.342
LF6	7.919	8.175	8.400
WSA9	0.287	0.295	0.305
PSI2	1.584	1.642	1.702
SMBZ	10.256	10.499	endogenous
IDR9	0.331	0.415	0.390
DMF	1.000	0.0	0.0
DKW	0.0	0.0	0.0
RME9R	0.088	0.097	0.100
API9R	1.317	1.650	1.675
PFX2	1.056	1.077	1.121
X9	16.735	18.320	19.547
GNW9	6.629	7.255	7.540

sentation of the set of alternatives makes it clear, we hope, that we are not engaged in unconditional forecasting. Indeed all forecasts are conditional upon some government policy either being continued or changed in a specific manner.

In making two alternative assumptions to the basic forecast, we attempted to bracket the basic forecast by assuming in alternative no. 1 an expansionary fiscal policy in conjunction with more buoyant external conditions. Alternative no. 2 assumes less expansionary fiscal policy in conjunction with less buoyant external conditions. The alternative forecasts are shown in Table 13. The basic forecast gave rise to a forecast of an average unemployment rate for 1970 of 5.9 per cent. Alternative no. 1 implied an unemployment rate of 5.4 per cent, while alternative no. 2 implied a rate of 6.2 per cent. The complete set of values of the forecasts of the exogenous variables is given in Table 16. Table 16 also presents the actual figures for 1968 and the "guestimates" for 1969.

Some of the forecasts of exogenous variables deserve further comment. In the model, agricultural output and farm inventory change are both exogenous variables.

We assumed that agricultural output in 1970 would remain at approximately the same level as 1969 and that the price index of agricultural output would also remain unchanged. We anticipated a slightly smaller rate of accumulation of farm inventories in 1970.

One assumption that generated considerable discussion was our forecast that housing starts would decrease by 12 per cent in 1970 over the 1969 level. We made this forecast on the basis of a belief that the unusually high level of housing starts in the first half of 1969 would not be repeated in 1970 and that, therefore, there would be a substantial decline in housing starts. At the time we made the forecast most observers were forecasting a decline of only 5 per cent.

A crucial pair of assumptions that entered into our forecast were that the population in 1970 would be 21,414 thousand persons (as of June 1) and that the labour force would increase in 1970 by 2.8 per cent from 8,175,000 persons to 8,400,000 persons.

In the money market, we assumed that the three-month treasury bill rate in the United States would decrease by approximately 50 basis points while the long-term rate on government bonds would decrease by approximately 10 basis points.

The residual error of estimate in the National Accounts was set at its actual value for the solutions for 1968 and 1969. For the 1970 forecast it was given a value of zero.[2] An autoregressive forecast might have been a better assumption.

There were two developments that we did not foresee and did not take into account in the forecast. One was that unforeseen strength in merchandise exports in 1970 together with substantial inflows of capital would result in such an upward pressure on the value of the Canadian dollar that the dollar was unpegged on May 31, 1970. By the end of 1970 the rate had risen from the previously pegged rate of $0.93 US to approximately $0.99 US. The second was a prolonged strike of workers at General Motors in both the United States and Canada which affected consumer durable expenditure and both exports and imports of automobiles and parts.

On the basis of all the above-mentioned assumptions, the TRACE model then forecast the remaining components of gross national expenditure at market prices in both constant and current dollars, various income components, tax revenue, and the balance of international payments.

Although the forecast was prepared on the basis of the "old" National Accounts, we realized that the forecast would be used by most business economists in conjunction with the new National Accounts. We therefore presented the forecast in the form of percentage changes as shown in Table 13. One major change in classification that was made in the new National Accounts was that some hospital and medical expenditures have been transferred from personal expenditure on services to government expenditure. We tried to take this into account in the figures shown in Table 13 by making an adjustment to the figures produced from the TRACE model. The percentage change shown for gross national product in Table 13 is based on the 1968 weights assigned to the various components in the new National Accounts rather than on the old National Accounts basis.

---

2   On the revised National Accounts basis, the residual error was close to one billion dollars in 1970. It was much smaller on the "old" basis.

Figures available in November, 1969 from a preliminary survey of anticipated expenditures on business plant and equipment by large corporations indicated a 14 per cent increase for 1970. This was substantially higher than the forecast from the equations in the TRACE model but we elected to stay with our forecast as given by our equations as modified by the constant adjustments listed in Table 14.

Before comparing the realization in 1970 with our forecast, it may be useful to summarize the various sources of error that may affect a forecast from an econometric model: (a) Errors in specification of the model, i.e., errors in the economic theory of the behaviour of the economy. This may take the form of an incorrect list of relevant variables or an incorrect mathematical form of the equation. (b) The disturbance term not taking on its expected value. (c) Sampling errors, i.e., the parameter estimates differ from their actual values because only a small number of observations are available to estimate the parameters. (d) Estimation errors, i.e., the parameters are estimated by methods which do not have the statistical property of consistency. If the sample is small, bias may still exist even if consistent estimators are used. (e) Structural shifts, i.e., the parameters may change over over time in a way not allowed for by the specification of the equation or the time period used for estimation. This may be regarded as an important but special case of (a). (f) Errors in data. This may be lack of conformity between the variable measured and the variable specified by economic theory or measurement errors. (g) Computational errors. (h) Errors in selecting appropriate alternative values of the policy instrument variables. (i) Errors in forecasting the values of the other exogenous variables. (j) The cumulative effect of errors in forecasting lagged endogenous variables when the forecast is for more than one period into the future. (k) Revisions to the official data so that the data used to estimate the parameters of the model are different form currently published data.

The task of forecasting gross national product is further complicated by the uncertainty about the actual values one is actually forecasting. National Accounts revisions and the long time lag before final figures are available mean that one is trying to hit a moving target. Should the model try to forecast the preliminary or the final GNP figure? The parameters are estimated using what are assumed to be final figures for previous years (but preliminary figures for the most recent years) but attention is usually focused on forecasting preliminary values for the forthcoming year as these are the ones used for stabilization policy decisions and managerial decisions. A model's performance is usually judged by a comparison of the forecast with the preliminary annual figures published in the spring of the following year.

In Table 13 we have shown the estimated actual values for 1970 as of December, 1970. Because of the revision to the National Accounts it is unfair to TRACE to make this comparison since the 1970 forecast was produced from a model based on the "old" National Accounts while the estimated actuals are based on the "new" National Accounts.[3] To some extent this may be responsible for the substantial errors in the components.

---

3 The estimated actuals for 1970 are based on a solution of TRACE 1970 which had constant adjustments made to 1969 and 1970 to make the solution consistent with data published in the third quarter 1970 National Accounts which were published at the end of November, 1970 and to take into account the automobile industry strike in the fourth quarter of 1970. A forecast for 1971 from TRACE 1970 was made by Sawyer and published in Jump, Sawyer, and Winder (1970) on December 18, 1970.

Whether the 1970 realization should be compared with the "basic forecast" or one of the two alternatives depends on the purpose of the comparison. If the purpose is to test the accuracy of the model, apart from the accuracy of the assumptions concerning the exogenous variables, then it should be matched against the forecast whose assumptions concerning exogenous variables most closely agree with the actual outcome.[4] Given the strength in exports and the continued high level of government expenditure, alternative no. 1 would appear most appropriate. The effects of the automobile strike on consumer durables and a generally poor year for automobile sales somewhat offset the export strength. The growth in the money supply was higher than that assumed for the forecast.

On the other hand, if the concern is whether our forecast would have given an accurate signal to government policy makers, we should examine the accuracy of the "basic" forecast since it received the most publicity and had the status of the "most probable" forecast. For policy analysis, attention focuses on the main aggregates: the percentage change in real gross national product, the implicit price of GNP, and the unemployment rate. From Table 13 we see that our "basic forecast" of the increase in nominal GNP was 6.5 per cent compared with an estimated actual of 6.2 per cent. The breakdown of the forecast into real and price components was 3.4 per cent and 3.0 per cent, respectively; the estimated actuals are 2.4 per cent and 3.7 per cent. Thus, we overestimated the real growth and underestimated the amount of inflation. We were correct, however, in forecasting that there would be a marked decrease in growth in real output over 1969 (when the rate was 4.6 per cent), a decrease in the rate of inflation (the rate of increase in the GNP deflator in 1969 was 4.3 per cent), and a sharp rise in the unemployment rate from 4.7 per cent in 1969 to about 6 per cent in 1970. The implications of our forecast for economic policy in 1970 were that during the year unemployment would replace inflation as the major problem and that a shift from a restrictive monetary-fiscal policy to an expansionary one would be appropriate.

4 Ideally the forecast should have been rerun using actual values of the exogenous variables to see the extent to which errors in forecasting these variables affected the forecast.

6 Conclusion

1. FURTHER DEVELOPMENT OF THE TRACE MODEL

TRACE is designed as a model to make conditional forecasts in order to assess the effects of alternative economic policies on the economy. We believe the test of such a model is its ability, in conjunction with the judgment of those using the model, to make accurate *ex ante* forecasts. We do not believe there is a dichotomy between forecasting models and policy-analytic models. Policy decisions involve conditional forecasts of the future. Moreover, as our simulations in Chapter 4 demonstrate, the results of economic policies depend in a non-linear world, as represented by our model, on the position of the economy. Policy decisions should therefore be based on conditional forecasts from the present position of the economy. To base policy decisions on conditional forecasts from an econometric model requires demonstrated ability of the model to make accurate forecasts and to simulate satisfactorily the behaviour of the economy under varying conditions.

TRACE 1968 was clearly not a suitable model for this purpose. TRACE 1969 is a substantial improvement over TRACE 1968. The *ex post* forecasts reported on in Chapter 3, the *ex ante* forecast discussed in Chapter 5, and the simulations of Chapter 4 indicate that the development of the model has proceeded to a stage where it can be used for policy analysis and forecasting with a considerable degree of confidence.

On the supply side, TRACE 1969 explains only the behaviour of the business non-agricultural sector. Agriculture, government, and the personal sector are exogenous. On the demand side, domestic demand for agricultural products is included in the consumption function but the major part of farm and fish exports is exogenous. Both government current expenditure and capital formation in nominal dollars are exogenous. Capital formation in agriculture and capital formation of private non-commercial institutions are also exogenous. Farm inventory change, most of the exports of services, and, in the labour market, the supply of labour, are exogenous.

The monetary sector also has large exogenous components. The total money supply is taken as exogenous and is used in simulations as a policy instrument although this is not in accordance with the evidence on Canadian monetary policy. Another shortcoming is the absence from the model of any reaction by the Exchange Fund Account to changes in foreign exchange reserves during periods of fixed exchange rates. Short-term capital flows are derived residually in the model on the assumption that changes in reserves are determined exogenously. (This may have been correct in some periods where the level of reserves was clearly a target variable.) A large part of the long-term capital flows are exogenous.

The tax and transfer payment mechanism requires further improvement and explicit incorporation of more tax and social security payment rates as variables in the model so that the effect of a wider range of fiscal policy instruments can be examined. Jutlah (1970) has contributed to a substantial improvement of the income tax relations which may be incorporated into future versions of the model.

Thus, a lengthy agenda for future development of the TRACE model exists. TRACE 1970 incorporates an improved export demand and export price sector for both goods and services and a comparable disaggregation of imports of goods and services. This disaggregation has been done to meet the needs of Project LINK, an international project designed to link together national econometric models of various countries in order to forecast levels of world trade. TRACE is the Canadian model in Project LINK.[1] An important by-product of Project LINK will be forecasts coming from other-country models of foreign activity variables which presently enter the TRACE model as exogenous variables in the foreign trade, price, and capital flows equations.

As variables which are currently exogenous are made endogenous, the model should develop into a model with a good capability for making medium-term projections, conditional upon sets of values for policy instruments and demographic and other mainly non-economic variables. At present, there are too many exogenous variables whose values cannot be projected more than one or two years into the future without either developing inconsistencies in the projection or, by keeping these variables exogenous, suppressing adjustment mechanisms which operate in the real world such as the reaction of the supply of labour to changing real wages and unemployment rates. The fact that the model incorporates short-run adjustment functions while being built around a production function (in the sense that the labour demand, supply price, and capital formation equations are derived from a production function) give it the capability of tracking the year-by-year movements of the economy so that medium-term projections made from the model reflect the short-run dynamic behaviour of the economy rather than merely projecting trends. We hope that TRACE will continue to evolve as a more and more reliable vehicle for making medium-term conditional projections of the behaviour of the Canadian economy which will be of policy-analytic value.

2. MONETARY AND FISCAL POLICY UNDER FIXED AND FLEXIBLE EXCHANGE RATES

The simulations of Chapter 4 add to the empirical evidence concerning the differing effects of monetary and fiscal policies under fixed and flexible exchange rate regimes. The principal conclusion is that different tradeoffs between prices and employment exist for monetary and for fiscal policies. The government may, therefore, through an appropriate combination of monetary and fiscal policies influence the possible range of employment-price configurations at the same time as making a choice among them. This is particularly true with flexible exchange rates. We illustrated this in Chapter 4 with a calculation from our 1957 simulation which showed that the inflationary tendencies of an expansionary fiscal policy could be partly offset by simultaneously pursuing a restrictive monetary policy and allowing the exchange rate to appreciate.

---

1   A preliminary report on this disaggregation was made by J.A. Sawyer in a paper "Foreign Trade in the TRACE Model" presented to the second annual meeting of Project LINK, London, England, September 1970.

The differing results obtained with different exchange rate regimes are now partic-ularly relevant since Canada again floated the exchange rate on June 1, 1970. It is essential that those who are in charge of economic policy be aware of the essential characteristics of a system of flexible exchange rates and know how to make use of its potentialities. Sohmen (1969, p. 236) states the opinion that the Canadian experience with flexible rates in the 1950s was a dismal failure because the monetary-fiscal au-thorities did not seem to be aware of these essential characteristics. As Sohmen points out "It is of little help to know that monetary policy is a highly effective policy tool under [a system of flexible rates] if the monetary authorities fail to make use of it or even use it perversely, thus intensifying stagnation at a time of general unemploy-ment." We hope that the empirical evidence provided by the simulations with TRACE 1969, and future analyses with later versions of TRACE, will contribute to the devel-opment of suitable stabilization policies for Canada which take advantage of the char-acteristics of a flexible exchange rate system.

Appendices

1. Names, definitions, and sources of variables

1. EXPLANATION OF TERMINOLOGY AND SOURCES

All variables have been given six-character Fortran names so that no change need be made in variable names for regression or simulation programs. The variable name has four components.

(a) Basic name

Up to three characters, which must all be alphabetic are used for the basic name, e.g., DUR for personal expenditure on consumer durables.

(b) Units

A numerical character in the fourth position indicates units of measurement. This digit is the power of ten by which the value of the variable must be multiplied to express its value in normal units. Normal units are defined to be dollars, persons, per cent, or base 100 for index numbers, e.g., if DUR values are in billions of dollars, the variable name becomes DUR9.

(c) Current value, constant dollars, or lagged values

The character in the fifth position may have the following values with the following meaning: 0 = current value, unlagged; 1 = current value, lagged one period; 2 = current value, lagged two periods; R = 1957 dollars, unlagged; S = 1957 dollars, lagged one period; T = 1957 dollars, lagged two periods. For United States variables, real values are in constant 1958 dollars. E.g., if DUR is in constant (1957) dollars, unlagged, it would be given the name DUR9R.

(d) Per person, per man hour, or differences

The character in the sixth position may have the following values with the following meaning: 0 = not per person, not differenced; 1 = not per person, first difference; 2 = not per person, second difference; C = per person, not differenced; D = per person, first difference; E = per person, second difference; M = per man hour, not differenced; N = per man hour, first difference; P = per man hour, second difference. E.g., if DUR is in constant (1957) dollars per person, unlagged, in thousands of dollars, it would be given the name DUR3RC. In the variable names, when a zero occurs in the last position it is suppressed; but not in other positions. E.g., unemployment, as a per cent of the labour force, lagged one period, is given the name U01.

Definitions are given for the variable in the basic form in which it appears in the model. The meaning of other forms can be obtained by consulting the rules for variable names. Endogenous variables are indicated by a Y, exogenous variables by an X.

Sources are given for all data obtained from published sources. Where it states that the variable is a "calculated variable," an explanation of the calculations is available from the authors.

Abbreviations are used for sources of data. They are as follows. *NA:* Dominion Bureau of Statistics, *National Accounts Income and Expenditure, 1926-1956* (Ottawa: Queen's Printer, 1958), and subsequent annual issues. *Investment Outlook:* Department of Trade and Commerce, *Private and Public Investment in Canada, Outlook* (Ottawa: Queen's Printer, annual). *Canadian Balance of Internation Payments:* Dominion Bureau of Statistics, *The Canadian Balance of International Payments: A Compendium of Statistics from 1946 to 1965* (Ottawa: Queen's Printer, 1967) and subsequent issues. *Canadian Housing Statistics:* Central Mortgage and Housing Corporation, *Canadian Housing Statistics* (Ottawa, annual.). *Bank of Canada: Bank of Canada Statistical Summary* (Ottawa, monthly). *Historical Statistics of Canada:* M.C. Urquhart and K.A.H. Buckley (eds), *Historical Statistics of Canada* (Toronto: Macmillan, 1965). *Index of Real Output:* Dominion Bureau of Statistics, *Indexes of Real Domestic Product by Industry of Origin, 1935-61* (Ottawa, Queen's Printer, 1963).

2. LISTING OF VARIABLE NAMES, DEFINITIONS, AND SOURCES

The listing follows on the next twenty-one pages.

2. LISTING OF VARIABLE NAMES, DEFINITIONS, AND SOURCES

SYMBOL	X=EXOG Y=ENDOG	DEFINITION	UNITS	SOURCE, TABLE	LINE
AGT9	X	ADJUSTMENT ON GRAIN TRANSACTIONS	$ BILL.	N.A.,12	28(D)
AME9	X	AGRICULTURE, FISHING, AND TRAPPING GROSS INVESTMENT IN MACHINERY AND EQUIPMENT	$ BILL	INVESTMENT OUTLOOK	
AME9R	Y	REAL AGRICULTURE, FISHING, AND TRAPPING GROSS INVESTMENT IN MACHINERY AND EQUIPMENT	$ BILL	AME9/PME2	
ANR9	X	AGRICULTURE, FISHING, AND TRAPPING GROSS INVESTMENT IN NONRESIDENTIAL CONSTRUCTION	$ BILL	INVESTMENT OUTLOOK	
ANR9R	Y	REAL AGRICULTURE, FISHING, AND TRAPPING GROSS INVESTMENT IN NON RESIDENTIAL CONSTRUCTION	$ BILL	ANR9/PNR2	
API9R	X	IMPORTS OF AUTOMOBILES AND PARTS FROM THE U. S. ATTRIBUTED TO THE U. S. – CANADA AUTO PACT	$ BILL	CALCULATED	
BCF9	Y	BUSINESS GROSS FIXED CAPITAL FORMATION IN NEW NON-RESIDENTIAL CONSTRUCTION,MACHINERY AND EQUIPMENT	$ BILL	N.A.,2	7+8
BCF9R	Y	REAL BUSINESS GROSS FIXED CAPITAL FORMATION IN NEW NON-RESIDENTIAL CONSTRUCTION,MACHINERY AND EQUIPMENT	$ BILL	N.A.,5	7+8
BME9	Y	BUSINESS NON-AGRICULTURE GROSS INVESTMENT IN MACHINERY AND EQUIPMENT	$ BILL.	INVESTMENT OUTLOOK	
BME9R	Y	REAL BUSINESS NON AGRICULTURE GROSS INVESTMENT IN MACHINERY AND EQUIPMENT	$ BILL	BME9/PME2	

SYMBOL	X=EXOG Y=ENDOG	DEFINITION	UNITS	SOURCE, TABLE	LINE
BNR9	Y	BUSINESS NON-AGRICULTURE GROSS INVESTMENT IN NON RESIDENTIAL CONSTRUCTION	$ BILL.	INVESTMENT OUTLOOK	
BNR9R	Y	REAL BUSINESS NON AGRICULTURE GROSS INVESTMENT IN NON RESIDENTIAL CONSTRUCTION	$ BILL.	BNE9/PNR2	
C9	Y	PERSONAL EXPENDITURE ON CONSUMER GOODS AND SERVICES	$ BILL	N.A.,2	1
C9R	Y	REAL PERSONAL EXPENDITURE ON CONSUMER GOODS AND SERVICES	$ BILL	N.A.,5	1
CAB9	X	CORPORATE CAPITAL CONSUMPTION ALLOWANCES	$ BILL.	N.A.,51	1
CAP9	Y	CAPITAL INFLOW (NET)	$ BILL.	LDU9 + CIF9 + S9 + LN9	
CAS9	X	CAPITAL ASSISTANCE	$ BILL.	N.A.,10	20(C)
CCA9	X	CAPITAL CONSUMPTION ALLOWANCES AND VALUATION ADJUSTMENTS	$ BILL.	N.A.,1	11
CCD9	X	CORPORATE CHARITABLE DONATIONS	$ BILL.	N.A.,50	11
CCP9	X	EMPLOYER AND EMPLOYEE CONTRIBUTIONS TO CANADA PENSION PLAN	$ BILL.	N.A.,42	9
CF9	Y	TOTAL GROSS INVESTMENT	$ BILL	N.A.,18	
CHA9	X	MORTGAGE APPROVALS NHA CMHC	$ BILL.	BANK OF CANADA S.S.	
CIF9	Y	NET LONG-TERM CAPITAL MOVEMENT IN SECURITIES, INCLUDING TRADE IN OUTSTANDING SECURITIES BETWEEN U.S. AND CANADA	$ BILL.	CANADIAN BALANCE OF INTERNATIONAL PAYMENTS TABLE 2	D3.1, D3.2, D4,AND D5
CNA9R	Y	CONVENTIONAL MORTGAGE APPROVALS DEFLATED BY PRS2	$ BILL	CANADIAN HOUSING STATISTICS (NOMINAL DOLLARS)	
CPG9	Y	CORPORATION PROFITS BEFORE CAPITAL CONSUMPTION ALLOWANCES	$ BILL.	N.A.,50 & N.A.,51	1+ 1

SYMBOL	X=EXOG Y=ENDOG	DEFINITION	UNITS	SOURCE, TABLE	LINE
CPN9	Y	CORPORATION PROFITS BEFORE TAXES	$ BILL.	N.A.,50	1
CR9	Y	CURRENT ACCOUNT BALANCE OF BALANCE OF INTERNATIONAL PAYMENTS	$ BILL	CANADIAN BALANCE OF INTERNATIONAL PAYMENTS TABLE 2	C4
CRA9	Y	BALANCE OF EXPORTS OVER IMPORTS (NATIONAL ACCOUNTS)	$ BILL.	N.A.,18	56
CT9	Y	CORPORATIONS INCOME TAX LIABILITIES	$ BILL	N.A.,50	2
DHA9	X	VALUE OF PHYSICAL CHANGE IN FARM INVENTORIES AND GRAIN IN COMMERCIAL CHANNELS	$ BILL.	N.A.,2	11
DHA9R	X	REAL VALUE OF PHYSICAL CHANGE IN FARM INVENTORIES AND GRAIN IN COMMERCIAL CHANNELS	$ BILL.	N.A.,5	11
DHB9	Y	VALUE OF PHYSICAL CHANGE IN NON-FARM BUSINESS INVENTORIES	$ BILL.	N.A.,2	10
DHB9R	Y	REAL VALUE OF PHYSICAL CHANGE IN NON-FARM BUSINESS INVENTORIES	$ BILL	N.A. 5	10
DIV9	Y	TOTAL DIVIDENDS PAID TO RESIDENTS AND NONRESIDENTS	$ BILL.	N.A.,50	8+10
DKW	X	1926-50 DKW=0 1951 DKW=1 1952 DKW=-1 1953- DKW=0			
DMA	X	1926-46 DMA = 0 1947-66 DMA = 1			
DMB	X	1926-40 DMB = 1 1941-66 DMB = 0			
DMF	X	1926-62 DMF=0 1963... DMF=1			
DMI	X	1926-62 DMI = 0 1963 DMI =.30 1964 DMI =.42 1965 DMI =.84 1966 DMI =1.0			

SYMBOL	X=EXOG Y=ENDOG	DEFINITION	UNITS	SOURCE, TABLE	LINE
CR9	X	CHANGES IN THE OFFICIAL GOLD AND FOREIGN EXCHANGE RESERVES, CHANGE IN INTERNATIONAL MONETARY FUND POSITION, AND OTHER INTERNATIONAL FINANCIAL ASSISTANCE	$ BILL.	CANADIAN BALANCE OF INTERNATIONAL PAYMENTS TABLE 1.1	H4
DUR3RC	Y	PERSONAL EXPENDITURE ON CONSUMER DURABLES IN CONSTANT DOLLARS PER PERSON	$ THOU.	DUR9R / POP6	
DUR9	Y	PERSONAL EXPENDITURE ON CONSUMER DURABLE GOODS	$ BILL.	N.A.,47	39
DUR9R	Y	REAL PERSONAL EXPENDITURE ON CONSUMER DURABLE GOODS	$ BILL.	N.A.,48	10
E6	Y	TOTAL CIVILIAN LABOUR FORCE EMPLOYED	MILL.	N.A.,APPENDIX TABLE II	4
EA6	Y	EMPLOYMENT IN AGRICULTURE, FISHING, AND TRAPPING	MILL.	N.A.,APPENDIX TABLE II	3
EB6	Y	EMPLOYMENT IN BUSINESS, NON-AGRICULTURE	MILL.	CALCULATED VARIABLE	
ECS9	Y	EMPLOYER AND EMPLOYEE CONTRIBUTIONS TO SOCIAL INSURANCE AND GOVERNMENT PENSION PLANS EXCLUDING CANADA AND QUEBEC PENSION PLANS	$ BILL.	SIP9-CCP9 -QCP9	
EG6	X	EMPLOYMENT IN THE PERSONAL AND GOVERNMENT SECTORS	MILL	E6-EB6-EA6	
EL3	X	BASIC FEDERAL PERSONAL INCOME TAX EXEMPTION LEVEL FOR A SINGLE INDIVIDUAL	$ THOU.	INCOME TAX STATISTICS	
EMA9	Y	WEIGHTED AVERAGE EMPLOYED MAN-HOURS PER ANNUM IN AGRICULTURE	BILL. MAN-HRS.	.052*HB*EA6	
EMB9	Y	WEIGHTED AVERAGE EMPLOYED MAN-HOURS PER ANNUM IN NON AGRICULTURE	BILL. MAN-HRS.	.052*HB*EB6	
ERA9	Y	STATISTICAL DISCREPANCY (IN NATIONAL EXPENDITURE)	$ BILL.	EQUATION E.3	
ERB9	Y	STATISTICAL DISCREPANCY (IN CAPITAL FORMATION)	$ BILL.	EQUATION E.3	

SYMBOL	X=EXOG Y=ENDOG	DEFINITION	UNITS	SOURCE, TABLE	LINE
EXC	Y	FOREIGN EXCHANGE RATE: NO. OF CDN DOLLARS PER U.S. DOLLAR (AVERAGE NOON SPOT RATE)	DOLLARS	BANK OF CANADA STATISTICAL SUMMARY	
EXG	X	RATE OF EXCHANGE: POUND STERLING PER U.S. DOLLAR	POUNDS	IMF INTERNATIONAL FINANCIAL STATISTICS	
EXS	X	RATE OF EXCHANGE: SWEDISH KRONA PER U.S. DOLLARS	KRONA	IMF INTERNATIONAL FINANCIAL STATISTICS	
F9	X	CURRENT ACCOUNT BALANCE MINUS EXPORTS, PLUS IMPORTS. I.E. NATIONAL ACCOUNTS ADJUSTMENT	$ BILL.	CANADIAN BALANCE OF INTERNATIONAL PAYMENTS TABLE 2	C4 LESS N.A.,2 LINE 12 PLUS LINE 13
G9	X	GOVERNMENT EXPENDITURE CN GOODS AND SERVICES	$ BILL.	N.A., 2	2
G9R	Y	GOVERNMENT EXPENDITURE ON GOODS AND SERVICES	$ BILL	N.A.,5	2
GAP	Y	UTILIZATION RATIO BUSINESS NON-AGRICULTURE	RATIO	YB9R / YBP9R	
GAPB	Y	GAPB=0 IF GAP<1.C1 GAPB=GAP-1.01 IF GAP>1.01			
GDF9	Y	TOTAL GOVERNMENT DEFICIT	$ BILL.	N.A.,37	26
GCU2	X	INDEX OF GROSS PRODUCTION IN MANUFACTURING IN CONSTANT 1958 DOLLARS IN THE UNITED STATES	1958=1.0	SURVEY OF BUS U.S. DEPT. OF COMMERCE TABLE 121	
GEX9	Y	TOTAL GOVERNMENT EXPENDITURE	$ BILL.	N.A., 37	22
GI9	X	GOVERNMENT INVESTMENT INCOME. (A) INTEREST, (B) PROFITS OF GOVERNMENT BUSINESS ENTERPRISES	$ BILL.	N.A.,9	16(A) 16(B)
GNW9	X	GOVERNMENT EXPENDITURES ON GOODS AND SERVICES, EXCLUDING WAGES AND SALARIES AND MILITARY PAY AND ALLOWANCES	$ BILL.	G9-WSG9-MPA9	

SYMBOL	X=EXOG Y=ENDOG	DEFINITION	UNITS	SOURCE, TABLE	LINE
GPC2	X	UNITED KINGDOM COMPETING PRICE OF CHEMICALS AND FERTILIZERS	1957=1.0	MONTHLY DIGEST OF STATISTICS (WHOLESALE)	
GPF2	X	U.K. COMPETING PRICE OF FARM AND FISH PRODUCTS	1957=1.0	MONTHLY DIGEST OF STATISTICS WHOLESALE PRICE OF MAT. AND FUEL USED IN FOOD MFG.	
GPI2	X	UNITED KINGDOM COMPETING PRICE OF OTHER MANUFACTURED GOODS	1957=1.0	MONTHLY DIGEST OF STAT. RETAIL PRICE OF MISCELLANEOUS GOODS	
GPM2	X	UNITED KINGDOM COMPETING PRICE OF MINERALS AND MINERAL PRODUCTS	1957=1.0	MONTHLY DIGEST OF STATISTICS WHOLESALE PRICE OF MAT. USED IN MECH. ENGINEERING	
GPP2	X	UNITED KINGDOM COMPETING PRICE OF FOREST PRODUCTS	1957=1.0	U.N. TIMBER STATISTICS	
GRV9	Y	TOTAL GOVERNMENT REVENUE	$ BILL.	N.A., 36	29
HB	Y	AVERAGE WEEKLY HOURS PER EMPLOYEE IN BUSINESS NON-AGRICULTURE	HOURS	CALCULATED VARIABLE	
HR2	X	HIGH CORPORATE PROFIT TAX RATE	RATIO	REVISED STATUTES OF CANADA	
HS2	X	LOW CORPORATE PROFIT TAX	RATIO	REVISED STATUTES OF CANADA	
IDP9	Y	INTEREST AND DIVIDENDS PAID ABROAD	$ BILL.	N.A.,4	5
IDP9R	Y	INTEREST AND DIVIDENDS PAID ABROAD IN CONSTANT 1957$	$ BILL.	IDP9/PX2	
IDR9	Y	INTEREST AND DIVIDENDS RECEIVED FROM ABROAD	$ BILL.	N.A.,4	4

SYMBOL	X=EXOG Y=ENDOG	DEFINITION	UNITS	SOURCE, TABLE	LINE
IDR9R	Y	INTEREST AND DIVIDENDS RECEIVED FROM ABROAD IN CONSTANT 1957$	$ BILL.	IDR9/PIM2	
IKB9R	Y	BUSINESS NON—AG STOCK OF INVENTORIES IN CONSTANT 1957$	$ BILL.	CALCULATED VARIABLE	
ILA9R	Y	INSTITUTIONAL LENDERS APPROVALS UNDER N.H.A. DEFLATED BY PRS2	$ BILL	CANADIAN HOUSING STATISTICS (NOMINAL DOLLARS)	
IMP9	Y	IMPORTS OF GOODS AND SERVICES	$ BILL.	N.A.,2	13
IMP9R	Y	IMPORTS OF GOODS AND SERVICES IN CONSTANT 1957$	$ BILL.	N.A.,5	13
IPD9	Y	INTEREST ON THE PUBLIC DEBT	$ BILL.	N.A., 37	9
IPG2	X	INDEX OF INDUSTRIAL PRODUCTION IN THE UNITED KINGDOM	1957=1.0	U.N. STATISTICAL YEARBOOK	
IPU2	X	INDEX OF INDUSTRIAL PRODUCTION IN THE UNITED STATES	1957=1.0	U.N. STATISTICAL YEARBOOK	
IPW2	X	INDEX OF INDUSTRIAL PRODUCTION FOR THE WORLD	1957=1.0	U.N. STATISTICAL YEARBOOK	
IRG9	X	IMPUTED RENT ON GOVERNMENT BUILDINGS	$ BILL.	N.A.,49	7
IRW2	X	INDEX OF INDUSTRIAL PRODUCTION FOR THE REST OF THE WORLD	1957=1.0	IPW2 − .315 IPU2 − .052 IPG2	
IT9	Y	TOTAL INDIRECT TAXES	$ BILL	N.A.,9	15
IT9R	Y	REAL TOTAL INDIRECT TAXES	$BILL.	IT9 / PSI2	
IVA9	X	INVENTORY VALUATION ADJUSTMENT	$ BILL.	N.A.,1	8
KAORM	Y	REAL CAPITAL STOCK IN AGRICULTURE, FISHING, AND FISHING PER MAN HOUR	$ BILL.	(KMA9S+KCA9S) / EMA9	
KA9R	Y	REAL CAPITAL STOCK IN AGRICULTURE, FISHING, AND TRAPPING	$ BILL.	KCA9R+KMA9R	

SYMBOL	X=EXOG Y=ENDOG	DEFINITION	UNITS	SOURCE, TABLE	LINE
KBORM	Y	REAL CAPITAL STOCK IN BUSINESS NON AGRICULTURE PER MAN HOUR	$ BILL. PER MAN-HR.	(KCB9S+KMB9S+ K9S9S)/EMB9	
KCA9R	Y	CAPITAL STOCK OF NON RESIDENTIAL CONSTRUCTION IN AGRICULTURE, FISHING, AND TRAPPING 1957$	$ BILL.	CALCULATED	
KCB9R	Y	CAPITAL STOCK OF NON RESIDENTIAL CONSTRUCTION IN BUSINESS NON AGRICULTURE	$ BILL.	CALCULATED	
KMA9R	Y	CAPITAL STOCK OF MACHINERY AND EQUIPMENT IN AGRICULTURE, FISHING, AND TRAPPING 1957$	$ BILL.	CALCULATED	
KMB9R	Y	CAPITAL STOCK OF MACHINERY AND EQUIPMENT IN BUSINESS NON-AGRICULTURE 1957$	$ BILL.	CALCULATED	
KRS9R	Y	CAPITAL STOCK OF HOUSING 1957$	$ BILL.	CALCULATED	
L3	X	CUTOFF POINT BETWEEN HIGH AND LOW CORPORATE TAX RATE	$ THOU.	STATUTES OF CANADA	
LDU9	Y	U.S. DIRECT INVESTMENT IN CANADA	$ BILL.	CANADIAN BALANCE OF INTERNATIONAL PAYMENTS, TABLE 2.	D1
LF6	Y	CIVILIAN LABOUR FORCE	MILL.		
LIC	Y	LONG-TERM INTEREST RATE IN CANADA,(AVERAGE WEDNESDAY MARKET YIELD, OVER THE YEAR, IN GOVERNMENT BONDS WITH 14 YEARS TO MATURITY)	PER CENT	BANK OF CANADA STATISTICAL SUMMARY AND HISTORICAL STATISTICS OF CANADA H605 H614	
LIU	X	U.S. GOVERNMENT LONG-TERM BOND INTEREST RATE	PER CENT	HISTORICAL STATISTICS OF U.S.	X330
LN9	X	NET LONG-TERM CAPITAL MOVEMENT BETWEEN CANADA AND THE REST OF THE WORLD	$ BILL.	CANADIAN BALANCE OF INTERNATIONAL PAYMENTS TABLE 2	E1 LESS LDU AND CIF

SYMBOL	X=EXOG Y=ENDOG	DEFINITION	UNITS	SOURCE, TABLE	LINE
M9	X	TOTAL CURRENCY AND CHARTERED BANK DEPOSITS HELD BY GENERAL PUBLIC INCLUDING PERSONAL SAVINGS DEPOSITS, AVG OF DEC WEDS.	$ BILL.	BANK OF CANADA STATISTICAL SUMMARY	
MHC3	Y	MULTIPLE HOUSING COMPLETIONS	THOU.	CANADIAN HOUSING STATISTICS TABLE 7	
MHS3	Y	MULTIPLE HOUSING STARTS	THOU.	CANADIAN HOUSING STATISTICS TABLE 7	
MIN9	Y	MISCELLANEOUS NATIONAL INCOME	$ BILL.		
MPA9	X	MILITARY PAY AND ALLOWANCES	$ BILL.	N.A.,19	11
ND3RC	Y	PERSONAL EXPENDITURE ON CONSUMER NON-DURABLES IN CONSTANT DOLLARS PER PERSON	$ THOU.	ND9R / POP6	
ND9	Y	PERSONAL EXPENDITURE ON CONSUMER NON DURABLE GOODS	$ BILL.	N.A.,47	42
ND9R	Y	PERSONAL EXPENDITURE ON CONSUMER NON DURABLE GOODS IN CONSTANT DOLLARS	$ BILL.	N.A.,48	11
NFC9	Y	NET NATIONAL INCOME AT FACTOR COST	$ BILL.	N.A.,1	9
NHA	X	MAXIMUM NHA MORTGAGE RATE	PERCENT	CANADIAN HOUSING STATISTICS	
NMP9R	Y	REAL IMPORTS OF GOODS AND SERVICES (DOMESTIC BASIS)	$ BILL.	IMP9R-IDP9R	
PAU2	X	PRICE OF AUTOMOBILES AND PARTS EXPORTED TO THE UNITED STATES	1957=1.0	UNOFFICIAL STATISTIC	
PBC2	Y	IMPLICIT PRICE INDEX FOR BCF9	1957=1.0	N.A.,6	(7+8)/2
PC2	Y	IMPLICIT PRICE INDEX OF PERSONAL EXPENDITURE ON CONSUMER GOODS AND SERVICES	1957=1.0	N.A.,6	1

SYMBOL	X=EXOG Y=ENDOG	DEFINITION	UNITS	SOURCE, TABLE	LINE
PCT2	Y	EXPORT PRICE OF CHEMICALS AND FERTILIZERS	1957=1.0	UNOFFICIAL STATISTIC	
PCU2	X	EXPORT PRICE TO THE UNITED STATES OF CHEMICALS AND FERTILIZERS	1957=1.0	UNOFFICIAL STATISTIC	
PD2	Y	PRICE LEVEL OF CONSUMER EXPENDITURE ON DURABLE GOODS	1957=1.0	N.A. TABLES 47 AND 48	39/10
PDI3RC	Y	PERSONAL DISPOSABLE INCOME PER PERSON AND IN CONSTANT 1957$	$ THOUS.	PDI9R/POP6	
PCI3RD	Y	PERSONAL DISPOSABLE INCOME PER PERSON, CONSTANT DOLLARS, 1ST DIFFERENCE	$ THOUS.	PDI3RC - PDI3SC	
PDI9	Y	PERSONAL DISPOSABLE INCOME	$ BILL.	N.A.,3	7
PEX2	Y	INDEX OF THE FOREIGN EXCHANGE RATE	1957=1.0	EXC/EXC57	
PFG2	X	PRICE OF FARM AND FISH PRODUCTS EXPORTED TO THE UNITED KINGDOM	1957=1.0	UNOFFICIAL STATISTIC	
PFR2	X	IMPLICIT PRICE INDEX OF IMPORTS OF GOODS AND SERVICES IN U.S. DOLLARS	1957=1.0	PIM2 / EXC	
PFU2	X	PRICE OF FARM AND FISH PRODUCTS EXPORTED TO THE UNITED STATES	1957=1.0	UNOFFICIAL STATISTIC	
PFW2	X	PRICE OF FARM AND FISH PRODUCTS EXPORTED TO THE REST OF THE WORLD	1957=1.0	UNOFFICIAL STATISTIC	
PG2	Y	IMPLICIT PRICE INDEX OF GOVERNMENT EXPENDITURES ON GOODS AND SERVICES	1957=1.0	N.A.,6	2
PGW2	X	DEFLATOR FOR WAGES AND SALARIES IN GOVERNMENT AND PERSONAL SECTORS	1957=1.0	(WSG9+MPA9)/ G9R-(G9-WSG9- MPA9)/PYI2	
PI9	Y	PERSONAL INCOME	$ BILL	N.A.,3	5
PIG2	X	PRICE OF OTHER MANUFACTURED GOODS EXPORTED TO THE UNITED KINGDOM	1957=1.0	UNOFFICIAL STATISTIC	

SYMBOL	X=EXOG Y=ENDOG	DEFINITION	UNITS	SOURCE, TABLE	LINE
PIM2	Y	IMPLICIT PRICE INDEX OF IMPORTS OF GOODS AND SERVICES IN CDN. DOLLARS	1957=1.0	N.A.,6	10
PIU2	X	PRICE OF OTHER MANUFACTURED GOODS EXPORTED TO THE UNITED STATES	1957=1.0	UNOFFICIAL STATISTIC	
PIT9	Y	PERSONAL INCOME TAX	$ BILL.	N.A.,38	1+5
PIW2	X	PRICE OF OTHER MANUFACTURED GOODS EXPORTED TO THE REST OF THE WORLD	1957=1.0	UNOFFICIAL STATISTIC	
PME2	Y	PRICE LEVEL OF GROSS INVESTMENT IN MACHINERY AND EQUIPMENT	1957=1.0	N.A. TABLE 6	8
PMG2	X	PRICE OF MINERALS AND METALS EXPORTED TO THE UNITED KINGDOM	1957=1.0	UNOFFICIAL STATISTIC	
PMU2	X	PRICE OF MINERALS AND METALS EXPORTED TO THE UNITED STATES	1957=1.0	UNOFFICIAL STATISTIC	
PMW2	X	PRICE OF MINERALS AND METALS EXPORTED TO THE REST OF THE WORLD	1957=1.0	UNOFFICIAL STATISTICS	
PND2	Y	PRICE LEVEL OF CONSUMER EXPENDITURES ON NON DURABLE GOODS	1957=1.0	N.A. TABLES 47 AND 48	42/11
PNR2	Y	PRICE LEVEL OF GROSS INVESTMENT IN NON RESIDENTIAL CONSTRUCTION	1957=1.0	N.A. TABLE 6	8
POP6	X	POPULATION IN CANADA	MILL.	N.A.,APPENDIX TABLE I	13
POT9	X	MISCELLANEOUS PERSONAL TAX	$ BILL.	PT9-PIT9	
PPA2	Y	DEFLATOR FOR OUTPUT IN THE GOVERNMENT AND PERSONAL SECTORS	1957=1.0	YPA9/YPA9R	
PPG2	X	PRICE OF FOREST PRODUCTS EXPORTED TO THE UNITED KINGDOM	1957=1.0	UNOFFICIAL STATISTIC	

SYMBOL	X=EXOG Y=ENDOG	DEFINITION	UNITS	SOURCE, TABLE	LINE
PPS2	X	PRICE OF EXPORTS OF NEWSPRINT FROM SWEDEN IN KRONA	1957=1.0	U.N. TIMBER STATISTICS	
PPU2	Y	PRICE OF FOREST PRODUCTS EXPORTED TO THE UNITED STATES	1957=1.0	UNOFFICIAL STATISTIC	
PPW2	X	PRICE OF FOREST PRODUCTS EXPORTED TO THE REST OF THE WORLD	1957=1.0	UNOFFICIAL STATISTIC	
PRC2	Y	RENT COST INDEX	1949=1.0	CANADIAN HOUSING STATISTICS	
PRS2	Y	PRICE LEVEL OF RESIDENTIAL CONSTRUCTION	1957=1.0	N.A. 6	6
PS9	Y	PERSONAL NET SAVING	$ BILL	N.A.,3	5
PSI2	Y	IMPLICIT DEFLATOR FOR INDIRECT TAX SUBSIDIES	1957=1.0	(IT9-SU9)/ (Y9R-YGD9R- IDR9R+IDP9R)	
PSR2	Y	PRICE LEVEL OF CONSUMER EXPENDITURE ON SERVICES	1957=1.0	N.A. 47 AND 48	43/12
PT9	Y	PERSONAL DIRECT TAXES	$ BILL.	N.A.,38	12
PX2	Y	IMPLICIT PRICE INDEX OF EXPORTS GOODS AND SERVICES	1957=1.0	N.A.,6	9
PXE2	Y	IMPLICIT PRICE INDEX OF A SUBTOTAL OF EXPORTS	1957=1.0	XE9/XE9R	
PY2	Y	IMPLICIT PRICE INDEX OF GROSS NATIONAL EXPENDITURE AT MARKET PRICES	1957=1.0	N.A.,6	12
PYA2	X	IMPLICIT PRICE INDEX OF GDP IN AGRICULTURE	1957=1.0	YA9/YA9R	
PYB2	Y	DEFLATOR FOR OUTPUT IN BUSINESS NON-AGRICULTURE	1957=1.0	(YGD9-YA9- YPA9)/YB9R	
PYG2	Y	DEFLATOR FOR GDP AT FACTOR COST	1957=1.0	YGD9/YGD9R	
PYI2	Y	PRICE LEVEL OF FINAL EXPENDITURE	1957=1.0	(Y9-X9+IMP9)/ (Y9R-X9R+ IMP9R)	

SYMBOL	X=EXOG Y=ENDOG	DEFINITION	UNITS	SOURCE, TABLE	LINE
PYU2	X	IMPLICIT PRICE DEFLATOR FOR GNP IN USA	1958=1.0	NATIONAL PRODUCT ACCOUNTS OF THE USA TABLE 8.1	1
QCP9	X	EMPLOYER AND EMPLOYEE CONTRIBUTIONS TO THE QUEBEC PENSION PLAN	$ BILL.	N.A.,42	10
RES9	Y	NEW RESIDENTIAL CONSTRUCTION EXPENDITURES	$ BILL.	N.A.,2	6
RES9R	Y	NEW RESIDENTIAL CONSTRUCTION EXPENDITURES IN CONSTANT 1957$	$ BILL.	N.A. 5	6
REY9	X	RESIDUAL ERROR OF ESTIMATE (EXPENDITURE)	$ BILL.	N.A. 2	14
REY9R	X	RESIDUAL ERROR OF ESTIMATE IN CONSTANT 1957 $ (EXPENDITURE)	$ BILL.	N.A. 5	14
RIT2	Y	IMPLICIT RATE OF INDIRECT TAX	RATIO	IT9/(DUR9 +ND9+(RES9+ BNR9+ANR9)* DMI+BME9+ AME9)	
RME9	X	INVESTMENT IN MACHINERY AND EQUIPMENT IN PRIVATE INSTITUTIONS AND ADJUSTMENT OF UTILITIES TO NATIONAL ACCOUNTS BASIS	$ BILL.	INVESTMENT OUTLOOK	
REM9R	X	REAL INVESTMENT IN MACHINERY AND EQUIPMENT IN PRIVATE INSTITUTIONS AND ADJUSTMENT OF UTILITIES TO NATIONAL ACCOUNTS BASIS	$ BILL.	RME9/PME2	
RNR9	X	INVESTMENT IN NONRESIDENTIAL CONSTRUCTION IN PRIVATE INSTITUTIONS AND ADJUSMENT OF UTILITIES TO NATIONAL ACCOUNTS BASIS	$ BILL.	INVESTMENT OUTLOOK	

SYMBOL	X=EXOG Y=ENDOG	DEFINITION	UNITS	SOURCE, TABLE	LINE
RNR9R	X	REAL INVESTMENT IN NONRESIDENTIAL CONSTRUCTION IN PRIVATE INSTITUTIONS AND ADJUSTMENT OF UTILITIES TO NATIONAL ACCOUNTS BASIS	$ BILL.	RNR9/PNR2	
RPT2	X	AVERAGE PERSONAL INCOME TAX RATE FOR $4,250 TAXABLE INCOME	RATIO	CALCULATED	
S9	Y	SHORT-TERM CAPITAL MOVEMENT,I.E.,CHANGE IN CANADIAN DOLLAR HOLDINGS BY FOREIGNERS PLUS OTHER CAPITAL MOVEMENTS	$ BILL	CANADIAN BALANCE OF INTERNATIONAL PAYMENTS TABLE 2	D14.1 D17.5
SAV9	Y	TOTAL SAVING	$ BILL.	N.A., 18	58
SCF9	Y	BUSINESS GROSS FIXED CAPITAL FORMATION	$ BILL.	N.A. 2	5
SCF9R	Y	REAL BUSINESS GROSS FIXED CAPITAL FORMATION	$ BILL.	N.A. 5	5
SER3RC	Y	REAL PERSONAL EXPENDITURE ON SERVICES PER PERSON	$ THOUS.	SER9R/POP6	
SER9	Y	PERSONAL EXPENDITURES ON SERVICES	$ BILL.	N.A.,47	43
SER9R	Y	REAL PERSONAL EXPENDITURES ON SERVICES	$ BILL.	N.A.,48	12
SHB	Y	STANDARD HOURS WORKED PER WEEK IN BUSINESS NONAGRICULTURE	HOURS	EQUATION H.3	
SHC3	Y	SINGLE HOUSING COMPLETIONS	THOU.	CANADIAN HOUSING STATISTICS TABLE 7	
SHS3	Y	SINGLE HOUSING STARTS	THOU.	CANADIAN HOUSING STATISTICS TABLE 7	
SIC	Y	TREASURY BILL RATE IN CANADA, AVERAGE YIELD IN THREE MONTH BILLS	PER CENT	HISTORICAL STATISTICS OF CANADA H604 BANK OF CANADA STATISTICAL SUMMARY	

SYMBOL	X=EXOG Y=ENDOG	DEFINITION	UNITS	SOURCE, TABLE	LINE
SIP9	Y	TOTAL EMPLOYER AND EMPLOYEE CONTRIBUTIONS TO SOCIAL INSURANCE AND GOVERNMENT PENSION FUNDS	$ BILL.	ECS9+CCP9+ QCP9	
SIU	X	TREASURY BILL RATE U.S.A. THREE MONTH BILLS	PER CENT	HISTORICAL STATISTICS U.S.A.	X311
SMB9	Y	STANDARD TOTAL MAN-HOURS WORKED IN BUSINESS NON AGRICULTURE	MILL.	EB6/(1.0- (U-4.0)/100.0 *SHB*.052	
SMBZ	X	STANDARD TOTAL MAN-HOURS WORKED IN BUSINESS NON AGRICULTURE	MILL.		
SME9	Y	BUSINESS GROSS FIXED CAPITAL FORMATION IN MACHINERY AND EQUIPMENT	$ BILL.	N.A. 2	8
SME9R	Y	REAL BUSINESS GROSS FIXED CAPITAL FORMATION IN MACHINERY AND EQUIPMENT	$ BILL.	N.A. 5	8
SNR9	Y	BUSINESS GROSS FIXED CAPITAL FORMATION IN NONRESIDENTIAL CONSTRUCTION	$ BILL.	N.A. 2	7
SNR9R	Y	REAL BUSINESS GROSS FIXED CAPITAL FORMATION IN NONRESIDENTIAL CONSTRUCTION	$ BILL.	N.A. 5	7
SU9	X	SUBSIDIES	$ BILL.	N.A.,10	21
SU9R	Y	REAL SUBSIDIES	$ BILL	SU9/PSI1	
T	X	1926-66 T=1,2,3,...,41			
TR9	X	TRANSFER PAYMENTS	$ BILL.	N.A.,10	20(B)
TTA	X	1928-40 = 1,....,13 1941-66 = 0			
TTB	X	1926-46 = 0 1947-66 = 1,....,20			
U	Y	UNEMPLOYMENT AS A PERCEN-TAGE OF LABOUR FORCE	PERCENT	N.A.,APPENDIX TABLE II	(5/6)* 100
UCP9	Y	UNDISTRIBUTED CORPORATE PROFITS	$ BILL	N.A.,50	12

SYMBOL	X=EXOG Y=ENDOG	DEFINITION	UNITS	SOURCE, TABLE	LINE
UPC2	X	UNITED STATES COMPETING PRICE OF CHEMICALS AND FERTILIZERS	1957=1.0	HIS. STAT. OF U.S. E32A	
UPF2	X	UNITED STATES COMPETING PRICE OF FARM AND FISH PRODUCTS	1957=1.0	HIST. STAT. OF U.S. E27R	
UPI2	X	UNITED STATED COMPETING PRICE OF OTHER MANUFACTURED GOODS	1957=1.0	HIST. STAT. OF U.S. E41A	
UPM2	X	UNITED STATES COMPETING PRICE OF MINERALS AND METAL PRODUCTS	1957=1.0	HIST. STAT. OF U.S. E36A	
UPP2	X	UNITED STATES COMPETING PRICE OF FOREST PRODUCTS	1957=1.0	CALCULATED VARIABLE	
VPC9	Y	VALUE OF THE PHYSICAL CHANGE IN INVENTORIES	$ BILL.	N.A.,2	9
VPC9R	Y	REAL VALUE OF THE PHYSICAL CHANGE IN INVENTORIES	$ BILL.	N.A.,5	9
WBA9	Y	WAGE BILL IN BUSINESS INCLUDING AGRICULTURE	$ BILL.	N.A.,19	4
WGP9	X	WAGES, SALARIES AND SUPPLEMENTARY LABOUR INCOME ARISING IN GOVERNMENT AND PERSONAL SECTORS (NON-MILITARY)	$ BILL.	N.A.,19	1+11
WPC2	X	REST OF THE WORLD COMPETING PRICE OF CHEMICALS AND FERTILIZERS	1957=1.0	U.N. STATISTICS	
WPF2	X	REST OF THE WORLD COMPETING PRICE OF FARM AND FISH PRODUCTS	1957=1.0	U.N. STATISTICS	
WPI2	X	REST OF THE WORLD COMPETING PRICE OF OTHER MANUFACTURED GOODS	1957=1.0	U.N. STATISTICS	
WPM2	X	REST OF THE WORLD COMPETING PRICE OF MINERALS AND METALS	1957=1.0	U.N. STATISTICS	
WPP2	X	REST OF THE WORLD COMPETING PRICE OF FOREST PRODUCTS	1957=1.0	U.N. STATISTICS	
WRB	Y	WAGE RATE IN THE BUSINESS NON-AGRICULTURAL SECTOR	DOLLARS	WSB9/EMB9	

SYMBOL	X=EXOG Y=ENDOG	DEFINITION	UNITS	SOURCE, TABLE	LINE
WRB001	Y	CHANGE IN BUSINESS NON-AGRICULTURAL WAGE RATE	DOLLARS	(WRB-WRB01)	
WSA9	Y	WAGE BILL IN AGRICULTURE	$ BILL.	N.A.,22	1+3
WSB9	Y	WAGE BILL IN BUSINESS NON-AGRICULTURE	$ BILL.	WBA9-WSA9	
WSG9	X	WAGES, SALARY AND SUPPLEMENTARY LABOUR INCOME IN THE GOVERNMENT SECTOR	$ BILL.	N.A.,19	11
WSP9	X	WAGES, SALARIES AND SUPPLEMENTARY LABOUR INCOME IN THE PERSONAL SECTORS	$ BILL.	N.A. 19	2
WSS9	Y	TOTAL WAGE BILL	$ BILL.	WSB9+WSA9+ WGP9	
WT9	X	WITHOLDING TAXES	$ BILL.	N.A.,9	14
X9	Y	TOTAL EXPORTS OF GOODS AND SERVICES	$ BILL	N.A.,2	12
X9R	Y	REAL TOTAL EXPORTS OF GOODS AND SERVICES	$ BILL	N.A.,5	12
XAU9	X	EXPORTS OF AUTOMOBILES AND PARTS TO THE UNITED STATES	$ BILL	BANK OF CAN. COMMODITY EXPORTS TABLE	
XCT9	X	TOTAL EXPORTS OF CHEMICALS AND FERTILIZERS	$ BILL	BANK OF CAN. COMMODITY EXPORTS TABLE	
XCT9R	Y	TOTAL EXPORTS OF CHEMICALS AND FERTILIZERS IN CONSTANT DOLLARS	$ BILL	XCT9/PCT2	
XE9	Y	SUBTOTAL EXPORTS	$ BILL	XFU9 + XEG9 + XFW9 + XPU9 + XPG9 + XPW9 + XMU9 + XMG9 + XMW9 + XIU9 + XIG9 + XIW9+ XCT9 + XRU9 + XTT9	

SYMBOL	X=EXOG Y=ENDOG	DEFINITION	UNITS	SOURCE, TABLE LINE
XE9R	Y	SUBTOTAL EXPORTS CONSTANT DOLLARS	$ BILL	XFU9R+XFG9R+ XFW9R+XPU9R+ XPG9R+XPW9R+ XMU9R+XMG9R+ XMW9R+XIU9R+ XIG9R+XIW9R+ XCT9R+XAU9/ PRU2+XTT9/ ((ND9+SER9)/ (ND9R+SER9R))
XFG9	X	EXPORTS OF FARM AND FISH PRODUCTS TO THE U.K.	$ BILL	BANK OF CAN. COMMODITY EXPORTS TABLE
XFS9	X	TOTAL EXPORTS OF FREIGHT AND SHIPPING	$ BILL	CAN BAL INT PAYMENTS TABLE 2-A.6
XFU9	X	EXPORT OF FARM AND FISH PRODUCTS TO THE U.S.	$ BILL	BANK OF CAN. COMMODITY EXPORTS TABLE
XFU9R	Y	EXPORT OF FARM AND FISH PRODUCTS TO THE U.S. IN CONSTANT DOLLARS	$ BILL	XFU9/PFU2
XFW9	X	EXPORTS OF FARM AND FISH PRODUCTS TO REST OF WORLD	$ BILL	BANK OF CAN. COMMODITY EXPORTS TABLE
XG9	Y	TOTAL EXPORTS OF GOLD AVAILABLE FOR EXPORT	$ BILL	(EXC/XXU)*XGZ
XG9R	Y	EXPORTS OF GOLD AVAILABLE FOR EXPORTS (IN CONSTANT DOLLARS)	$ BILL	=XG9
XGZ	X	EXPORT OF GOLD AVAILABLE FOR EXPORT (EXOGENOUS)	$ BILL	BANK OF CAN. EXTERNAL TRADE
XIG9	X	EXPORTS OF OTHER MANUFACTURED GOODS TO THE UNITED KINGDOM	$ BILL	BANK OF CAN. COMMODITY EXPORTS TABLE
XIG9R	Y	EXPORT OF OTHER MFG. GOODS TO THE U.K. IN CONSTANT DOLLARS	$ BILL	XIG9/PIG2
XIU9	Y	EXPORTS OF OTHER MANUFACTURED GOODS TO THE UNITED STATES	$ BILL	BANK OF CAN. COMMODITY EXPORTS TABLE (XAU9 IS NOT INCLUDED)

SYMBOL	X=EXOG Y=ENDOG	DEFINITION	UNITS	SOURCE, TABLE	LINE
XIU9R	Y	EXPORT OF OTHER MFG. GOODS TO THE U.S. IN CONSTANT DOLLARS	$ BILL	(XIU9+XAU9-(PIU2/PAU2 * XAU9))/PIU2	
XIW9	X	EXPORTS OF OTHER MANUFACTURED GOODS TO THE REST OF THE WORLD	$ BILL	BANK OF CAN. COMMODITY XPORTS TABLE	
XIW9R	Y	EXPORT OF OTHER MFG. GOODS TO THE REST OF THE WORLD IN CONSTANT DOLLARS	$ BILL	XIW9/PIW2	
XMG9	X	EXPORST OF MINERALS AND METALS TO THE UNITED KINGDOM	$ BILL	BANK OF CAN. COMMODITY EXPORTS TABLE	
XMG9R	Y	EXPORTS OF MINERALS AND METALS TO THE U.K. IN CONSTANT DOLLARS	$ BILL	XMG9/PMG2	
XMU9	X	EXPORTS OF MINERALS AND METALS TO THE UNITED STATES	$ BILL	BANK OF CAN. COMMODITY EXPORTS TABLE	
XMU9R	Y	EXPORTS OF MINERALS AND METALS TO THE U.S. IN CONSTANT DOLLARS	$ BILL	XMU9/PMU2	
XMW9	X	EXPORTS OF MINERALS AND METALS TO THE REST OF THE WORLD	$ BILL	BANK OF CAN. COMMODITY EXPORTS TABLE	
XMW9R	Y	EXPORT OF MINERAL AND MINERAL PRODUCTS TO THE REST OF THE WORLD IN CONSTANT DOLLARS	$ BILL	XMW9/PMW2	
XPG9	X	EXPORTS OF FOREST PRODUCTS TO THE UNITED KINGDOM	$ BILL	BANK OF CAN. COMMODITY EXPORTS TABLE	
XPG9R	Y	EXPORTS OF FOREST PRODUCTS TO U.K. IN CONSTANT DOLLARS	$ BILL	XPG9/PPG2	
XPU9	X	EXPORTS OF FOREST PRODUCTS TO THE UNITED STATES	$ BILL	BANK OF CAN. COMMODITY EXPORTS TABLE	
XPU9R	Y	EXPORT OF FOREST PRODUCTS TO THE U.S. IN CONSTANT DOLLARS	$ BILL	XPU9/PPU2	
XPW8	X	EXPORTS OF FOREST PRODUCTS TO THE REST OF THE WORLD	$ BILL	BANK OF CAN. COMMODITY EXPORTS TABLE	

SYMBOL	X=EXOG Y=ENDOG	DEFINITION	UNITS	SOURCE, TABLE	LINE
XPW9R	Y	EXPORT OF FOREST PRODUCTS TO THE REST OF THE WORLD IN CONSTANT DOLLARS	$ BILL	XPW9/PPW2	
XSD9	X	EXPORT STATISTICAL DISCREPANCY	$ BILL	CALCULATED VARIABLE	
XSD9R	X	REAL EXPORTS STATISTICAL DISCREPANCY	$ BILL	CALCULATED VARIABLE	
XTT9	X	TOTAL EXPORTS OF TOURIST AND TOURIST TRAVEL	$ BILL	NAT. ACCOUNT TABLE 14	38B
XXU	X	FOREIGN EXCHANGE RATE: CDN DOLLARS PER UNITED STATES DOLLAR	DOLLARS	BANK OF CANADA, STATISTICAL SUMMARY	
Y9	Y	GROSS NATIONAL EXPENDITURE AT MARKET PRICES	$ BILL	N.A.,2	15
Y9R	Y	REAL GROSS NATIONAL EXPENDITURE AT MARKET PRICES	$ BILL	N.A.,5	15
YAORM	Y	REAL OUTPUT PER MAN HOUR IN AGRICULTURE, FISHING, AND TRAPPING	$ BILL	YA9R/EMA9	
YA9	Y	OUTPUT IN AGRICULTURE, FISHING, AND TRAPPING	$ BILL	N.A.,21	1
YA9R	X	REAL GDP IN AGRICULTURE, FISHING, AND TRAPPING	$ BILL.	INDEX OF REAL OUTPUT * YA9 (1957)	
YBORM	Y	REAL OUTPUT PER MAN HOUR IN BUSINESS NON FARM	$ BILL	YB9R/EMB9	
YB9	Y	OUTPUT IN BUSINESS NON FARM AT FACTOR COST	$ BILL	YGD9-YA9-YPA9	
YB9R	Y	REAL OUTPUT IN BUSINESS NON FARM AT FACTOR COST	$ BILL	YGD9R-YA9R-YPA9R	
YBP9R	Y	POTENTIAL REAL OUTPUT IN BUSINESS NON-FARM AT FACTOR COST	$ BILL	EQN. F.10	
YGD9	Y	GROSS DOMESTIC PRODUCT AT FACTOR COST	$ BILL.	N.A.,21	16
YGD9R	Y	REAL GROSS DOMESTIC PRODUCT AT FACTOR COST	$ BILL.	INDEX OF REAL OUTPUT * YA9 (1957)	

SYMBOL	X=EXOG Y=ENDOG	DEFINITION	UNITS	SOURCE, TABLE	LINE
YPA9	Y	OUTPUT IN GOVERNMENT AND PERSONAL SECTORS	$ BILL.	WGP9 + MPA9 + IRG9	
YPA9R	Y	REAL OUTPUT IN GOVERNMENT AND PERSONAL SECTORS	$ BILL.	EQUATION F.4	

2. Method of estimating stock of capital

Since no estimates of capital stock in place were available for the whole Canadian economy, or for major component parts, on a continuing basis, it was necessary to construct our own series.

There are two basic approaches one can take here: (*a*) Perpetual Inventory method, utilized by T.K. Rymes in his estimates of capital stock for manufacturing. [See Dominion Bureau of Statistics, (1967).] (*b*) A geometrically declining depreciated net stock, utilized by T.M. Brown (1964b) in estimating total capital stock for the economy.

The first approach is conceptually superior, as it takes account of discardments, as well as depreciation, and thus enables one to separate declining productivity of capital stock (e.g., depreciation) from length of life of the equipment to discardment. Unfortunately, this approach requires reliable data on investment going back at least 15 years for equipment and 40 years for buildings beyond the initial year of the stock estimate. These data did not exist. We were therefore compelled to use the second approach.

This approach assumes that capital stock depreciates in productive efficiency at the rate of D per year and has a theoretically infinite life. Empirically, of course, the stock declines into an insignificant level after a large number of years, depending on the assumed rate of depreciation. Thus the effective length of life of capital is tied to its depreciation rate, and no discardment is possible independent of the rate of depreciation. Thus a rate of depreciation may be chosen, which is different from the true rate of decline in productivity of capital, in order to insure a proper length of life. This error is equivalent to assuming a given rate of embodied technical progress (if discardment is ignored), which may distort the estimate of "capital augmenting technical progress."

Thus capital stock estimates (K_t) at the end of any period "t":

$$K_t = K_{t-1}(1 - D) + I_t = \sum_{i=1}^{\infty}(1 - D)^{i-1}I_{t-i+1} \tag{1}$$

where I_t = gross investment in constant prices during period "t".

If the true level of depreciation is "d" and no embodied technical progress occurs:

$$K_t = \sum_{i=1}^{\infty}(1 - D)^{i-1}I_{t-i+1} = \sum_{i=1}^{\infty}[(1 - D)[(1 - D)/(1 - d)]]^{i-1}I_{t-i+1}$$

$$= \sum_{i=1}^{\infty}(1 - d)^{i-1}I_{t-i+1}[(1 - D)/(1 - d)]^{i-1}. \tag{2}$$

If the embodied technical progress of $[1 - (1 - D)/(1 - d)] = [(D - d)/(1 - d)]$ per year is assumed, then the estimated capital stock is equivalent to the true capital stock.

If the age of the capital stock does not change or changes at a constant rate this implicit value of embodied technical progress will be equivalent to an opposite error in the disembodied-capital augmenting rate of technical change.[1]

As values of investment for a long period back are not available, we used a benchmark estimate of capital stock K_0 and expanded from it by using the relation:

$$K_t = K_{t-1}(1 - D) + I_t = K_0(1 - D)^t + I_1(1 - D)^t + ... + I_t \tag{3}$$

We experimented with different years for our benchmark and found that forward calculation from an early benchmark was better than the other way around, because the error in the estimate of the benchmarks tends to expand as we move back, and contract as we move forward. So that as one moves forward, the series becomes less sensitive to a mismeasurement of the benchmark, which is likely to be present.

Benchmark estimates of net capital stock for 3 sectors were derived from Hood and Scott (1957, Table 6b) for the earliest year available. These were then extended backward to 1926 and forward by equation 3. The sectors are: agriculture and fishing, business non-agriculture (including housing), and government and institutions. Different rates of depreciation were applied to machinery and equipment and to structures. Some experimentation with slightly different rates was tried but they performed almost identically in the Cobb-Douglas form of the production function. As the capital coefficient tended to be relatively high (higher than capital share), we chose those depreciation rates which gave the lowest value to the coefficient of the logarithm of K/L in the relevant production functions. However, the differences were quite minor. We chose $D_1 = 0.035$, $D_2 = 0.14$, $D_3 = 0.035$, $D_4 = 0.12$, $D_5 = 0.035$, $D_6 = 0.12$, $D_7 = 0.02$ where: D_i = depreciation rates for (1) agricultural buildings, (2) agricultural machinery and equipment, (3) business non-agricultural structures, (4) business non-agricultural machinery and equipment, (5) government structures, (6) government machinery and equipment, and (7) housing. These are close to the values used by Hood and Scott.

---

1   It is interesting to note that this analysis completely invalidates all the tests of embodiment. They may simply be interpreted as experiments in finding the appropriate rate of depreciation.

3. Estimates of interindustry input-output coefficients, 1956 and 1959

by T.I. Matuszewski, P.R. Pitts, and J.A. Sawyer*

In order to produce the import content coefficients given in Appendix 4, it was necessary to update the 1949 interindustry input-output coefficients published by the Dominion Bureau of Statistics (1960). It had been demonstrated in Matuszewski, Pitts, and Sawyer (1963a, pp. 424-71) that these coefficients change over time.[1]

To explain the techniques used for updating the coefficients it is convenient to set out the input-output model used by the Dominion Bureau of Statistics for the 1949 table. This table divides the production sector of the Canadian economy into forty-two industry groups. Each industry group represents a grouping of industries from the DBS Standard Industrial Classification (1948 edition). These industry groups[2] are shown in Table 17.

Table 18 depicts the balancing system of inter-industry flows. The set of symbols used to refer to the various flows in the system and for various analytical coefficients derived from them are as follows. X_j is the output of the jth domestic industry; Y_j is the amount of competitive imports[3] which compete with the output of the jth domestic industry; X_{ij} is that part of the output of the ith industry which is used as an input in the jth industry; Y_{ij} is that part of imports which are competitive with output of the ith domestic industry and which are used in the jth industry; X_{if} is the final output of the ith domestic industry; Y_{if} is the portion of imports which are competitive with the output of the ith industry which were not used as inputs into industry; that is, which enter without further processing or assembly in Canada into final demand sectors; W is total non-competitive imports; W_j is non-competitive imports used by the jth industry; W_f is non-competitive imports entering directly into final demand sectors; V is total indirect taxes less subsidies; V_j is indirect taxes less subsidies on inputs into the jth industry; V_f is indirect taxes less subsidies on goods and services used by final demand sectors, excluding those taxes or subsidies included in V_j; Z is total primary input and equals gross domestic product at factor cost; Z_j is primary input into the jth industry; Z_f is primary input entering directly into a final demand sector; Q is the total final output of the domestic industries plus imports and indirect taxes entering directly into final demand. It is equal to gross domestic product at market prices plus total imports of goods and services.

---

* The first two authors are respectively, Professeur, Laboratoire d'économétrie, Université Laval, and Senior Advisor, Input-Output Research, Dominion Bureau of Statistics.
1 These updated coefficients were also used by Rosenbluth (1967, pp. 24-31) and by Robinson (1967 and 1968).
2 One change must be noted. The 1949 table included "public administration and defence" in industry group 42. The updated table includes it and enters the inputs into this industry directly into final demand as components of "government expenditure on goods and services."
3 See Matuszewski, Pitts, and Sawyer (1965) for a definition of competitive imports.

TABLE 17

The forty-two industries.

Industry no.	Industry
1	Agriculture
2	Forestry
3	Fishing, hunting and trapping
4	Metal mining and smelting and refining
5	Coal mining, crude petroleum and natural gas
6	Non-metal mining, quarrying, and prospecting
7	Meat products
8	Dairy products
9	Fish processing
10	Fruit and vegetable preparations
11	Grain mill products
12	Bakery products
13	Carbonated beverages
14	Alcoholic beverages
15	Confectionery and sugar refining
16	Miscellaneous food preparations
17	Tobacco and tobacco products
18	Rubber products
19	Leather products
20	Textile products (except clothing)
21	Clothing (textile and fur)
22	Furniture
23	Wood products (except furniture)
24	Paper products
25	Printing, publishing, and allied industries
26	Primary iron and steel
27	Agriculture implements
28	Iron and steel products, n.e.s.
29	Transportation equipment
30	Jewellery and silverware (including watch repair)
31	Non-ferrous metal products, n.e.s.
32	Electrical apparatus and supplies
33	Non-metallic mineral products
34	Products of petroleum and coal
35	Chemicals and allied products
36	Miscellaneous manufacturing industries
37	Construction
38	Transportation, storage, and trade
39	Communication
40	Electric power, gas, and water utilities
41	Finance, insurance, and real estate
42	Service industries (excluding public administration and defence)

Note: For the relation of these industries to the DBS Standard Industrial Classification (1948) see Dominion Bureau of Statistics (1960, Table 10 and pages 26-34).

The final demand vector can be subdivided into eight component vectors: (1) personal expenditure on consumer durables, (2) personal expenditure on consumer non-durables, (3) personal expenditure on consumer services, (4) government expenditure on goods and services, (5) new construction, (6) business expenditure on new machinery and equipment, (7) value of physical change in inventories, and (8) exports of goods and services.

TABLE 18

Scheme of inter-industry flow of goods and services matrix

| | | Disposition of output or supply | | | | |
| | | Industry | | | Final | |
Input into industry		1	2	...	42	Final Output	Total
Output of industry	1	$X_{1,1}$	$X_{1,2}$	...	$X_{1,42}$	$X_{1,f}$	X_1
	2	$X_{2,1}$	$X_{2,2}$	...	$X_{2,42}$	$X_{2,f}$	X_2
		.	.		.	.	.
		.	.		.	.	.
		.	.		.	.	.
	42	$X_{42,1}$	$X_{42,2}$	...	$X_{42,42}$	$X_{42,f}$	X_{42}
Imports competitive with industry	1	$Y_{1,1}$	$Y_{1,2}$	...	$Y_{1,42}$	$Y_{1,f}$	Y_1
	2	$Y_{2,1}$	$Y_{2,2}$	...	$Y_{2,42}$	$Y_{2,f}$	Y_2
		.	.	.	.	.	.
		.	.		.	.	.
	42	$Y_{42,1}$	$Y_{42,2}$	...	$Y_{42,42}$	$Y_{42,f}$	Y_{42}
Non-competitive imports		W_1	W_2	...	W_{42}	W_f	W
Indirect taxes less subsidies		V_1	V_2	...	V_{42}	V_f	V
Primary input		Z_1	Z_2	...	Z_{42}	Z_f	Z
Total		X_1	X_2	...	X_{42}	Q	

Let us define the following input-output coefficients:

$$a_{ij} = X_{ij}/X_j \quad \text{and} \quad m_{ij} = Y_{ij}/X_j.$$

Matrices of input coefficients can then be defined.[4]

$$A = [a_{ij}] \quad \text{and} \quad M = [m_{ij}].$$

Vectors of output, imports and final demand can also be defined:

$$X = [X_j], Y = [Y_i], X_f = [X_{f,i}] \quad \text{and} \quad Y_f = [Y_{f,i}].$$

4 The matrix of competitive import input coefficients (M) was estimated for 1949 by Mr A.A.
Tooms of the Dominion Bureau of Statistics but was not published in DBS (1960). Matrix A for
1949 (apart from the difference in classification in industry 42 noted above) was published as
Table 2 of DBS (1960). It should be noted, however, that in that publication the coefficients are
normalized on industry output *excluding* intra-industry consumption.

To update the 1949 estimates of the A and M matrices required updated estimates of the components of the X, Y, and X_f vectors.[5] The A matrix for 1949 was adjusted to make it consistent with output and final output totals for 1959 (in 1949 dollars) and the M matrix for 1949 adjusted to make it consistent with estimates of total competitive imports and final demand for these inputs in 1956 (in 1949 dollars). Data were not readily available to update the M matrix to 1959 but an M matrix adjusted to 1956 was preferable to the 1949 matrix for use in conjunction with an A matrix adjusted to 1959.[6] Both years had disadvantages. Foreign exchange controls existed in 1949 whereas 1956 was a year in which some Canadian industries were operating at close to capacity and imports may have therefore been at relatively higher levels than in 1959.

A number of coefficients in both the A and M matrices had been estimated directly for 1956. This was done to allow for the gradual replacement of natural fibres by man-made fibres in the textile industry, the partial replacement of imported oil by Canadian oil, and the growing importance of natural gas in comparison with manufactured gas. For industries 20, 21, and 34, the total imports used were estimated and the competitive portion assumed to be the same as in 1949. These estimates were used in the adjustment procedure. In addition, the import of competitive iron and steel products by the iron and steel industry, n.e.s., was estimated directly.

Superscripts 49 and 56 will be used to denote flows or coefficients relating to the years 1949 and 1956, respectively. The procedure for adjusting M^{49} to M^{56} is as follows.[7] The independently estimated coefficients were "blocked" in the adjustment procedure by setting them equal to zero and adding the total blocked flows for a row of the matrix to final output. Using B_i to designate the blocked flow, then final output $= Y_{if} + B_i$, $i = 1, \ldots, 42$.

For industries 20, 21 and 34 where the total imports used in an industry had been estimated directly, the coefficients in these columns (excluding blocked coefficients) were adjusted to add to the proper total.

For the other industries, an adjustment factor e_i was calculated for each row of the M matrix.

$$e_i^{56} = [Y_i^{56} - (Y_{if}^{56} + B_i^{56})] / \sum_{j=1}^{42} m_{ij}^{49} X_j^{56}$$

A new matrix $E^{56} M^{49}$, where E^{56} is a diagonal matrix whose principal elements are e_i^{56}, and where the elements in columns 20, 21, and 34 of the M matrix are zero, was then calculated. The proper value of the blocked coefficients and of columns 20, 21 and 34 were put into place and the resulting matrix accepted as an estimate of M^{56} (in 1949 dollars).

---

5   These estimates were made by Miss B.J. Emery and Paul R. Pitts of the Dominion Bureau of Statistics, using direct import data and coefficients from the 1949 input-output table.
6   This is also preferable to using both an A and an M matrix updated to 1956 since the procedure we used produces coefficients closer to more recent values, if, as the evidence suggests, there is a time-time trend in the change in coefficients.
7   This procedure was developed by Matuszewski, Pitts, and Sawyer (1963a, 1963b). An alternative adjustment procedure is described by Matuszewski, Pitts, and Sawyer (1964) but it was not used because of some of its arbitrary features.

Estimates of non-competitive imports used in each industry in 1956 were obtained by applying the 1949 coefficients (W_j/X_j) to the 1956 levels of output and adjusting all flows upward on a proportionate basis to add to an independently-made estimate of total non-competitive imports used in all industries.

Since a number of coefficients had been estimated directly for 1956, a procedure involving two steps was used to arrive at an estimate of A^{59}. Estimates of total industry output for 1956 and 1959 were made, utilizing detail from the DBS Index of Industrial Production, and estimates of final demand directed towards domestic industry made in a manner similar to that described above for competitive imports. Blocked coefficients were set at zero and the blocked flows added to final output. Designating blocked flows relevant to the A matrix by C_i, $i = 1, ..., 42$, the adjustment factors d^{56} were calculated as follows

$$d_i^{56} = [X_i^{56} - (X_{if}^{56} + C_i^{56})]/\sum_{j=1}^{42} a_{ij}^{49} \, X_j^{56} \, .$$

A new matrix $D^{56} \, A^{49}$ was then formed, where D is a diagonal matrix whose principal elements are d_i^{56} and the blocked coefficients put in their proper places. The resulting matrix was accepted as an estimate of A^{56}.

The procedure was repeated for 1959, except that no coefficients had been estimated independently for that year. A new set of adjustment factors d_i^{59} were obtained.

$$d_i^{59} = (X_i^{59} - X_{if}^{59})/\sum_{j=1}^{42} a_{ij}^{56} \, X_j^{59} \, .$$

A new matrix $D^{59} \, A^{56}$ was computed and accepted as an estimate of A^{59} (in 1949 dollars).

The above computations were complicated by the presence of statistical discrepancies (including outputs and inputs which could not be allocated to using industries or final demand sectors) in the 1949 DBS study. Some of these unallocated output items were allocated for the present study. The unallocated output of each of the 42 industries was distributed proportionately over the several final demand categories.

Unallocated imports amounting to $318 million in 1949 (and a small amount of indirect taxes) were omitted from the computations. This represented a large portion of the "other current payments" item of $315 million in the balance of international payments plus a relatively small amount of merchandise imports. (Some of the other current payments item is closer to an income or a transfer payment flow than to flows of goods and services). The procedure of adjusting the non-competitive import coefficients to 1956 probably resulted in unallocated imports for that year being too low; that is, non-competitive imports were too high.

The statistical discrepancy between the total final demand allocated to the various industries, direct imports, direct indirect taxes less subsidies, and direct wages and salaries, and the total final demand as derived from the National Accounts totals was also ignored in the computations; that is, unallocated final demand was omitted.

4. Import content of gross domestic product, 1959

The updated estimates of input-output coefficients described in Appendix 3 were used to estimate the import content of gross domestic product at market prices. This content function was then utilized in the import demand function of the TRACE model (equation D.35).

Following the notation of Appendix 3 the method of computing the import content coefficients is as follows.[1] Let us assume that the relationship of inputs to outputs is proportional. That is, let us assume that to produce one unit of output of the jth industry, the input from the ith industry is $a_{ij} = X_{ij}/X_j$. Let us make a similar assumption about competitive imports; that is, to produce a unit of output of the jth industry an input of imports competitive with the ith industry equal to $m_{ij} = Y_{ij}/X_j$ is used. Similar proportionality assumptions can be made with respect to the other inputs. Then, in matrix notation, where $A = [a_{ij}]$, X is a vector of industry output, and X_f a vector of final output.

$$X_f = (I - A) X, \text{ hence } X = (I - A)^{-1} X_f.$$

Thus the industry outputs, direct and indirect, implied in a given vector of final ouput, given the proportionality assumption, can be obtained. The implied import content can then be obtained, again on the basis of the proportionality assumption.

Let $M = [m_{ij}]$, the competitive import matrix. Then the indirect competitive import content of final output of the forty-two domestic industries is given by $M(I - A)^{-1} X_f$. Total competitive imports of each type is obtained by adding the direct content, Y_{if}, $i = 1, ..., 42$.

Total non-competitive imports are obtained by post-multiplying the row vector $[(W_1/X_1), (W_2/X_2), ..., (W_{42}/X_{42})]$ by $(I-A)^{-1} X_f$ and adding W_f.

The computations for 1959 used non-competitive and competitive import coefficients for the year 1956. Competitive imports may have been relatively higher in 1956 than in 1959 because of the high levels of economic activity in Canada in the former year. These two factors probably resulted in an overestimation of the import content of final demand in 1959. This tends to be confirmed by the fact that the residual estimate of unallocated imports for 1959 was in the neighbourhood of $100 million, about one-sixth of the other current payments for 1959 (in 1949 dollars).

The calculation resulted in the *indirect* import content coefficients shown in Table 19. Table 20 gives the percentage distribution of final demand categories for 1959. In this table, rows 43–46 refer to the following inputs: 43, direct imports of goods and services; 44, indirect taxes on direct imports of goods and services; 45, indirect taxes on domestically-produced goods and services; 46, direct labour input (wages, salaries

---

1 This method was used in Dominion Bureau of Statistics (1960, Table 4).

TABLE 19

Indirect import content of final demand expenditures directed towards the jth industry, 1959.

Industry	Imports in 1949 dollars per dollar of final demand
1	0.076157
2	0.035428
3	0.089209
4	0.124075
5	0.030808
6	0.050641
7	0.106913
8	0.073621
9	0.091228
10	0.174548
11	0.139753
12	0.154320
13	0.238860
14	0.156882
15	0.447774
16	0.555344
17	0.120498
18	0.350961
19	0.322738
20	0.367339
21	0.338644
22	0.193412
23	0.074012
24	0.109051
25	0.085890
26	0.291952
27	0.278964
28	0.215861
29	0.348132
30	0.447887
31	0.154009
32	0.276354
33	0.199251
34	0.362793
35	0.333644
36	0.279570
37	0.150505
38	0.070767
39	0.040144
40	0.059622
41	0.026008
42	0.070251

and supplementary labour income). The column symbols are defined as: DUR9, personal expenditure on consumer durable goods; ND9, personal expenditure on consumer nondurable goods; SER9, personal expenditure on consumer services; G9, government expenditure on goods and services; SME9, business gross fixed capital for-

TABLE 20

Composition of $100 million of final demand directed towards industries by categories, 1959 (1949 dollars).

Industry	DUR9	ND9	SER9	G9	SME9	RES9+ SNR9	X9	VPC9
				Final demand categories				
1	–	10.09	–	0.99	0.42	–	15.19	–155.94
2	–	0.06	–	–	–	–	1.03	–7.42
3	–	0.12	–	–	–	–	1.12	–
4	–	–	–	0.04	–	–	20.26	–29.70
5	–	0.32	–	0.10	–	–	1.57	–
6	–	–	–	–	–	–	1.30	–
7	–	8.22	–	0.09	–	–	2.06	21.29
8	–	5.47	–	0.05	–	–	0.77	–
9	–	0.54	–	0.01	–	–	1.56	–
10	–	2.17	–	0.02	–	–	0.18	–10.15
11	–	1.05	–	0.03	–	–	1.88	–
12	–	3.66	–	0.05	–	–	0.01	–
13	–	1.08	–	0.02	–	–	–	–
14	–	2.61	–	0.02	–	–	1.39	–
15	–	1.96	–	0.02	–	–	0.03	–
16	–	2.20	–	0.02	–	–	0.43	19.80
17	–	1.85	–	0.06	–	–	0.41	15.35
18	–	0.85	–	0.04	–	–	0.23	–
19	0.82	1.42	0.38	0.04	–	–	0.18	–
20	5.68	0.59	–	0.23	–	–	0.71	52.97
21	–	7.86	0.25	0.44	–	–	0.08	25.00
22	5.64	–	0.13	0.19	0.97	–	0.01	–
23	0.20	0.06	–	0.09	0.44	–	7.61	26.73
24	–	0.27	–	0.26	–	–	17.18	–
25	–	1.12	–	0.96	–	–	0.13	–
26	–	–	–	0.02	–	–	2.29	–
27	–	–	–	0.03	1.85	–	1.32	–
28	6.05	0.05	–	1.81	10.11	–	1.60	79.20
29	16.94	0.43	0.87	5.17	15.28	–	1.48	47.03
30	0.99	–	0.04	–	–	–	0.08	24.01
31	1.00	0.01	–	0.04	0.40	–	1.18	–
32	7.66	0.13	0.15	1.92	9.34	–	0.54	32.18
33	0.99	0.11	–	0.18	–	–	1.06	–
34	–	3.41	–	0.99	–	–	0.30	–
35	0.01	1.39	–	0.31	–	–	4.16	–40.35
36	1.17	0.37	–	0.58	1.02	–	0.24	–
37	–	–	–	27.37	–	100.00	–	–
38	31.52	17.33	10.33	3.83	8.59	–	8.46	–
39	–	–	3.90	1.27	–	–	–	–
40	–	3.61	0.67	0.56	0.23	–	0.07	–
41	–	–	42.67	0.68	–	–	–	–
42	–	–	30.37	15.40	–	–	–	–
43	11.35	7.07	10.23	1.50	43.36	–	1.91	–
44	2.14	1.18	–	–	4.19	–	–	–
45	7.83	11.32	–	–	3.73	–	–	–
46	–	–	–	34.56	–	–	–	–
Total	100.00	100.00	100.00	100.00	100.00	100.00	100.00	100.00

TABLE 21

Primary direct and indirect import content of an expenditure of $100,000 (1949 $) by a final demand category, assuming the 1959 industrial distribution (dollars of 1949 purchasing power)

Industry	DUR9	ND9	SER9	G9	SME9	RES9+SNR9	X9	VPC9
				Final demand categories				
1	–	768.4	–	75.4	32.0	–	1156.8	–11875.9
2	–	2.1	–	–	–	–	36.5	–262.9
3	–	10.7	–	–	–	–	99.9	–
4	–	–	–	5.0	–	–	2513.8	–3685.0
5	–	9.9	–	3.1	–	–	48.4	–
6	–	–	–	–	–	–	65.8	–
7	–	878.8	–	9.6	–	–	220.2	2276.2
8	–	402.7	–	3.7	–	–	56.7	–
9	–	49.3	–	0.9	–	–	142.3	–
10	–	378.8	–	3.5	–	–	31.4	–1771.7
11	–	146.7	–	4.2	–	–	262.7	–
12	–	564.8	–	7.7	–	–	1.5	–
13	–	258.0	–	4.8	–	–	–	–
14	–	409.5	–	3.1	–	–	218.1	–
15	–	877.6	–	9.0	–	–	13.4	–
16	–	1221.8	–	11.1	–	–	238.8	10995.8
17	–	222.9	–	7.2	–	–	49.4	1849.6
18	–	298.3	–	14.0	–	–	80.7	–
19	265.0	458.3	122.6	12.9	–	–	58.1	–
20	2086.0	216.7	–	84.5	–	–	260.8	19457.9
21	–	2661.7	84.7	149.0	–	–	27.1	8466.1
22	1091.0	–	25.1	36.7	187.6	–	1.9	–
23	14.8	4.4	–	6.7	32.6	–	563.2	1978.3
24	–	29.4	–	28.4	–	–	1873.5	–
25	–	96.2	–	82.5	–	–	11.2	–
26	–	–	–	5.8	–	–	668.6	–
27	–	–	–	8.4	516.1	–	368.2	–
28	1306.0	10.8	–	390.7	2182.4	–	345.4	17096.2
29	5897.4	149.7	303.4	1799.8	5319.5	–	515.2	16372.6
30	443.4	–	17.9	–	–	–	35.8	10753.8
31	154.0	1.5	–	6.2	61.6	–	181.7	–
32	2116.9	35.9	41.5	530.6	2581.1	–	149.2	8893.1
33	197.3	21.9	–	35.9	–	–	211.2	–
34	–	1237.1	–	359.2	–	–	108.8	–
35	3.3	463.8	–	103.4	–	–	1388.0	–13462.5
36	327.1	103.4	–	162.2	285.2	–	67.1	–
37	–	–	–	4119.3	–	15050.5	–	–
38	2230.6	1226.4	731.0	271.0	607.2	–	598.7	–
39	–	–	156.6	51.0	–	–	–	–
40	–	215.2	39.9	33.4	13.7	–	4.2	–
41	–	–	1109.8	17.7	–	–	–	–
42	–	–	2133.5	1081.9	–	–	–	–
Total indirect	16133.7	13432.7	4766.0	9539.5	11819.0	15050.5	12674.3	67081.6
Direct	11350.0	7070.0	10230.0	1500.0	43360.0	–	1910.0	–
Total	27483.7	20502.7	14996.0	11039.5	55179.0	15050.5	14584.3	67081.6

TABLE 22

Import content coefficients for components of final demand, 1959

Component	1949 dollars	1957 dollars
DUR9	0.274837	0.285281
ND9	0.205027	0.212408
SER9	0.149960	0.120268
G9	0.110395	0.087874
SME9	0.551790	0.463504
RES9 + SNR9	0.150505	0.123264
X9	0.145843	0.146135

mation in machinery and equipment; RES9 + SNR9, construction; VPC9, value of the physical change in inventories; X9: exports of goods and services (excluding interest and dividends received from abroad).

Rows 1 - 42 of Table 21 are derived by multiplying each element of each column of Table 20 by the corresponding element of Table 19 times 1000. The direct import content shown in Table 21 is taken directly from row 43 of Table 20. The last row of Table 21 gives the total direct and indirect content of each category of final demand (in 1949 dollars).

The last column of Table 21 shows VPC9 (value of the physical change in inventories). Because of the great lack of precision associated with these estimates they were not used in subsequent analysis.

The import content coefficients were converted from 1949 dollars to 1957 dollars by the following method. Each coefficient was multiplied by the ratio of the implicit price index (1949 = 100) of imports of goods and services to the implicit price index for the appropriate component of gross national expenditure for 1957 and 1964, respectively. Thus, the coefficients in Table 22 were obtained.

A few comments on Table 22 may be helpful. Direct imports into the final demand category SER9 include tourist expenditure abroad and other miscellaneous current payments abroad classed as personal expenditure. The input-output table distinguished only a construction sector. No breakdown was made for residential, non-residential, and government construction and the RES9 column is an average for these two types of construction activity. The X9 column includes re-exports. The proportion of re-exports is shown in row 43 of Table 20. For use in an import demand equation, the import content coefficient of X9 was adjusted downward to 0.142 to reflect the fact that the aggregate exports of goods and services in the National Accounts (in contrast to the input-output model) include interest and dividends received from abroad which have zero import content.

References

Agarwala, R., J.R. Downs, W.M. Illing, and H.S. Tjan (1970), "A Medium-Term Macro-Model of Canada: A Progress Report," Discussion Paper No. 9, Econometrics Group, Economic Council of Canada (Ottawa).

Aitchison, J., and J.A.C. Brown (1957), *The Lognormal Distribution* (Cambridge: Cambridge University Press).

Ball, R.J., and R.G. Bodkin (1963), "Income, the Price Level, and Generalized Multipliers in Keynesian Economics," *Metroeconomica*, XV (1963), 59-81; reprinted in R.G. Bodkin, *The Wage-Price-Producitivity Nexus* (Philadelphia: University of Pennsylvania, 1966), and in R.J. Ball and Peter Doyle (eds.), *Inflation: Selected Readings* (Middlesex: Penguin Books, 1969).

Bank of Canada, *Statistical Summary* (Ottawa, monthly).

Bodkin, R.G., E.P. Bond, G.L. Reuber, and T.R. Robinson (1967), *Price Stability and High Employment: The Options for Canadian Economic Policy* (Ottawa: Queen's Printer for the Economic Council of Canada).

Bodkin, R.G. (1970), "Wage and Price Formation in Selected Econometric Models," a paper given at a Conference on Inflation held at Queen's University in June 1970 and available as Research Report 7023 of the Department of Economics of the University of Western Ontario.

Brittain, J.A. (1964), "The Tax Structure and Corporate Dividend Policy," *American Economic Review*, LIV (May, 1964), 272-87.

Brown, T.M. (1952), "Habit Persistence and Lags in Consumer Behaviour," *Econometrica*, XX (July, 1952), 355-371.

Brown, T.M. (1964a), "A Forecast Determination of National Product, Employment, and Price Level in Canada, from an Econometric Model," in *Models of Income Determination*, Studies in Income and Wealth, vol. XXVIII (Princeton: Princeton University Press).

Brown, T.M. (1964b), *Canadian Economic Growth* (Ottawa: Queen's Printer).

Brown, T.M. (1970), *The Specification and Use of Econometric Models* (London: Macmillan).

Caves, R.E., and G.L. Reuber (1969), *Canadian Economic Policy and the Impact of International Capital Flows* (Toronto: University of Toronto Press).

Caves, R.E., and G.L. Reuber (1971), *Capital Transfers and Economic Policy: Canada 1951-1962* (Cambridge, Mass.: Harvard University Press).

Choudhry, N.K., Y. Kotowitz, J.A. Sawyer, and J.W.L. Winder (1968), "An Annual Econometric Model of the Canadian Economy, 1928-1966," Working Paper 6818, Institute for the Quantitative Analysis of Social and Economic Policy, University of Toronto.

Choudhry, N.K., Y. Kotowitz, J.A. Sawyer, and J.W.L. Winder (1969), "TRACE, 1969 – An Econometric Model of the Canadian Economy," Working Paper 6908, Institute for the Quantitative Analysis of Social and Economic Policy, University of Toronto.

Choudhry, N.K., Y. Kotowitz, J.A. Sawyer, and J.W.L. Winder (1970), "Some Simulation Results from the TRACE Econometric Model of the Canadian Economy," a paper presented at the Second World Congress of the Econometric Society, Cambridge, England, Sept. 8-14, 1970.

Christ, Carl F. (1968), "A Simple Macroeconomic Model with a Government Budget Restraint," *Journal of Political Economy*, LXVII (Jan.-Feb., 1968), 53-67.

Courchene, T.J. (1967), "Inventory Behaviour and the Stock-order Distinction: An Analysis by Industry and Stage of Fabrication with Empirical Application to the Canadian Manufacturing Sector," *Canadian Journal of Economics and Political Science*, XXXIII (Aug., 1967), 325-57.

de Leeuw, F. (1962), "The Demand for Capital Goods by Manufacturers: A Study of Quarterly Time Series," *Econometrica*, XXX (July, 1962), 407-23.

Dernberg, T.F. (1970), "Exchange Rates and Co-ordinated Stabilization Policy," *Canadian Journal of Economics*, III (Feb., 1970), 1-13.

Dominion Bureau of Statistics, *National Accounts, Income and Expenditure* (Ottawa, monthly and quarterly).

Dominion Bureau of Statistics, (1948), *Standard Industrial Classification* (Ottawa, Queen's Printer).

Dominion Bureau of Statistics (1960), *Supplement to the Inter-Industry Flow of Goods and Services, Canada, 1949* (Ottawa: Queen's Printer).

Dominion Bureau of Statistics (1963), *Indexes of Real Domestic Product by Industry of Origin, 1935-1961* (Ottawa: Queen's Printer).

Dominion Bureau of Statistics (1967), *Fixed Capital Flows and Stocks, Manufacturing, Canada, 1926-1960, Methodology* (Ottawa: Queen's Printer).

Duesenberry, J.S., G. Fromm, L.R. Klein, and E. Kuh (1965), *The Brookings Quarterly Econometric Model of the United States* (Chicago: Rand-McNally).

Eastman, H.C., and S. Stykolt (1969), "The Performance of Two Protected Oligopolies in Canada" in S. Stykolt, *Efficiency in the Open Economy* (Toronto: Oxford University Press), 81-102.

Evans, M.K. (1969a), "Reconstruction and Estimation of the Balanced Budget Multiplier," *Review of Economics and Statistics*, LI (Feb. 1969), 14-26.

Evans, M.K. (1969b), *Macroeconomic Activity* (New York: Harper and Row).

Evans, M.K., and L.R. Klein (1968), *The Wharton Econometric Forecasting Model* (Philadelphia: Department of Economics, University of Pennsylvania, revised edition).

Evans, R.G., and J.F. Helliwell (1969), *Quarterly Business Capital Expenditures* (Ottawa: Bank of Canada).

Hall, R.E., and D.W. Jorgenson (1967), "Tax Policy and Investment Behavior," *American Economic Review*, LVII (June, 1967), 391-414. Comment in *ibid.*, LVIX (June, 1969), 370-401.

Helliwell, John F. (1968), *Public Policies and Private Investment* (Oxford: Oxford University Press).

Helliwell, J.F., L.H. Officer, H.T. Shapiro, and I.A. Stewart (1969a), *The Structure of* RDX*1* (Ottawa: Bank of Canada).

Helliwell, J.F., L.H. Officer, H.T. Shapiro, and I.A. Stewart (1969b), *The Dynamics of* RDX*1* (Ottawa: Bank of Canada).

Helliwell, J.F., L.H. Officer, H.T. Shapiro, and I.A. Stewart (1969c), "Econometric Analysis of Policy Choices for an Open Economy," *Review of Economics and Statistics*, LI (Nov., 1969), 383-98.

Hood, Wm. C., and A.D. Scott (1957), *Output, Labour and Capital in the Canadian Economy* (Ottawa: Queen's Printer).

Houthakker, H.S., and L.D. Taylor (1966), *Consumer Demand in the United States, 1929-1970* (Cambridge: Harvard University Press).

Johnson, Harry G. (1966), "Some Aspects of the Theory of Economic Policy in a World of Capital Mobility," in T. Bagiotti (ed.) *Essays in Honor of Marco Fanno* (Padua: Cedam).

Johnson, H.G., and J.W.L. Winder (1962), *Lags in the Effects of Monetary Policy in Canada,* (Royal Commission on Banking and Finance, Ottawa).

Jones, Ronald W. (1968), "Monetary and Fiscal Policy for an Economy with Fixed Exchange Rates," *Journal of Political Economy*, LXXVI (July-Aug., 1968), 921-43.

Jorgenson, D.W. (1965), "Anticipations and Investment Behavior" in J.S. Duesenberry *et. al., The Brookings Quarterly Econometric Model of the United States* (Chicago: Rand-McNally), 35-92.

Jorgenson, D.W. (1967), "The Theory of Investment Behavior" in R. Ferber (ed.), *Determinants of Investment Behavior* (New York: National Bureau of Economic Research), 129-55.

Jorgenson, D.W., and C.D. Siebert (1968), "A Comparison of Alternative Theories of Corporate Investment Behavior," *American Economic Review,* LVIII (Sept., 1968), 681-712.

Jump, Gregory V. (1970), "Policy Choices for an Open Economy: An Evaluation," Working Paper 7006, Institute for the Quantitative Analysis of Social and Economic Policy, University of Toronto.

Jump, Gregory V., J.A. Sawyer, and J.W.L. Winder (1970), "The Economic Outlook for 1971, Canada," Policy Paper No. 8, Institute for the Quantitative Analysis of Social and Economic Policy, University of Toronto.

Jutlah, C.B. (1970), "Income Tax Relationships: Estimation and Role in Economic Stabilization," PhD thesis, University of Toronto.

Keynes, J.M. (1936), *General Theory of Employment, Interest and Money* (London: Macmillan).

Kotowitz, Yehuda (1968a), "Production and Distribution in an Econometric Model of Canada." A paper presented to the Tokyo meetings of the Econometric Society, June 1968.

Kotowitz, Yehuda (1968b), "On the Estimation of a Non-Neutral CES Production Function," *Canadian Journal of Economics,* I (May 1968), 429-39.

Kotowitz, Yehuda (1968c), "Capital-Labour Substitution in Canadian Manufacturing, 1926-39 and 1946-61," *Canadian Journal of Economics,* I (Aug. 1968), 619-32.

Kotowitz, Yehuda (1969), "Technical Progress, Factor Substitution and Income Distribution in Canadian Manufacturing, 1926-39 and 1946-61," *Canadian Journal of Economics,* I (Feb. 1969), 106-114.

Kotowitz, Y., J.A. Sawyer, and J.W.L. Winder (1969), "Economic Outlook for 1970, Canada," Policy Paper No. 6, Institute for the Quantitative Analysis of Social and Economic Policy, University of Toronto, December 12, 1969.

Lintner, John (1962), "Dividends, Earnings, Leverage, Stock Prices and the Supply of Capital to Corporations," *Review of Economics and Statistics*, XLIV (Aug. 1962), 243-69.

Lipsey, Richard G. (1960), "The Relation between Unemployment and the Rate of Change of Money Wage Rates in the United Kingdom, 1862-1957; A Further Analysis," *Economica*, XXVII (Feb. 1960).

Matuszewski, T.I., P.R. Pitts, and J.A. Sawyer (1963a), "Alternative Treatments of Imports in Input-Output Models: A Canadian Study," *Journal of the Royal Statistical Society*, A, CXXVI (1963), 410-32.

Matuszewski, T.I., P.R. Pitts, and J.A. Sawyer (1963b), "L'ajustement périodique des systèmes de relations interindustrielles Canada, 1949-1958," *Econometrica*, XXXI (1963), 90-110.

Matuszewski, T.I., P.R. Pitts, and J.A. Sawyer (1964), "Linear Programming Estimates of Changes in Input Coefficients," *Canadian Journal of Economics and Political Science*, XXX (May 1964), 203-10.

Matuszewski, T.I., P.R. Pitts, and J.A. Sawyer (1965), "The Impact of Foreign Trade on Canadian Industries," *Canadian Journal of Economics and Political Science*, XXXI (May 1965), 206-21.

May, S.J. (1966), "Dynamic Multipliers and their Use for Decision-Making," in *Conference on Stabilization Policies* (Ottawa: Queen's Printer, for the Economic Council of Canada).

Meiselman, D. (1962), *The Term Structure of Interest Rates* (Englewood Cliffs: Prentice-Hall).

Miller, M.H. and Modigliani, F. (1967), "Estimates of the Cost of Capital Relevant for Investment Decisions under Uncertainty," in R. Ferber (ed.), *Determinants of Investment Behavior* (New York: National Bureau of Economic Research), 179-213.

Mundell, R.A. (1962), "The Appropriate Use of Monetary and Fiscal Policies for Internal and External Stability," *IMF Staff Papers*, IX (1962), 70-77.

Mundell, R.A. (1963), "Capital Mobility and Stabilization Policy under Fixed and Flexible Exchange Rates," *Canadian Journal of Economics and Political Science*, XXIX (Nov., 1963), 475-85.

Mundell, R.A. (1964), "Capital Mobility and Size: Reply," *Canadian Journal of Economics and Political Science*, XXX (Aug. 1964), 421-31.

Officer, L.H. (1968), *An Econometric Model of Canada under the Fluctuating Exchange Rate* (Cambridge: Harvard University Press).

Officer, L.H., and J.R. Hurtubise (1969), "Price Effects of the Kennedy Round on Canadian Trade," *Review of Economics and Statistics*, LI (Aug. 1969), 320-33.

Report of the Royal Commission on Taxation (1966) (Ottawa: Queen's Printer).

Rhomberg, R.R. (1964), "A Model of the Canadian Economy under Fixed and Fluctuating Exchange Rates," *Journal of Political Economy*, LXXII (Feb., 1964), 1-31.

Robinson, T.R. (1967), *Foreign Trade and Economic Stability* (Ottawa: Queen's Printer, for the Royal Commission on Taxation).

Robinson, T.R. (1968), "Canada's Imports and Economic Stability," *Canadian Journal of Economics*, I (May, 1968), 401-28.

Rosenbluth, Gideon (1967), *The Canadian Economy and Disarmament* (Toronto: Macmillan of Canada).

Sawyer, John A. (1969), "Policy-Oriented Econometric Models of the Canadian Economy," *Canadian Operational Research Journal,* VII (Nov. 1969), 177-92.

Sawyer, John A. (1970a), "Models for Forecasting Gross National Product," in M.G. Kendall (ed.), *Mathematical Model Building in Economics and Industry,* Series 2 (London: Griffin), 231-40.

Sawyer, John A. (1970b), "Foreign Trade in the TRACE Model," a paper presented at the second annual meeting of Project LINK, London, England, September 2-7, 1970.

Schweitzer, T.T. (1970), *Personal Consumer Expenditures in Canada, 1926-75,* Part I (Ottawa: Queen's Printer).

Scott, Anthony (1959), "Canada's Reproductive Wealth," in *The Measurement of National Wealth,* Income and Wealth, Series VIII (London: Bowes and Bowes).

Shapiro, H.T. (1967), "Distributed Lags, Interest Rate Expectations, and the Impact of Monetary Policy: An Econometric Analysis of Canadian Experience," *American Economic Review* (May 1967), 444-61.

Smith, D.C. (1963), "Corporate Saving Behavior," *Canadian Journal of Economics and Political Science,* XXIX (Aug. 1963), 297-310.

Smith, L.B. (1969a), "A Model of the Canadian Housing and Mortgage Markets," *Journal of Political Economy,* LXXVII (Sept./Oct. 1969), 795-816.

Smith, L.B. (1969b), "A Bi-Sectoral Housing Market Model," *Canadian Journal of Economics,* II (Nov. 1969), 557-69.

Smith, L.B. and G.R. Sparks (1970), "The Interest Sensitivity of Canadian Mortgage Flows," *Canadian Journal of Economics,* III (Aug. 1970), 407-21.

Sohmen, Egon (1969), *Flexible Exchange Rates* (Chicago: University of Chicago Press, revised edition).

Suits, D.B. (1962), "Forecasting with an Econometric Model," *American Economic Review,* LII (March 1962), 104-32, reprinted in R.A. Gordon and L.R. Klein, *Readings in Business Cycles* (Homewood: Irwin, 1965), 597-625.

Takayama, Akira (1969), "The Effects of Fiscal and Monetary Policies under Flexible and Fixed Exchange Rates in Canada," *Canadian Journal of Economics,* II (May 1969), 190-209. See also the corrections, *ibid.,* III (Feb. 1970), 167-8.

Tsurumi, Hiroki (1970), "A Four-Sector Growth Model of the Canadian Economy,," Discussion Paper No. 8, Institute for Economic Research, Queen's University.

Tsurumi, H., and M.F.J. Prachowny (1968), "A Four-Sector Growth Model of the Canadian Economy," a paper presented at the meetings of the Econometric Society, Evanston, 1968.

Walters, A.A. (1963), "Production and Cost Functions: An Econometric Survey," *Econometrica,* XXXI (Jan., 1963), 1-66.

Wilson, T.A. (1967), *Capital Investment and the Cost of Capital* (Ottawa: Queen's Printer for the Royal Commission on Taxation).

Winder, J.W.L. (1971), "A Note on the Houthakker-Taylor Demand Analysis," *Journal of Political Economy* (forthcoming).